Courting Justice

Rivergate Regionals

Rivergate Regionals is a collection of books published by Rutgers University Press focusing on New Jersey and the surrounding area. Since its founding in 1936, Rutgers University Press has been devoted to serving the people of New Jersey, and this collection solidifies that tradition. The books in the Rivergate Regionals Collection explore history, politics, nature and the environment, recreation, sports, health and medicine, and the arts. By incorporating the collection within the larger Rutgers University Press editorial program, the Rivergate Regionals Collection enhances our commitment to publishing the best books about our great state and the surrounding region.

Courting Justice

Ten New Jersey Cases That Shook the Nation

PAUL L. TRACTENBERG, EDITOR

FOREWORD BY DEBORAH T. PORITZ

RUTGERS UNIVERSITY PRESS

NEW BRUNSWICK, NEW JERSEY, AND LONDON

LIBRARY OF CONGRESS CATALOGING-IN-PUBLICATION DATA

Courting justice : ten New Jersey cases that shook the nation / Paul L. Tractenberg, editor; foreword by Deborah T. Poritz.

p. cm.

Includes bibliographical references and index.

ISBN 978–0–8135–6159–2 (pbk. : alk. paper) — ISBN 978–0–8135–6160–8 (e-book)

Trials—New Jersey. 2. Law—New Jersey—Popular works. 3. Civil rights—New Jersey—Popular works. I. Tractenberg, Paul L., 1938–

KF220.N486 2013

347.749'07—dc23   2012038530

A British Cataloging-in-Publication record for
this book is available from the British Library.

Visit our website: http://rutgerspress.rutgers.edu

Manufactured in the United States of America

For my wife, Neimah,
who has been my joy, my partner, and my rock

CONTENTS

FOREWORD

DEBORAH T.PORITZ

This book and each of its chapters tell a fascinating and important story, a story about the origins of New Jersey's modern judiciary, about the framework within which the state's highest court functions, and about the cases that stand as examples of the court's finest work. It is a story of an independent court system and the search for justice as the peculiar and specific charge of the judicial branch within a framework of three powerful, coequal branches of government.

In "New Jersey's 1947 Constitution and the Creation of a Modern State Supreme Court," the concluding chapter by John B. Wefing, we learn about the unique history of this court system, born in the constitution of 1947 and lauded as a model for efficient court administration by those who study courts and those who run them. In 1947, the year the judicial article of the constitution became effective, New Jersey moved from an antiquated complex of overlapping courts mired in jurisdictional disputes, possibly the worst system in the country, to a unified and streamlined judiciary administered by an independent chief justice acting in partnership with the other members of the state's supreme court through the exercise of the court's rule-making authority.

The new system was revolutionary when it was approved; it has remained independent and strong into the twenty-first century. And that independence and strength have provided the basis for the New Jersey Supreme Court's preeminence among its peers over these past sixty-five years. During the period encompassed by the cases discussed in this book (from 1960 to 2011), the court was known for its careful and scholarly exploration of the issues before it and for its willingness to adapt traditional legal principles to reflect changing social attitudes and the complexities of modern life, including the enormous technological revolution that so altered the world the justices once knew. I have previously characterized the court's approach in such cases, "[W]hen the law is not clear or the facts do not fit the legal paradigm or recent legislative enactments reflect changed attitudes or norms, then the court must mine deeply and creatively for the principles that sustain its work. That experience affects the members of the court profoundly; it alters their understanding of the world around them and forces them to consider anew the values that shape the law."[1]

As is well known, courts are constrained in respect to the issues they can or must, or cannot, entertain. A legislature may require convicted sex offenders to register with the police on release from prison, or a legislature may duck a politically difficult issue, but a court cannot decline to decide a case properly before it, or take the initiative in any matter it chooses. Only when litigants bring such questions to the courts and, in New Jersey, only when those issues arise out of a genuine case or controversy, can the court issue an opinion. Yet, in New Jersey and elsewhere, controversial and unpopular issues do come to the states' highest courts and, when they do, the courts decide them.

Often, then, the New Jersey Supreme Court is asked to decide issues that are controversial, that sit at the outer edge of what we know, and that do not fit the legal paradigm so useful in other cases. Then, the court will look for analogies in existing law, for precedents and legal rules that may shed some light on the difficult questions before it, for indications of social attitudes and new understandings—and will answer those questions as best it can. On occasion, the court's critics will claim that "activist" justices have intruded on the prerogatives of the other branches of government. Those who object to particular decisions of the court will raise concerns about the court's role in our tripartite form of government and question the legitimacy of those rulings.

This book allows us to examine a series of seminal cases decided by the court so that we can determine for ourselves whether the court has overstepped its bounds. Each of the cases discussed here tells a story about the people before the court and about the problems that brought them there, but each case also tells us something about how the court works, how it comes to grips with seemingly intractable problems, and how it advances the argument for the policy decisions it makes in support of constitutional and common law values. So, for example, we learn in chapter 4 that Chief Justice Richard J. Hughes, writing the court's groundbreaking decision in *In re Karen Ann Quinlan*, determined that "the right of privacy under the New Jersey state constitution encompasses the right to refuse life sustaining treatment" in circumstances where technological advances permit machines to keep patients alive who, on their own, would not survive.[2] We also learn that courts across the country followed the chief justice's reasoning and "embraced the core principles of *Quinlan* to establish rights, processes and boundaries for decisions near the end of life."[3] This was a modern problem and the court, using principles derived from earlier cases, balanced the state's interest in preserving life against principles of personal autonomy and the "voice" of the patient to develop processes that would protect the patient and respect her wishes whenever possible.

In chapter 6 on *State v. Hunt*, we come to understand the concerns that are raised when a state court of last resort relies on its state constitution to provide more expansive rights than those provided under the federal Constitution, even when the language of the two constitutions is similar. We observe various members of the court grappling with the standards that should be applied to guide judges when they are deciding whether the state constitution should be interpreted differently from its federal counterpart and we understand that a dialogue on the principles for state constitutional decision making has begun.

Or we read in chapter 1 about the court's decision in *Henningsen v. Bloomfield Motors* and we see how the justices reshape the common law to meet changing circumstances in the marketplace to protect consumers who have little bargaining power. We discover that a wave of consumer protection legislation followed *Henningsen*, placing the responsibility for the harms caused by manufacturers' products on the manufacturers themselves.

Each chapter provides insights into the court's approach and into how the court reached its decision. When the court holds that the state's funding for urban school districts does not comply with the state constitutional mandate, we observe in chapter 10 the tension between the court and the legislature as, in case after case over a period of nearly forty years, the court first accepts legislative action and later rejects the state's implementation as inadequate. It is a tension that may be inevitable when the court requires legislative action to implement constitutional values.

Each chapter deals with a seminal decision of the court. Whether or not readers agree with the results in each case, they will develop an understanding not only of how the court does its work but also about the law, and about how, in a variety of contexts and when the system is at its best, the law expands and develops to meet new challenges.

NOTES

1. Deborah T. Poritz, "The New Jersey Supreme Court: A Leadership Court in Individual Rights," *Rutgers Law Review* 60 (2008): 708.
2. See chapter 4, "*In Re Karen Ann Quinlan* (1976): Establishing a Patient's Right to Die in Dignity," xx.
3. Ibid.

Courting Justice

Introduction

PAUL L. TRACTENBERG

The New Jersey Supreme Court is consistently ranked "as one of the leading state supreme courts in the United States."[1] A critical assessment of American courts in the early 1990s said that it "appears on every list of innovative or prestigious courts."[2] By 2000, when the California courts fell from the short list of top state court systems, one writer urged them to "model . . . the Garden [State]" in its courts' commitment to activist decisions.[3]

This high regard was not always the case. Until 1947, when New Jersey adopted its pathbreaking state constitution, the state's court system was bulky and antiquated, hardly a model of independence and activism. One commentator described the shift from old to new constitution as an "exchange [of] America's worst court system for America's best" as "New Jersey goes to the head of the class."[4]

In celebrating the 1947 constitution's fiftieth anniversary, prominent New Jersey legal scholars joined in the accolades. They praised the state courts for addressing "urgent public needs left unattended by the other branches" and enumerated the factors that enabled the courts to be so independent and activist.[5]

By focusing on ten decisions the New Jersey Supreme Court rendered in a variety of fields over a period of more than fifty years starting in 1960 and ending in 2011, this book tells the story of how the court has exercised its widely touted independence and activism. These decisions shook the nation as well as the state of New Jersey. They provide dramatic support for those who laud the court.

Perhaps these decisions also provide support for those who decry what they see as the court's overreaching and intrusion into the functions of the other governmental branches. That debate in New Jersey mirrors a broad national debate about the proper role of courts. Should they be "activist," adapting the law to meet new and evolving circumstances, or should they be limited to "strict construction" of constitutional and statutory provisions that date back decades or centuries? Should the judiciary absolutely defer to decisions of the elected branches of government or should it be, in the words of the New Jersey Supreme Court, "the designated last-resort guarantor of the Constitution's command?"[6]

Selecting ten decisions of the New Jersey Supreme Court since 1947, out of the thousands it has issued, to tell that story and illuminate that debate was a formidable challenge. The process actually began in 1999, long before this book was even a twinkle in anyone's eye. Anticipating the new millennium, the *New Jersey Lawyer*, a publication of the state bar association, surveyed New Jersey judges and lawyers about the most important decisions of the twentieth century by New Jersey state courts and by federal courts and published the results.

The top state cases, in the order selected, were the tandem of *Robinson v. Cahill* and *Abbott v. Burke, Mount Laurel, Henningsen v. Bloomfield Motors, In re Karen Ann Quinlan*, and *Lepis v. Lepis*.

Love or hate the results of these cases, they and many other decisions by the modern New Jersey Supreme Court have had a profound effect not only on New Jersey but also on the rest of the nation and even, in some cases, on the world.[7] They tend to be, in the vernacular of some, liberal or activist decisions. That means they tend to find for the less powerful and influential against the more powerful and influential, for the public good against private interests.

In *Robinson/Abbott*, the beneficiaries of the court's decisions over four decades were millions of poor and minority students living in depressed urban areas. In *Mount Laurel*, the beneficiaries were those excluded from meaningful access to affordable housing in many parts of New Jersey by municipalities' exclusionary zoning practices. In *Henningsen*, those who benefited had been severely injured by defective automobiles where the precise cause of the defects could not be proven. In *Quinlan*, it was parents who wanted their daughter to die in dignity rather than be kept alive indefinitely by artificial means. In *Lepis*, it was a divorced wife who sought to reopen an alimony award based on substantially changed circumstances.

My long and deep involvement with the New Jersey Supreme Court in *Robinson/Abbott* and other educational cases, coupled with my expanded view of the court's pathbreaking work, led me to the idea of a book about the court's most important "modern" (post-1947) decisions. I started with the *New Jersey Lawyer*'s list of the five most important twentieth-century decisions and then decided to expand the list to ten. That made the selection of the cases to be included much more complicated. With the aid of several talented and diligent law student research assistants,[8] I developed a wide range of criteria for determining how influential decisions of the New Jersey Supreme Court were not only in New Jersey but also in the rest of the nation. Among these criteria was the frequency with which the cases were cited by other courts, in legal casebooks, in law review articles, and in the general press. With input from distinguished members of the bench, the bar, and the legal academy, I was able to identify dozens of important decisions that were considered candidates for inclusion to which the criteria were systematically applied. Finally, there were more qualitative judgments, including whether the cases lent themselves to interesting "stories" and whether, as a collection, they covered a wide variety of subject matter areas. Ultimately, the choice was mine and, although there were some close calls, I stand behind them.

The result was that I settled on four of the five *New Jersey Lawyer* decisions (*Lepis* was excluded because its impact, while substantial, was primarily limited to matrimonial lawyers) and six others: *Marini v. Ireland, State v. Hunt, Right to Choose v. Byrne, In the Matter of Baby M, Lehmann v. Toys 'R' Us*, and *Doe v. Poritz*.

From the start, my concept of the book was that each author should write a chapter telling the story of the case in a way and from a perspective that he or she preferred. I never sought to impose a uniform structure, style, or approach. Rather, I wanted ten flowers to bloom. All I asked of the authors was that they produce relatively brief chapters, with a modest number of endnotes, written in a way that would be accessible to a general readership. Despite the fact that law professors predominate, and that the authors who were directly involved in litigating the cases tended to write chapters delving into the cases in greater technical detail, I believe they did so brilliantly, but you, the readers, will be the ultimate judges of that.

Closing the circle is the book's concluding chapter. It tells the tale, in much greater detail than this introduction, of New Jersey's 1947 constitution, the potential it created for judicial independence and national leadership, and the chief justices of the New Jersey Supreme Court who led the way to the realization of that potential. The stories of the ten cases that come in between add the illustrative flesh and blood. These cases are presented in chronological order based on when the New Jersey Supreme Court rendered its most significant doctrinal decision or, in the case of *Abbott v. Burke*, its most recent decision.

The period since the 1947 constitution became a reality has been a remarkable six and a half decades, and the ten cases span five and a half of those decades. But, as some of the chapters suggest, the political climate of 2012 has raised questions about whether the court will be able to continue on that long and strong path. Beyond that, not all the chapters sing the praises of the court in unqualified terms. Some recognize that the New Jersey Supreme Court's push into relatively uncharted waters, perhaps inspired by a social as well as a legal vision, came at the expense of doctrinal purity. And, in some cases, for "political" reasons, the court stopped short of directly confronting the underlying problem, especially as it might relate to race.

NOTES

1. John B. Wefing, "The New Jersey Supreme Court 1948–1998: Fifty Years of Independence and Activism," *Rutgers Law Journal* 29 (1998): 701; see also Leigh B. Bienen, "A Good Murder," *Fordham Urban Law Journal* 20 (1993): 590 ("[T]he New Jersey Supreme Court has had a history of being a leader in the development of state constitutional doctrine").

2. John B. Gates and Charles A. Johnson, *The American Courts, A Critical Assessment* (Washington, DC: CQ Press, 1991), 111.

3. Kevin M. Mulcahy, "Modeling the Garden: How New Jersey Built the Most Progressive State Supreme Court and What California Can Learn," *Santa Clara Law Review* 40 (2000): 863 (outlining New Jersey's activists decisions on criminal procedure, right to refuse medical treatment, sexual assault/rape standard, and education reform).

4. Glenn R. Winters, "New Jersey Goes to the Head of the Class," *Journal of the American Judicature Society* 31 (1948): 131.

5. Jack Sabbatino, "Assertion and Self-Restraint: The Exercise of Governmental Powers Distributed Under the 1947 New Jersey Constitution," *Rutgers Law Journal* 29 (1998): 800; Wefing, "The New Jersey Supreme Court 1948–1998," 710; see also Brendan T. Byrne, "The Role of the Judiciary in the Modern Institutional State," *Seton Hall Law Review* 11 (1980): 653; Worrall F. Mountain, "Role of Judicial Activism," *Seton Hall Law Review* 10 (1979): 6; "Robinson v. Cahill: A Case Study in Judicial Self-Legitimization," *Rutgers Law Journal* 8 (1977): 508.

6. *Robinson v. Cahill*, 69 N.J. 133, 154 (1975).

7. Although this book's focus is on decisions by the modern New Jersey Supreme Court created by the 1947 state constitution, it is interesting, perhaps even prophetic, that in 1780 the New Jersey Supreme Court (not then the state's highest court) rendered what was ostensibly the first judicial decision in the newly formed United States striking down a legislative enactment. The decision preceded by twenty-three years the United States Supreme Court's landmark decision in *Marbury v. Madison* to the same effect. For more on the fascinating history and importance of *Holmes v. Walton*, see Bernard Schwartz, *A History of the Supreme Court* (New York: Oxford University Press, 1995), 7; Austin Scott, "Holmes v. Walton: The New Jersey Precedent," *American History Review* 4 (1899): 456; and Paul Axel-Lute, "Holmes v. Walton: Case File Transcriptions and Other Materials," *New Jersey Digital Legal Library* (October 2009), http://njlegallib.rutgers.edu/hw/. Special thanks are due Paul Axel-Lute, collection development librarian of the Rutgers School of Law–Newark law library, for bringing this case and the materials about it to my attention, and for writing a substantial paper on the subject.

8. I owe a great debt of gratitude to Danielle Weslock, Sarah Koloski, Guillermo Artiles, and Tarik Shah for their exemplary research and editorial assistance while they were students at, and, in one case, a recent graduate of, Rutgers School of Law–Newark.

1

Henningsen v. Bloomfield Motors, Inc. (1960)

Promoting Product Safety by
Protecting Consumers of Defective Goods

JAY M. FEINMAN AND CAITLIN EDWARDS

Ford Motor Company announced the culmination of the largest series of recalls in its history in October 2009: sixteen million cars, trucks, and minivans contained a faulty switch that created a risk of fire even when the vehicle was turned off. The toy in a McDonald's Happy Meal contains no dangerous lead paint, and the box warns parents that the toy contains small parts and is unsuitable for children under three years of age.

Safety recalls, child-safe toys, and other consumer protections are taken for granted today, but there was a time not so long ago when everyday products were dangerous and consumers who were injured by cars, toys, or other products faced a difficult road to recover compensation from manufacturers. About fifty years ago all of this changed, drastically and in a short period of time. The catalyst for this dramatic change was an unlikely source—a woman from Keansburg, New Jersey, who was injured when her new Plymouth sedan suddenly veered into a brick wall. When she initially sued the dealer who had sold her the car and Chrysler, the manufacturer, the state of the law posed roadblocks to her recovery. The New Jersey Supreme Court recognized that change was needed and issued an opinion that quickly would change the world of products liability and consumer protection.

The Case

On May 7, 1955, Helen Henningsen was "very happy" and "running around like a madwoman."[1] She and her husband, Claus, had gone from their home in Keansburg to nearby Bloomfield Motors, a Chrysler and DeSoto dealership, to buy a car that would be her Mother's Day present from Claus; it would be the first new car they had owned in seventeen years of marriage. Claus signed a contract for a Plymouth Club Sedan and put down a $1,000 deposit. (In a sign of the times, even though it was to be Helen's car, the couple always put major purchases in Claus's name.) The next day the dealer prepared the car for delivery, and they picked up their new car on May 9.

Over the next week Helen only used the car a couple of times to go to the store and around town. On May 19, she drove to Asbury Park. While driving home on Route 36 at about twenty miles per hour, she suddenly heard a "terribly loud noise . . . as if something cracked" under the hood; the steering wheel spun out of her hands, and the car veered sharply to the right and crashed into a highway sign and a brick wall.[2] The impact threw Helen's face into the steering wheel, knocking loose her teeth so they all had to be pulled out. The crash also broke five of her ribs and injured her left knee and ankle, requiring emergency treatment, two subsequent hospitalizations, and surgery to her left kneecap.

Breck Jones, the insurance appraiser who inspected the damaged vehicle, could not pin down the exact cause of the accident but concluded there must have been a mechanical defect, something "wrong from the steering wheel down to the front wheels."[3]

The Henningsens sued Bloomfield Motors and Chrysler Corporation, Helen for her injuries and Claus for damage to the car, the medical expenses he paid, and the loss of Helen's "society and services." Their legal theories were that Bloomfield and Chrysler were negligent in manufacturing or preparing the car and that they had made express or implied warranties—promises about the quality of the car. However, because of the state of the law in the late 1950s, in New Jersey and across the United States, the Henningsens faced some formidable obstacles.

First, they could not point to how Bloomfield or Chrysler had been negligent, or even what the defect in the car was. The Henningsens' lawyer argued that the Plymouth was new, the road where the accident occurred was smooth, Helen was not at fault, and Jones had acknowledged that something had gone wrong with the car. From this, the jury could infer that the accident must have been caused by a defect in the car's steering. But Chrysler and Bloomfield each pointed out that there was no proof that they had been negligent. Chrysler argued that the Henningsens had not demonstrated that Chrysler failed to use reasonable care in making the car. Bloomfield argued in turn that it had done nothing to the car other than the ordinary preparation for delivery. As Samuel Weitzman, Bloomfield's lawyer, put it, "We do not know what we should have done that they say we didn't do, and we do not know whether we didn't do something that we should have done. That is normally the definition of negligence."[4] The lack of proof was fatal to the negligence claim. Chrysler pointed out that in each of the precedents cited by the Henningsens' lawyer, there had been stronger, often direct, evidence of negligence.

Second, the sale of the car was accompanied by several warranties of quality, expressly made and implied by law, such as the warranty of merchantability—a promise that the car would perform the way cars normally should, including not suddenly veering off the road. But, in enforcing the warranties, the Henningsens faced yet another problem. Helen was injured in the Plymouth that Claus bought from Bloomfield who bought it from Chrysler. Could she enforce a warranty when she was not the purchaser? If so, who made what warranty, Bloomfield or Chrysler?

Under existing law, Helen's suit would be blocked by what Benjamin Cardozo, legendary chief judge of the New York Court of Appeals and later associate justice of the United States Supreme Court, had described as the "citadel of privity." Privity was a legal doctrine that barred claims for breach of warranty between persons who had not contracted with each other, just as Helen had not contracted with Bloomfield and neither she nor Claus had contracted with Chrysler. At the time, New Jersey decisions had ruled that warranty "is the creature of contract" and could only be asserted by one contracting party against another. Therefore, under settled law, Bloomfield argued that it had no legal obligation to Helen, and Chrysler argued that it had no obligation either to her or to Claus.

Third, even if Helen could sue to enforce the warranties, the sales documents that Claus had signed effectively forfeited their protections. Paragraph seven of the fine print on the back of the document stated that Chrysler guaranteed the car would be "free from defects in material or workmanship." Chrysler's responsibility in honoring that warranty, however, required it only to replace defective parts at the factory within the first ninety days or four thousand miles of ownership. Most importantly, it stated, "It is expressly agreed that there are no warranties, express or implied, made by either the dealer or the manufacturer" except for the ninety-day replacement warranty.

Claus had read the front page of the contract, but not the fine print on the back. Under the law, his ignorance of the fine print did not matter; having signed it, he was presumed to have agreed to all its terms. Therefore, the argument went, neither Chrysler nor Bloomfield owed any further obligation to the Henningsens.

When the case came to trial, many people testified: Claus; Helen; Harold Roman, Bloomfield's president; police officers and witnesses to the accident; one of Helen's doctors and other witnesses from the hospital where she was treated; and Breck Jones, the Henningsens' expert about the purchase of the car, the accident, and Helen's injuries. The trial judge agreed with Chrysler and Bloomfield that the negligence claim could not stand under existing law, and he dismissed it.

The warranty claims were a different story. When the judge instructed the jury on the law, he presented the steps by which it could surmount the privity barrier and the contract's disclaimer of warranty. Although he left the final decision to the jurors, he strongly suggested what their conclusion should be. As to the existence of a warranty, he said:

> When the defendant Chrysler Corporation manufactured the Plymouth car which the plaintiffs bought, it would be for you to say whether or not there was an implied warranty. . . . In fact, that is what they warranted. When they made the car, they said, "that car is reasonably suited for ordinary use."
>
> When the Bloomfield Motors . . . displayed the automobile for sale to the plaintiffs and sold it to them, that defendant also warranted that the automobile was reasonably suited for ordinary use.[5]

The warranty also would extend to Helen even though she was not the purchaser, because the car was purchased for her use. And the disclaimer would not bar the claim because, under the trial judge's novel theory, a disclaimer would not be effective "unless its inclusion in the contract was fairly procured or obtained."[6]

The jury found in favor of Helen and Claus and against both defendants, awarding Helen $26,000 and Claus $4,000 in damages. The defendants appealed to the appellate division, New Jersey's intermediate appeals court, complaining that the trial judge had erred on the warranty and other issues. Ordinarily, the case would be briefed and argued before a three-judge panel of the appellate division, the panel would decide the case, and, if the loser appealed further, the supreme court would decide whether to hear the case. Not here. The New Jersey Supreme Court, recognizing the importance of the issue, used its authority to reach down and take the case away from the appellate division and hear it right away.

The Arguments

Each of the parties began by submitting briefs—written arguments—to the court. The Henningsens went first, represented by Carmen Rusignola of Newark, aided by lawyers from the Hoboken firm of Baker, Garber & Chazen.[7] The negligence claim had been dismissed by the trial court, so the focus was on the warranty claims. Despite prevailing in the trial court, the plaintiffs faced the same obstacles as before. Existing law was against them on the extension of the warranty from Chrysler, through Bloomfield, to Claus and from the actual purchaser, Claus, to the injured party, Helen. They also had to confront the issue of effectiveness of the disclaimer in barring any claim.

To overcome these problems, they tried two approaches. First, they attempted either to distinguish the Henningsens' case from prior unfavorable decisions or to reinterpret prior decisions so they supported the Henningsens' position. This approach was untenable, though, and the defendants exposed it in their briefs, pointing out that the prior cases just did not say what the plaintiffs argued they did.

The second approach was more successful, however, and the court ultimately adopted it; the Henningsens' lawyers shifted ground. The case should be decided, they argued, not by drawing on precedents from dusty law books but by responding to the needs of the times. Accordingly, the lawyers placed as much emphasis on the work of legal scholars as on prior cases.

Most significant were citations to the two major tort law treatises of the times. William L. Prosser's text had predicted, enthusiastically if prematurely, that strict liability for defective products would be "the law of the future."[8] Fleming James viewed the primary function of tort law to be "social insurance," providing compensation for the victims of accidents by spreading the losses to manufacturers and society at large.[9] The scholars' theories provided the Henningsens' lawyers with authority to present to the court in support of their suggestion that the court reshape the law.

As to the making of the warranty, the Henningsens' brief argued that the dealer and the manufacturer were an economic unit as far as the public was concerned. The warranty extended to Helen because the car was really bought jointly in all but name; even more telling, the plaintiffs' lawyers encouraged the court to "consider the broader legal problems involved in warranty cases rather than decide the issue on the narrower factual matters in the record," so any user of a product would benefit from an implied warranty.[10]

The same approach dictated that the disclaimer of warranty was invalid:

> Anyone who has had the experience of purchasing a new car knows that the average purchaser, in the excitement generated by such a substantial purchase, does not look for the fine print on the back of the sheet. . . . If the manufacturer and dealer do not stand fully and completely behind the safety of their highly advertised product they should be required to state this fact clearly. . . . The sale of an automobile involves the public interest. Not only is the safety of the purchaser and his passengers involved, but also the safety of the public. . . . It is not in the public interest to permit the manufacturer and dealer to absolve themselves from responsibility for the safety of their products.[11]

The bottom line:

> In view of the economic "setup" in the industry and the fact that the manufacturers go to great expense to invite reliance by the public on their own reputations and in view of the fact that the manufacturers do exercise control over their dealers, it is only fair and equitable that the industry rather than the consumer be required to bear the loss resulting from defective products.[12]

The Henningsens' lawyers cited an even broader proposition from Prosser: "Social policy demands that the burden of accidental injuries caused by defective chattels be placed upon the producer, since he is best able to distribute the risk to the general public by means of prices and insurance."[13]

The defendants' lawyers mostly responded by pounding on the gap between the trial judge's jury charge and the established law. Chrysler, for example, criticized the charge's statement of implied warranty as ignoring "well settled" New Jersey law, pointing out that "plaintiff's brief is conspicuous by its absence of any authority to the contrary." (One of Chrysler's lawyers was Sidney M. Schreiber; fifteen years later Schreiber would be appointed to the New Jersey Supreme Court, where he would author several notable products liability opinions in the wake of the *Henningsen* decision.) On the effectiveness of the disclaimer, "the law is clear and has been well settled for over fifty years."[14] Bloomfield added, in response to Helen's argument, that she was not bound by a disclaimer she did not sign, that "*[n]o authority is cited*," which they emphasized with the italics. On the lack of privity between Helen and Bloomfield, "The law, in these circumstances, is firmly established in this State."[15]

The defendants did not ignore the Henningsens' argument that the times demanded a new approach, but they vehemently dismissed it. Bloomfield rejected the need for new law and argued that at most it applied only to a manufacturer and not to a middleman such as a car dealer. Chrysler, which had the most to lose because an adverse decision would affect every one of its car sales, was bolder. Point 10 of its brief was direct: "To change the settled law is not warranted or established by the facts adduced" in this case. Its lawyers derided "the thought thrown out by Dean Prosser and Professors Harper and James that perhaps a manufacturer should be the 'guarantor of his product.'" Such liability, they argued, was at odds with the precedents and, worse, beyond the court's competence to decide. "Reflection on the 'social policy' which motivates the concept that a manufacturer should be a guarantor opens up a large vista of questions . . . , questions which must be considered and resolved before adopting the law suggested by text book writers. Should not such a radical change, if it is made, be one for the legislature?"[16]

Chrysler's brief asserted that "the trial court was bound by the settled law."[17] Maybe so, but the New Jersey Supreme Court was not. The supreme court opinion by Justice John Francis on May 9, 1960—five years to the day after the Henningsens had picked up their new car—creatively wove together precedent and policy to reshape the law of products liability.

The Court's Opinion

The court first examined the warranty claim against Chrysler. It traced two developments that led it to conclude that, even though Claus did not buy the car from Chrysler directly, the manufacturer's warranty that the car would be safe was available to the consumer.

The first development was in the law. Legislatures and courts over the past fifty years had recognized that the ancient rule of caveat emptor ("let the buyer beware") did not fit, as the court described it, "a rapidly expanding commercial society."[18] As a result, rules had developed that an implied warranty of merchantability accompanied every sale. Particularly important was the right to recover damages for injuries caused by an unsafe product without having to prove that the seller was negligent or knew of the product defect.

The second development was in the economy. "With the advent of mass marketing, the manufacturer became remote from the purchaser, sales were accomplished through intermediaries, and the demand for the product was created by advertising media," Justice Francis wrote.[19] Indeed, automobile manufacturers exploited the use of intermediaries—their dealers such as Bloomfield Motors—to invoke the privity doctrine; by using dealers, they could claim that they had no direct contract with the buyers. And they drafted warranty disclaimers like the one given to the Henningsens that denied what their advertising promised. The court described the warranty terms as "a sad commentary upon the automobile manufacturers' marketing practices."[20]

The practice was not unique to Chrysler—the warranty was a standard term promulgated by the Automobile Manufacturers Association and used by all carmakers, giving buyers no choice. Although it guaranteed parts and workmanship, the warranty only provided for the replacement of a defective part, and then only if the part was sent back to the factory and if the manufacturer determined it to be defective. There was no remedy at all provided for defective workmanship. As the court pointed out, as in this case, if a defective part caused an accident, but was itself destroyed in the accident, there would be nothing left to examine and no remedy for the injured consumer. Even worse, the warranty disclaimed liability for personal injuries caused by the defect.

The court carried forward the legal development in light of the economic circumstances and held that Chrysler was liable for breach of warranty. Citing dozens of cases from across the country (and, like the trial court, scholars including Prosser and Harper and James), it identified a movement that was "most certainly gathering momentum" to remove the privity barrier in order to render the manufacturer liable.[21]

The movement began in food products, then extended to other products for personal use such as detergents and clothing, and further beyond to rope, cinder blocks, and other items. "We see no rational doctrinal basis for differentiating between a fly in a bottle of beverage and a defective automobile," Justice Francis wrote. "The unwholesome beverage may bring illness to one person, the defective car, with its great potentiality for harm to the driver, occupants, and others, demands even less adherence to the narrow barrier of privity."[22] The consequences would be a better allocation of the cost of injuries and an incentive to make safer products. "In that way the burden of losses consequent upon use of defective articles is borne by those who are in a position to either control the danger or make an equitable distribution of the losses when they do occur."[23]

The same approach led the court to strike down the limits Chrysler tried to impose in its warranty disclaimer. Acknowledging the rule that one who signs a document is presumed to have agreed to its terms, the court recognized the limits of this rule in a society dominated by mass marketing.

> In the framework of modern commercial life and business practices, such rules cannot be applied on a strict, doctrinal basis. The conflicting interests of the buyer and seller must be evaluated realistically and justly, giving due weight to the social policy evinced by the [statute defining a warranty], the progressive decisions of the courts engaged in administering it, the mass production methods of manufacture and distribution to the public, and the bargaining position occupied by the ordinary consumer in such an economy.[24]

While not abandoning "freedom of contract," the court recognized the ubiquity of "the standardized mass contract" presented to consumers on a take-it-or-leave-it basis. Other courts had increasingly scrutinized the reasonableness of warranty disclaimers on claim checks, parking lot tickets, leases, contracts between banks and their customers, and flight insurance policies. In the Henningsens' case, the salesman did not draw Claus's attention to the warranty disclaimer in fine print on the back of the document, nor is it likely that Claus would have understood that he was forfeiting claims for personal injury.

In short, the court concluded, part of its job is "to protect the ordinary man against the loss of important rights through what, in effect, is the unilateral act of the manufacturer."[25] The automakers all used the same warranty provision, leaving the car buyer no choice but to be exposed to "the grave danger of injury to himself and others that attends the sale of such a dangerous instrumentality as a defectively made automobile."[26] That choice was no choice at all, and the result was so inimical to the public good that the warranty disclaimer could not be enforced.

With that, the other issues in the case followed as of course. Bloomfield was held to an implied warranty under the same logic that led to Chrysler's liability. The burden on Bloomfield would likely not be too great, however. Quoting a

New York decision by Chief Judge Cardozo, the court predicted that the damages ultimately "will be borne where it is placed by the initial wrong."[27] If Bloomfield was held liable, it could pass that liability on to Chrysler, who was really responsible for the defect.

The defendants argued that the proof as to the cause of the accident was inadequate to demonstrate a breach of warranty. However, the Henningsens' evidence that they had done nothing wrong with the car and that the road conditions were good was enough to raise an inference that the steering was defective, because the purpose of warranty liability was to make the sellers liable even if they were not proven to be at fault.

Finally, just as the lack of a formal contractual relationship between Claus and Chrysler did not bar the warranty claim, so Helen's status as a user of the car was enough to allow her claim. Henceforth, not only the purchaser of the car but also members of his family and others using it with his consent, and perhaps others, would benefit from the implied warranty.

Henningsen Spreads across the Nation

On the day the opinion in Henningsen was announced, the Yale Law Journal was preparing to print an article by Prosser entitled "The Assault Upon the Citadel (Strict Liability to the Consumer)." In it he described the attack on the privity doctrine that immunized manufacturers from liability to injured users of their products. In typically colorful prose, Prosser reported that "War correspondents with the beleaguering army are issuing daily bulletins, proclaiming that the siege is all but over."[28] All but over, indeed. Prosser would write a successor article—"The Fall of the Citadel (Strict Liability to the Consumer)"—in which he announced that "the date of the fall of the citadel of privity can be fixed with some certainty. It was May 9, 1960, when the Supreme Court of New Jersey announced the decision in Henningsen v. Bloomfield Motors, Inc."[29]

As the subtitle of Prosser's articles indicates, the citadel that Henningsen breached was more than the hoary doctrine of privity. The New Jersey court's opinion sparked changes in the law that made manufacturers strictly liable to injured consumers, without proof of negligence and even in the absence of a contract. Moreover, the decision spurred an era in which consumer safety moved to the forefront of public consciousness and government policy.

The effects of the court's decision in New Jersey were immediate. Nineteen-year-old Alphonse Pabon was driving his new Ford along Route 4 in Paramus when his steering wheel locked and the car veered off the road and into a pole. Alphonse sued Ford Motor Co. and its dealer, Hackensack Auto Sales. The case came to trial before the Henningsen decision, so the trial judge dismissed Alphonse's breach of warranty claim; because the car had been bought for his sister, Maxine, by their father, Alphonse lacked privity with Ford and the dealer. When Alphonse's appeal was heard in October 1960, the appellate division applied the supreme court's new law and held that Alphonse had a claim for breach of an implied warranty that the car was safe to drive.[30]

The decision's effects in other states were even more important. If *Henningsen* caused the citadel of privity to fall, a decision of the California Supreme Court three years later erected a new structure on the rubble. William Greenman's wife gave him a Shopsmith Home Workshop (a combination wood lathe, saw, and drill) for Christmas in 1955. One day while turning a piece of wood on the lathe, the wood flew off and struck him in the forehead, fracturing his skull. Ten and a half months later Greenman sued the Hayseeds Corporation, the dealer from whom his wife had bought the Shopsmith, and Yuba Power Products, its manufacturer, arguing that poor design of the set screws allowed the piece of wood to fly off. Hayseeds and Yuba defended on the ground that Greenman had waited too long to notify them of the defect; the statute governing warranties required notice to be given within "a reasonable time."[31]

In *Greenman v. Yuba Power Products, Inc.*, which Prosser described as "one of the twin landmarks"[32] of the new law along with *Henningsen*, the California Supreme Court concluded that the issue of notice was irrelevant. Instead, it formulated a simple rule: "A manufacturer is strictly liable in tort when an article he places on the market, knowing that it is to be used without inspection for defects, proves to have a defect that causes injury to a human being."[33] The court pointed out that manufacturers had been held liable without proof of negligence and without privity in a chain of cases, beginning with the food and drink cases and extending through *Henningsen*. Although these were technically cases involving breach of warranty, the liability they imposed was not assumed by the manufacturer's contract, nor could it be limited by a contractual disclaimer (again citing *Henningsen*).

The California court stated a simple reason in support of its simple rule: "The purpose of such liability is to insure that the costs of injuries resulting from defective products are borne by the manufacturers that put such products on the market rather than by the injured persons who are powerless to protect themselves."[34] This statement reflected the view in *Henningsen* that "the burden of losses consequent upon use of defective articles is borne by those who are in a position to either control the danger or make an equitable distribution of the losses when they do occur."[35]

The New Jersey Supreme Court recognized that imposing an implied warranty of safety on the manufacturer and seller constituted "strict liability," liability that arose without the need for a contractual relationship and liability that could not be avoided through a broad disclaimer. The California Supreme Court took the next logical step and imposed liability in tort—the law of personal injuries—rather than in contract law, which was burdened by the legal fiction and complications of warranty law. For example, Greenman could sue for breach of an express warranty only because he had actually read the manufacturer's brochure touting the machine's quality; in tort it would not matter whether he read the brochure or not because the Shopsmith's presence on the market constituted a representation that it would be safe in normal use. As Prosser wrote, warranty "had been from the outset only a rather transparent device to accomplish the desired result of strict liability. . . . Why not, then, talk of the strict liability in tort?"[36]

And that is exactly what happened. Two years after *Greenman*, the New Jersey Supreme Court agreed that a "sound expression" for the principles of *Henningsen* was found in the concept of strict liability in tort.[37] The same year the prestigious American Law Institute adopted strict liability for defective products as part of its second "Restatement" of the law of torts. The much cited section 402A of the Restatement held manufacturers and sellers strictly liable for the distribution of products "in a defective condition unreasonably dangerous to the user or consumer."[38]

Courts in half the states responded to *Henningsen, Greenman*, and section 402A almost immediately, and most of the rest later followed suit, signaling, according to Prosser, "the most rapid and altogether spectacular overturn of an established rule in the entire history of the law of torts."[39]

This rich body of products liability law expanded protections for consumers. In *Henningsen* and *Greenman*, the defendants were the manufacturer and the retailer of a new product. Over time, the pool of potentially responsible parties expanded. In New Jersey, for example, liability was extended to a company that leased trucks for commercial use, a commercial builder of houses, a beauty parlor for injuries caused by giving a permanent wave, a used car dealer for failing to properly inspect or repair a car it sold, and a corporation that had bought all the assets of a predecessor that had made a defective product.

The content of their responsibility also was fleshed out. The accident that injured Helen Henningsen likely was caused by a manufacturing defect; that is, the car was improperly made. The precise problem with the steering was never identified, but the "terribly loud noise" she heard probably was the result of the failure of a defective part or defectively installed part. William Greenman, on the other hand, was injured by the defective design of the Shopsmith. His tool was manufactured properly according to the way it was designed, but the design created an unreasonable risk of injury because of the inadequate set screws. Courts also expanded liability for defects in warning notices; a prescription drug, for example, needs to be accompanied by warnings about who should take it, proper dosage, and possible side effects.

As the law developed, controversies naturally arose about how far each of these elements should be expanded. For example, every product design carries some risk of injury; a car cannot be made perfectly safe. When does a design present such an unreasonable risk that it should be labeled defective and subject the manufacturer to liability? Courts developed a variety of tests and a range of interpretations of those tests.

One test focused on the consumer's expectations: Does the design render the product more dangerous than the ordinary user of it would expect? Another test balanced the risks created by the design with the utility of the product as designed: Do the dangers created by its design outweigh the benefits?

As court decisions and legislative enactments on this issue ebbed and flowed, however, *Henningsen* remained vital. The injuries produced by defective products should be borne by the manufacturers that produce them without regard to contracts or their absence; the debate is how far to go in labeling a product "defective."

The Consumer Safety Revolution

The products liability revolution ignited by *Henningsen* marked three changes in the law. First, law became recognized as a mechanism for addressing social problems. Second, tort law and contract law—the bodies of law implicated in the case—were transformed. Third, the role of the courts as policy-making institutions was recognized. In each, the New Jersey Supreme Court was a leader.

The first change was a shift from law as a realm of *corrective* justice to law as an instrument of *collective* justice. In times past, law was seen as a mechanism for resolving disputes between individuals. It still does that, of course. But, in times past, scholars and judges saw the sole purpose of law as providing a remedy for wrongs between individuals. The court in *Henningsen* made clear that on important issues each case is not singular but representative of a larger class of cases, and the resolution of each case ought to take account of the larger class of cases as a social problem. The court's decision was not animated by sympathy for Helen Henningsen or a judgment about the wrongfulness of the behavior of Chrysler or Bloomfield Motors. Instead, the court recognized the case as an example of the broader problem of injury caused by mass-produced and mass-marketed automobiles, where manufacturers promoted their products by vigorous advertising, but attempted to insulate themselves from liability through the establishment of middlemen dealers and the presentation of severe warranty disclaimers.

The use of law as a tool to solve social problems had particular significance for tort law and contract law. In considering resolutions to the social problem of injury, tort law serves the social goals of producing safer products and compensating accident victims. The *Henningsen* court's principle for doing so, which became widely adopted, was enterprise liability.

Enterprises and activities ought to bear their true costs, including the costs of injuries they produce. When an enterprise is liable for the injuries it produces, it has an incentive to reduce injuries to the lowest reasonable level. By shifting the costs of an injury to all who benefit from an activity, enterprise liability effectively provides insurance as compensation against catastrophic losses otherwise suffered by individuals.

Enterprise liability is fair because it imposes the costs of an activity, including the costs of injuries it produces, on those who profit from it, and it promotes safety because it encourages them to reduce the incidence of injuries and therefore their costs. As the court stated in *Henningsen*, "in that way the burden of losses consequent upon use of defective articles is borne by those who are in a position to either control the danger or make an equitable distribution of the losses when they do occur."[40]

The New Jersey court also expanded protections for injured parties in areas beyond products liability. Landlords were held to have a duty to protect their tenants from the foreseeable criminal acts of others.[41] Doctors who failed to diagnose a pregnant woman's condition that created a possibility of birth defects in her unborn child are liable and were held to have a duty to pay extraordinary medical expenses incurred after the child was born.[42] When the court abrogated the ancient principle that "the king can do no wrong," municipalities and the state were held liable for their torts just as private parties.[43] Homeowners who served their guests alcohol were held liable in some cases for accidents caused by their guests on the way home.[44]

The vision of contract law changed as well. The traditional approach to contracts envisioned two independent individuals bargaining on an equal footing about contract terms that would be to their individual advantage. In holding Chrysler's warranty disclaimer ineffective, the court recognized that that conception no longer fit an economy of mass distribution. As the court pointed out, the disclaimer "is a standardized form designed for mass use. It is imposed upon the automobile consumer. He takes it or leaves it, and he must take it to buy an automobile. No bargaining is engaged in with respect to it."[45] The traditional model of bargaining no longer applied, so rather than simply enforcing a contract, the court had to "protect the ordinary man against the loss of important rights through what, in effect, is the unilateral act of the manufacturer."[46]

The recognition spread that the new mode of contracting required regulation rather than simple enforcement. Courts scrutinized more carefully terms in all sorts of standardized consumer contracts, and they expanded their authority to invalidate contracts they found to be "unconscionable" when they were the product of one-sided bargaining resulting in grossly unfair terms. Legislatures enacted many statutes that required clear disclosure of contract terms of the sort that was lacking in Chrysler's warranty disclaimer and regulated the content of terms in many different transactions.

In *Henningsen*, as in other cases, the court was not modest about its need to make policy. Chrysler argued that any change in the law as dramatic as the Henningsens sought and the court eventually accomplished should be made by the legislature, not the court. The issue was too complex for the court to resolve, and it was not the court's job to make social policy, Chrysler contended.

As every case discussed in this book makes clear, the New Jersey Supreme Court has been a leader in rejecting this limited approach. The court necessarily makes policy when it decides cases; there are no secret books it can consult to divine the true answers to legal questions so all it can do is weigh precedents, principles, and social policies to reach what it believes to be a just conclusion.

The court did recognize the need to consider a range of sources and the tenor of the times. "Public policy is a term not easily defined. Its significance varies as the habits and needs of a people may vary. It is not static and the field of application is an ever increasing one. . . . Public policy at a given time finds expression in the Constitution, the statutory law and in judicial decisions."[47]

What *Henningsen* and its aftermath also make clear is that the court does not act alone in making social changes. As political science professors G. Alan Tarr and Mary Porter explain, the court "has invited the legislature to enter into a dialogue on policy development."[48] The legislature has not been shy about participating in the dialogue. When the court abrogated sovereign immunity and made government actors liable for their torts, the legislature established the presumption that government actors were not liable and created a more limited list of situations in which liability could be imposed.[49] The legislature also limited the liability of homeowners who served alcohol to their guests.[50]

The court's partnership with other institutions also is demonstrated by the way in which the transformation of the law sparked by the New Jersey Supreme Court's decision in *Henningsen* coincided with other changes that promoted consumer protection. The public became more aware of the need for consumer safety and more active in pursuing it, and government regulation of unsafe products expanded greatly.

The most dramatic event spurring a consumer movement for safer cars was the furor surrounding the publication in 1965 of Ralph Nader's book *Unsafe at Any Speed*.[51] The book was best known for its attack on the Chevrolet Corvair, a sporty car that unfortunately was what *Car and Driver* magazine described as "one of the nastiest-handling cars ever built." Nader revealed that the car had a rear engine and suspension system that required punctilious maintenance and remarkable driving skills to prevent loss of control, facts that its manufacturer General Motors knew but ignored in the design and marketing of the car. Even worse for GM, the company responded to Nader's message by trying to discredit the messenger; its tactics included spying on him and tapping his telephone, interviewing his acquaintances about his religious beliefs, personal habits, and sexual proclivities, and having women try to entrap him into illicit relationships. When its tactics came to light, GM's president James Roche was forced to appear before a U.S. Senate committee and apologize. Ironically, the damages Nader collected in a suit against GM for invading his privacy funded more of his consumer-oriented activities.

Today Nader's activism has been taken up by numerous organizations. The Center for Auto Safety, which he cofounded, publicizes safety problems and lobbies for laws protecting consumers. *Consumer Reports* tests vehicles and provides recommendations, positive and negative, to auto buyers. The media regularly report crash test results, recalls, and problems with unsafe cars.

Government responded, too. Increased regulation on behalf of consumers was spurred by President John F. Kennedy's 1962 message to Congress announcing a Consumer Bill of Rights. Foremost among the rights was "the right to safety—to be protected against the marketing of goods which are hazardous to health or life."[52] Over the next few years legislation would create federal agencies to collect information and regulate the safety of consumer products, notably what is now called the National Highway Traffic Safety Administration (NHTSA) in 1966 and the Consumer Products Safety Commission in 1972. NHTSA conducts research, promulgates vehicle standards, works with manufacturers to recall defective vehicles, and occasionally even orders recalls.

With consumer organizations, the media, and government agencies acting as watchdogs for consumer safety, some have argued that lawsuits by injured victims like the one brought by Helen and Claus Henningsen are no longer necessary to ensure product safety. Auto manufacturers, pharmaceutical companies, insurance companies, medical groups, and trade associations from big business marching under the banner of tort reform have complained that we have too many lawsuits and too many lawyers.[53]

The lesson of *Henningsen* is just the opposite. Ralph Nader's book begins with the tale of Rose Pierini, whose left arm was severed when her Corvair flipped over while she was driving in Santa Monica, California, in 1961. Pierini sued General Motors, which paid her $70,000 precisely because an adverse jury verdict "would have profoundly shaken even this goliath of American industry. And what about the possible spillover into that dreaded chasm, public regulation?"[54]

The point remains true today. Litigation brings attention to dangers to the public, spurs other agencies to action, and fills the gaps left when other agencies do not act. Dangerous consumer products, medical negligence, nursing home abuses, dumping of toxic waste, and industrial products such as asbestos all have become the subjects of public concern and government regulation because of lawsuits brought by injured parties.

Even the creation of government agencies to improve auto safety has not obviated the need for private litigation. Tort law scholar Carl Bogus points out that "NHTSA has not only been captured, exhausted, besieged, ossified, cycled, demoralized, and co-opted but starved as well," subject to political influence and control by the industry it was meant to regulate, and systematically under-funded.[55] Accordingly, the agency has become less aggressive in ordering recalls and promulgating safety standards. Where it does act, it is often spurred by private litigation; where it does not, the legal system must fill the gap.

What is required is a partnership among the courts, other government agencies and private institutions. In the area of product safety initiated by *Henningsen*, the partnership has been enormously successful. Cars are better designed, better built, and contain abundant safety devices. The toy in a McDonald's Happy Meal is safe for most children, and parents are warned when it poses even the slightest danger to small children. The revolution begun by the New Jersey Supreme Court in *Henningsen* continues to bear fruit in greater safety and better lives for New Jerseyans and all Americans.

NOTES

1. Testimony of Helen Henningsen, Plaintiff on Direct Examination, *Henningsen v. Bloomfield Motors, Inc.*, 161 A.2d 69 (N.J. 1960) (No. A-185–58).
2. Ibid.
3. Brief for Plaintiffs as Cross-Appellants, *Henningsen*, 161 A.2d.
4. Transcript of Opening Statement on Behalf of Defendant, Bloomfield Motors, *Henningsen*, 161 A.2d.
5. Transcript of Court's Charge, *Henningsen*, 161 A.2d.
6. Ibid.
7. Brief for Plaintiffs as Cross-Appellants, *Henningsen*, 161 A.2d. Actually, Bernard Chazen, rather than Rusignola, argued the case on behalf of the Henningsens in the New Jersey Supreme Court.
8. William L. Prosser, *The Law of Torts* (St. Paul, MN: West, 1941), 692.
9. Fowler V. Harper and Fleming James Jr., *The Law of Torts* (Boston: Little, Brown, 2006); see also George L. Priest, "Invention of Enterprise Liability: A Critical History of the Intellectual Foundations of Modern Tort Law," *Journal of Legal Studies* 14 (1985): 461.
10. Brief for Plaintiffs as Cross-Appellants, *Henningsen*, 161 A.2d.
11. Ibid.
12. Ibid.
13. Ibid. (quoting William L. Prosser, The *Law of Torts*, 2nd ed. (St. Paul, MN: West, 1955), 506).
14. Brief for Defendant, Chrysler Corp. as Cross-Respondent and Appellant, *Henningsen*, 161 A.2d.
15. Brief for Defendant, Bloomfield Motors, Inc., as Cross-Respondent and Appellant, *Henningsen*, 161 A.2d.

16. Brief for Defendant, Chrysler Corp. as Cross-Respondent and Appellant, *Henningsen*, 161 A.2d.

17. Ibid.

18. *Henningsen*, 161 A.2d at 77.

19. Ibid. at 80.

20. Ibid. at 78.

21. Ibid. at 81.

22. Ibid. at 83.

23. Ibid. at 81.

24. Ibid. at 84.

25. Ibid. at 94.

26. Ibid. at 95.

27. Ibid. at 96.

28. William L. Prosser, "The Assault Upon the Citadel (Strict Liability to the Consumer)," *Yale Law Journal* 69 (1960): 1099.

29. William L. Prosser, "The Fall of the Citadel (Strict Liability to the Consumer)," *Minnesota Law Review* 50 (1965–1966): 791.

30. *Pabon v. Hackensack Auto Sales, Inc.*, 164 A.2d 773 (N.J. Super. App. Div. 1960).

31. *Greenman v. Yuba Power Products, Inc.*, 377 P.2d 897, 899 (Cal. 1963).

32. Prosser, "Fall of the Citadel," 803.

33. *Greenman*, 377 P.2d at 900.

34. Ibid. at 901.

35. *Henningsen*, 161 A.2d at 81.

36. Prosser, "Fall of the Citadel," 802.

37. *Santor v. A & M Karagheusian, Inc.*, 207 A.2d 305 (N.J. 1965).

38. Restatement (Second) of Torts: Special Liability of Seller of Product for Physical Harm to User or Consumer § 402A(1) (1965).

39. Prosser, "Fall of the Citadel," 793–94.

40. *Henningsen*, 161 A.2d at 81.

41. *See Braitman v. Overlook Terrace Corp.*, 346 A.2d 76 (N.J. 1975).

42. *See Procanik v. Cillo*, 478 A.2d 755 (N.J. 1984).

43. *See Willis v. Department of Conservation. and Economic Development*, 264 A.2d 34 (N.J. 1970).

44. *See Kelly v. Gwinnell*, 476 A.2d 1219 (N.J. 1984).

45. *Henningsen*, 161 A.2d at 87.

46. Ibid. at 94.

47. Ibid. at 94–95.

48. G. Alan Tarr and Mary Cornelia Aldis Porter, *State Supreme Courts in State and Nation* (New Haven: Yale University Press, 1988), 233.

49. New Jersey Statutes Annotated, sec. 59:1 (West 2012).

50. Ibid., sec. 2A:15–5.7 (West 2012).

51. Ralph Nader, *Unsafe at Any Speed* (New York: Grossman, 1965).

52. Special Message to the Congress on Protecting the Consumer Interest, 1962, *Public Papers of the Presidents of the United States* 93 (March 15, 1962).

53. See Jay M. Feinman, *Un-making Law: The Conservative Campaign to Roll Back the Common Law* (Boston: Beacon Press, 2004).

54. Nader, *Unsafe at Any Speed*, 8.

55. Carl T. Bogus, *Why Lawsuits Are Good for America* (New York: NYU Press, 2001), 157.

2

Marini v. Ireland (1970)

Protecting Low-Income Renters
by Judicial Shock Therapy

RICHARD H. CHUSED

Within a thirty-four-day period in 1970, courts in Illinois, Washington, D.C., and New Jersey announced decisions that dramatically altered a central aspect of landlord-tenant law—the ability of landlords to summarily dispossess tenants for failure to pay rent. Each decision reached essentially the same conclusion: tenants were entitled to defend against summary dispossession if conditions in their residences endangered health and safety or if there were other unfair conditions imposed on their tenancies. These decisions opened the floodgates of change. Other reformist court decisions or legislative enactments followed in almost every state. The stories of the Illinois and D.C. decisions, *Rosewood v. Fisher* and *Javins v. First National Realty, Corp.*, have been told elsewhere in great detail,[1] and most first-year law students around the nation read *Javins* in their property law courses. But, surprisingly, the New Jersey Supreme Court's decision in *Marini v. Ireland* has received much less attention.[2] Placing that decision more solidly on the historical record is long overdue.

The importance of a major case is difficult to measure without knowing something about the social, cultural, and historical background of the dispute. *Marini* arose out of the maelstrom that was New Jersey in the 1960s. When I arrived at Rutgers University School of Law in Newark during the summer of 1968 to begin my teaching career, Newark was in chaos. The Reverend Martin Luther King Jr. had been assassinated on April 4. From July 12 to July 17 the summer before, rioting had left the core of the city in shambles. Whites had already left the city in large numbers to move to the suburbs, and the flight accelerated after 1967. Within a few years of my arrival, many of the main businesses in the downtown core downsized or closed, leaving empty building hulks behind. Driving up Springfield Avenue—the main 1967 riot corridor—was to go through a depressing stretch of poverty, gutted buildings, empty lots, and littered streets.

Crime rates skyrocketed. The city, in short, was a wreck—the butt end of tragic jokes on television and devastating commentaries in the media. It routinely was placed on lists of the worst cities in America.[3]

Camden, Newark's sister city in distress to the south and the site of the building that gave rise to *Marini*, also was in terrible condition. Riots sparked by the police beating and death of a Puerto Rican motorist erupted in August 1971, not quite a year after *Marini* was decided by the New Jersey Supreme Court. Major industrial facilities, including large plants run by RCA and the New York Shipbuilding Corporation, downsized or closed during the 1960s.[4] Between 1950 and 1970 the town's population declined by about 17 percent, and by an equal amount from 1970 to 1980.[5]

The alarming situations in Newark, Camden, and other inner-city areas of the nation's most densely populated state had a palpable impact on the New Jersey Supreme Court's desire to bring landlord-tenant disputes before it and on its overtly reformist resolution of the legal issues. Just as the relationships among poverty, politics, urban disturbances, and the law in Washington, D.C., profoundly influenced the decision in *Javins*, so too the desperate situations in Newark and other cities deeply affected judicial developments in New Jersey.[6]

In this chapter, I reconstruct some of that history—presenting a portrait of the times and describing some of the reasons the courts responded aggressively to the problems they perceived. To do that, I will take a four-stage journey. First, I will provide a few intimate, personal stories to bring to life how desperately bad the situation in Newark, and by implication other New Jersey cities, was in the late 1960s. Second, I will present a portrait of how the New Jersey Supreme Court responded to the crisis. That will entail a trek through landlord-tenant law as it was prior to the decision in *Marini*, as well as a look at the court's decision in *Reste Realty v. Cooper*[7]—a crucial opening gambit in the reforms *Marini* instituted a year later. That tour should make it easier to understand why, as a matter of traditional legal logic, the *Reste* and *Marini* opinions were partly untenable, if not incoherent. The extraordinary nature of the opinions symbolized the level of desperation felt by the New Jersey Supreme Court and the compelling power of demands among urban residents for change in the operation of the state's landlord-tenant courts. The court must have concluded that eviction law needed some shock therapy. Third, I do not want to leave the impression that New Jersey's high court behaved much differently or more irrationally than courts in other states. A very brief description of events elsewhere will make that clear. Finally, you might be curious about whether all the hoopla actually accomplished very much. I will end with a few brief thoughts on that issue.

Setting the Stage

The atmosphere at Rutgers Law School when I arrived in 1968 to join the faculty was tense and frenetic. You could cut the anxiety with a knife. After the riot in 1967 and the assassination of Martin Luther King Jr. in 1968, the school was the site of negotiations among representatives of the city, county, and state governments with members of Newark's black community over what various government entities, including the law school, should do. Those discussions led to a decision by Willard Heckel, then dean of the law school and a remarkable human being, and others in the law school community to seek approval from the faculty to establish three clinics—the Constitutional Litigation Clinic, the Administrative Process Project (a law school–run bureau in the state attorney general's office to create new methods to enforce fair housing laws), and the Urban Legal Clinic—in that order at the rate of one a year.[8] At my first faculty meeting, the vote was taken and, not without controversy, the clinics were approved. The Constitutional Litigation Clinic was established immediately and the other two followed. I was quickly thrust into discourse about the depth of need in the Newark community for law reform and action, a discourse that deeply affects the structure of legal education in New Jersey to this day.

Other events were even more telling. Two stand out, both related to control of the government of Newark by a corrupt, deeply racist white power structure. Shortly after my arrival in Newark, lawyers and law teachers were asked to participate in a court-watching project at the city's municipal court. Stories about mistreatment of black citizens by the court were legion. Various community groups, as well as the local chapters of the American Civil Liberties Union and the National Lawyers Guild, wanted to document them. Lawyers were sought out for the court-watching task to reduce the likelihood that court personnel would push the visitors around.

Down Broad Street I went with my yellow pad and pencil. I arrived early and sat near the back—the only white person in the public seating area. White court personnel—bailiff, clerks, and others—milled around at the front. The mood got ugly as those having business before the court began to arrive. The white court personnel, speaking quite loudly to ensure that those in the black audience heard their remarks, began spouting verbal harangues about niggers, welfare queens, absent fathers, and criminals. My jaw dropped in amazement. My yellow pad began to fill up.

After a few minutes of this, one of the court officials came over and asked me in a less than kindly manner what I was doing there. For the first time in my life, I pulled rank, saying I had just arrived in town to take a job teaching at Rutgers Law School and commenting that I wanted to see how things worked in the city. He coolly stared at me for a moment and left me alone. But even after the court personnel knew who I was, their nasty verbal assaults continued. They must have thought their power was unchallengeable.

The judge's attitude toward the litigants was not much better. Although he did not use any overtly nasty language, his demeanor could be characterized at best as curt. Anger among the court's clients was clearly visible in their body language, tone of voice, and demeanor. The experience made clear to me more than anything else could why the city had exploded in violence the year before.

Two years later much of the black political community supported Kenneth Gibson's campaign to become the first black mayor of the city. White out-migration and black in-migration over the previous twenty years had increased the possibility that a black candidate could win the seat. On Election Day in 1970, law faculty and students were asked by the Gibson campaign to serve as poll watchers. A group was assigned to a spot in the all-white North Ward. They were not greeted with open arms at the polling place. A law student and I were asked to pick them up when their shift was over. We went to the polling place to meet the team and walked as a group back to the car. A group of thugs chased us. We got away by the skin of our teeth—scrambling into a Volkswagen Beetle as our pursuers bent the hinges of one door out of shape just as we sped away. The drive back to the law school was frenetic as we raced down the streets with one door unable to be fully closed. Our testimony at an emergency chancery court hearing a short time later led to the impoundment of the ballot boxes. Newark, like other cities in the state with deeply felt racial tensions, was a very nasty place. Although Gibson won the election, the campaign's rough edges left an indelible impression on those living in both Newark and the rest of New Jersey.

Such personal anecdotes only touch the surface of Newark's troubles in the late 1960s and early 1970s. The rapidity and depth of the city's decline were remarkable. Between 1950 and 1970, the population of the city fell by 13 percent. But that single data point hides an incredible flow of humanity into and out of Newark. In that same twenty years, the city was transformed from a majority-white to a majority-black metropolis—the white population of Newark declined 54 percent, while the nonwhite population increased by 183 percent.[9]

Such dramatic shifts were accompanied by wholesale disruptions in the fabric of urban life, striking changes in commuting patterns and job locations, and a significant drop in the number of middle-class residents and resident property owners. As middle-class whites left, they were not replaced by either a similar number of people or a population as financially capable of buying property, maintaining businesses, and reconstructing a framework of social and economic life designed for the needs of the new residents. The transition was made more difficult by the unwillingness of many majority-white financial and other institutions to provide assistance or support to the incoming urban dwellers. Social service organizations, nonprofit support groups, religious institutions, and other establishments closed and often were not replaced.

TABLE 2.1.

Changing Demographics of Newark

Year	Newark total population	White population	% population white	% decline in white population	Nonwhite population
1950	438,776	363,149	82.8		75,627
1960	405,220	265,889	65.6	26.8	139,331
1970	382,417	168,382	44.0	36.7	214,035
1980	329,248	101,417	30.8	39.8	227,831
1990	275,221	78,771	28.6	22.3	196,450
2000	273,546	72,490	26.5	8.0	201,056

Source: U.S. Census data, 1950–2000.

As George Sternlieb summarized the situation in his classic study, the decline in Newark's housing stock was due in significant part to the decline of resident ownership of leasehold property:

> [T]here is no question of the significance of landlord residence, particularly single-parcel landlords, as insurance of property maintenance of slum tenements. Given the priority accorded by multiple-parcel owners to tenant problems as an inhibitor [to upkeep] . . . the lack of feeling on this score by resident landlords, coupled with their good record in maintenance, is most significant. It is the resident landlord, and only the resident landlord, who is in a position to properly screen and supervise his tenantry. No one-shot wave of maintenance and paint up-sweep up campaign can provide the day-to-day maintenance which is required in slum areas. Given the relatively small size of Newark tenement units, and others like them, this can only be accomplished by a resident landlord. The record of these landlords . . . is such as to inspire confidence in their future behavior on this score.[10]

The vast scope of problems confronting urban New Jersey was catalogued by two reports issued in 1968—the Kerner Commission Report, assembled by the National Advisory Commission on Civil Disorders convened by President Lyndon Johnson in response to the nationwide stream of riots between 1965 and 1967, and the Report for Action, the lengthy commentary issued by the Governor's Select Commission on Civil Disorder in the State of New Jersey.

The Kerner Commission spent a great deal of time studying the situations in Detroit and New Jersey—sites of two of the worst outbursts of urban disorder.[11] In both the federal and state reports, concerns were expressed about tensions between largely white police departments and residents of black communities, poor housing conditions, the impact of urban renewal and highway construction programs, unemployment, dysfunctional schools, poor health care, and the widespread perceptions that courts operated arbitrarily and unfairly.

Anyone living and working in New Jersey in the late 1960s knew that major portions of the state were in deep trouble. Both politicians and courts sensed a need for urgent action. Whether that sense of urgency emerged from fears about additional racial disorders or heartfelt desires to begin solving deep social wounds made little difference. There was both a local and a national consensus that something had to be done. For a brief historical moment, major legislative reforms were adopted and courts took risks by joining the efforts. Congress adopted Civil Rights Acts in 1964, 1965, and 1968.[12] The Office of Economic Opportunity was created in 1964 as part of President Johnson's War on Poverty.[13] Among many community-based initiatives, that agency developed the still-extant Head Start and national legal services programs.

The Judicial Response

Given the distressing events occurring across the nation and in New Jersey, as well as the growing restiveness and voting power of black citizens, it is easy to understand why those sitting on the New Jersey Supreme Court felt there was an urgent need to grapple with some of the issues within their control. They certainly sensed that "rebellion" was brewing outside, that one of the commonly articulated reasons for the riots in Newark and elsewhere in the state was the perception among black and poor people that judicial forums they frequented were unfair, and that reforms in some areas were long overdue.[14] The New Jersey Supreme Court then had a well-deserved reputation for initiating major reforms in noncriminal legal doctrine,[15] and the justices sitting on the court in the late 1960s and early 1970s, as a group, were generally open to arguments for changing existing law.[16]

When presented with an opportunity to decide two landlord-tenant cases shortly after Martin Luther King's assassination, the court moved forward with its law reform agenda. On May 14, 1968, only forty days after King's death, the justices agreed to review the appellate division decision in a commercial lease dispute—*Reste Realty Corp. v. Cooper.* Arguments were heard on November 18, and the decision was rendered the following year on March 17, 1969.[17] The *Reste* dispute, though not directly about the ability of residential tenants to raise defenses when landlords sought their eviction for nonpayment of rent, still provided the court with an opportunity to weaken or remove a series of old legal obstacles to reforming landlord-tenant courts.

About six months after *Reste* was decided, the court, aware that *Marini v. Ireland* was pending in the appellate division, certified the case on its own motion for immediate review. That action was unusual and spoke volumes about the court's determination to deal with landlord-tenant issues. Arguments were heard in short order on February 16, 1970, and the decision was issued only three months later—on May 18, 1970—while the Gibson mayoral campaign was gearing up.[18]

Preexisting Eviction Law

Why did landlord-tenant law become such a focus of attention for both those agitating in the streets of Newark and those sitting on the New Jersey Supreme Court? The state of the legal doctrine just before the justices heard arguments in *Reste* was horribly outmoded. Its impact—deeply felt in impoverished urban communities all across the nation—is best described by another tale. While in law school, I went to visit the landlord-tenant court in Chicago as part of a 1967 summer internship working with a tenants' union on the near north side of the city. I watched the long call of cases at the beginning of the court day. Most of the calls went unanswered by tenants, leading to the issuance of default judgments for landlords.

When cases finally began to be called for "hearings" where tenants had shown up, they were handled in remarkably rapid fashion. The cases of a single landlord were called in sequence so that lawyers representing different landlords would not have to constantly shuffle back and forth to the dais. Before the landlords' lawyers could say anything, the judge usually asked the tenants, "Have you paid the rent?" The answer generally was no. Without waiting for an explanation, the judge would say, "Judgment for possession for [name of the landlord]. Call the next case." In short, tenants were summarily evicted for not paying rent no matter what the circumstances.

One particularly poignant case has stuck in my mind for these last forty-five years. I wrote about it in a 2007 article.

> The cases were being called by the clerk when an elderly, thin, white woman rose from her seat in response to hearing her name. Her gait was quite slow—stooped over and supported by a wooden cane. She was dressed in a frilly, long white dress and a white hat with a veil. It struck me that she had picked out her finest clothes to wear that morning. Perhaps her generation thought it appropriate to dress up for a court appearance—like going to church. But this was no church. When she was about half way to the front of the court—even before she passed the bar—the judge impatiently asked, "Have you paid the rent?" She

looked up at him as best she could and began softly speaking. "No, but. . . ." She was cut off in mid-sentence by the court curtly saying, "Judgment for landlord. Call the next case." The woman continued to slowly approach the bench, raising her right hand—her left still resting on the cane—as if she was trying to get the judge's attention. The room became unusually quiet. Her apparent desire to continue talking was stopped by the judge who without a hint of emotion leaned forward and said, "Ma'am, your case has been decided. You can go now." Crestfallen, she slowly turned and with small, careful steps, worked her way toward the rear of the room. The next case was called and decided before she reached the courtroom door. A few tenants watched her sadly. Attention to her quickly faded as additional cases were called and quickly disposed of. I was stunned. I often wonder what happened to her. Where did she go?[19]

What sort of theater was I watching? This was a courtroom where only one bit of information was deemed important—whether the rent had been paid. No other aspects of the landlord-tenant relationship were allowed to disturb the march of "justice." The Chicago result was callous at best, but the court followed the existing "law" to the letter—just as New Jersey courts did for decades in deciding cases in exactly the same fashion. Two sets of legal rules combined to produce these results—one dealing with the substantive nature of a lease and the other with the procedures used to evict residential tenants. The combination produced tribunals that urban tenants viewed as blatantly favorable to landlords and devoid of sympathy for the plight of even the most impoverished tenants residing in deplorable conditions.

The early substantive law of land leases arose in largely agricultural settings. In return for virtually unchecked authority to use land, a tenant agreed to pay rent, to maintain the land, and to return it in its original condition to the owner when the lease expired. In those days, the most important asset leased was usually the land itself. Requiring the tenant to maintain it was probably sensible. As a result, English law provided for an "action in waste"—an action by the true owner for damage to the property or to its value occurring during possession by a nonowner like a tenant,[20] a position absorbed into New Jersey's statutes in 1795.[21] If, during the nineteenth century, a tenant destroyed a barn or cut down all the timber (rather than just the amount needed to cook or keep warm) on a parcel of land, the landlord could recover damages.

As New Jersey began to industrialize, the old rules were applied to commercial tenants without much thought about whether changing circumstances should lead to changes in the rules. In *Moore v. Townshend*, the first leasehold repair case decided by New Jersey's highest court, a landlord claimed that a glassworks factory tenant failed to maintain the facilities, including the molds and tools which came with it.[22] The tenant was required to pay $550 to the land-lord in damages.

This rule of waste law worked in tandem with limitations imposed by nineteenth-century contract law and civil procedure rules. Traditionally, con-tract claims were limited to those arising from a single covenant or contrac-tual provision. Defendants could raise only defenses specifically related to that claim. What we now know as a counterclaim—the right to respond to a lawsuit by filing another one back against the plaintiff—was barred. If a landlord sued a tenant for the rent, the tenant could not defend by arguing that the landlord had breached a promise to maintain the premises. Such a claim could only be resolved in a separate case brought for that purpose. The claims by landlord and tenant were independent of one another.

This is demonstrated well by the early twentieth century case of *Stewart v. Childs Co.*[23] Childs Company agreed to lease a building from Stewart for a res-taurant and a "steam apparatus that perfects the coffee" in the basement. The twenty-year term began in 1902. The lease agreement contained express cov-enants providing that the tenant would pay the $3,000 yearly rent when it fell due and that the landlord would "at all times during the said lease keep the said cellar waterproof at his own expense." The basement turned out not to be waterproof. The landlord did not make repairs or install adequate pump-ing equipment. As a consequence, Childs Company abandoned the premises in 1909, and the landlord sued for rent. The court ruled that the covenant to pay rent and the covenant to keep the basement dry were independent, that "breach of the covenant to keep the cellar waterproof was not a defense to an action for rent," and that the tenant had to pay the rent when it fell due despite the fact that the landlord violated the terms of the lease.

The Childs Company attempted to defend the action for rent not only by claiming that the dry basement covenant and the covenant to pay rent were interdependent, but also that Childs had been "constructively evicted" from the premises. Constructive eviction excused a tenant from the obligation to pay rent when the landlord failed to deliver possession to the tenant or took actions that deprived the tenant of all ability to use the premises. Even though a ten-ant's promise to pay rent was independent of virtually all the landlord's prom-ises in a lease, a landlord still was obligated to leave the tenant in undisturbed possession for the full term of the lease. That minimal level of mutuality was required in order to prevent landlords from renting property, kicking tenants out, and suing them for the rent.

Even though Childs Company was not able to operate its coffee equipment or store goods in the basement, the court refused to find that it was construc-tively evicted. "We are unable to find," the court wrote, "any evidence that shows that the landlord . . . did anything with the intention of depriving the tenant of the enjoyment of the premises." The tenant's right to possession of the building was not disturbed. The tenant, after all, was free to arrange for the water to be pumped out of the basement! While the lessee was free to file another case in contract alleging breach of the dry basement covenant, the rent had to be paid in the meantime.[24]

The final piece of the nineteenth-century legal structure was put in place in 1847 when New Jersey adopted a statute permitting the summary dispossession of nonpaying tenants. As towns and cities grew, pockets of poverty emerged, transiency became more common, and migration to western areas of the nation increased, and landlords began to complain about their inability to arrange for speedy transitions from one tenant to another. Ejectment, the traditional claim for possession of land, was slow, cumbersome, and laden with requirements that sometimes protected tenants.[25] The same issues had arisen in New York earlier in the century, resulting in adoption of "summary dispossess" legislation in 1820.[26] The New York statute became the model for New Jersey twenty-seven years later. A provision barring all appeals from summary actions was tossed in for good measure.[27]

As a result, New Jersey tenants not only were barred by substantive contract rules from raising virtually all contractual defenses or filing any counterclaims to suits seeking payment of overdue rent, but they also could be removed quickly if they failed to pay. Those tenants with valid claims were forced to either continue paying rent while they pursued their claims or cede possession and pursue their issues later. In general, summary dispossess courts required quick responses by tenants, barred use of counterclaims, and allowed removal of tenants in as little as a month. The lack of legal assistance for poor urban tenants made it virtually impossible to mount a sustained judicial challenge to those practices or to lobby legislatures for change. As a result, nineteenth-century eviction practices remained intact until the New Jersey Supreme Court decided *Reste* and *Marini*. There is no need to put a polite gloss on the situation. Landlord-tenant courts in Newark and every other large city in the nation were ugly places. My experience watching that elderly woman walk out of the courtroom in Chicago symbolized the anguish of the era—a sometimes seething anger in minority and poor communities at the unwillingness of people in positions of authority to see unfairness even when it was literally staring them in the face.

Intervention of the New Jersey Supreme Court

Reste Realty v. Cooper was a surprising vehicle for the initiation of reforms in New Jersey's residential landlord-tenant law. It was, after all, a commercial case. After the landlord's oral promise to repair a leak allowing rainwater to seep into the rented space went unfulfilled, the tenant moved out. On its face, it was a simple constructive eviction dispute—one the court could easily have decided for the tenant without much ado. But the justices saw a chance to make some pronouncements and, given the historical circumstances, took it. The court's resolution of the litigation, a suit for rent against a tenant forced to relocate her business because of rainwater leaking into the lower level of Reste's building, led to two important changes.

First, the court concluded that a lease was a modern contract, with its covenants and clauses part of a unified legal instrument structuring a relationship between two people or entities. The residue of the old independent covenant idea was washed away. Second, the test for constructive eviction was substantially eased. Rather than requiring tenants to show that they were permanently deprived of possession by actions of the landlord, the court ruled that tenants only had to show a material breach of the leasehold contract or some substantial interference with their right to possess the premises.

Highlighting the three kinds of legal verbiage used in the opinion makes it easier to understand how extraordinary the court's results were. The first change in the old constructive eviction requirement that a tenant be "permanently deprived of possession" involved property-law talk about the covenant of quiet enjoyment—the boilerplate clause in every lease guaranteeing that a tenant's property right to possession will not be disturbed by the landlord during the term of the lease. The second form of verbiage about "material breach" was contract-law talk and took explicit advantage of the contract law concept favoring interdependence of the various clauses of a lease. The third form of verbiage about "substantial interference with possession" was tort-law talk and placed duties of care on landlords. Put more simply, the court pulled ideas from an array of legal areas in its effort to modify preexisting rules. It suggests strongly that the justices were searching for all available tools to support their landlord-tenant law reform efforts.

Putting these ideas together, the tenant Cooper was allowed to use the breach of the landlord's express promise to fix the water seepage problems as a defense to the action for rent. She no longer had to file an independent action in another court. She was able to claim that the breach so substantially interfered with her possessory interest that she could either claim constructive eviction or the right to cancel the lease contract because of a material breach. And she was able to invoke the landlord's violation of its express duty of repair to justify her decision to leave the premises. Along the way, the court also made liberal use of exceptions to the parole evidence rule barring use of oral promises to modify written agreements and the statute of frauds requiring that leases longer than a year must be in writing to allow the tenant to use the landlord's oral promise to repair for her benefit.[28] In reaching these conclusions, however, the court issued a stream of dicta—statements in opinions not necessary to the decision. Rather than deciding the case using the simplest and most traditional constructive eviction formula, the justices went out of their way to make pronouncements reforming landlord-tenant law and signaling to the property bar that, as Bob Dylan sang in 1964, "The times they are a-changin'."

The case actually involved two successive leases. The water leakage problems emerged during the first lease. When Cooper's business grew and she wanted more space she negotiated a new lease agreement for a larger space. During negotiations for the second lease, the landlord orally promised to fix the water seepage problems that had arisen during the first lease term. Most of the dicta arose from the court's handling of the first lease. Before the landlord made the express oral promise to fix the water problems, Cooper had signed the first lease acknowledging that she had inspected the premises and promised to carry the burden of making repairs. The court first wrote a long paragraph outlining the skimpy learning on tenant remedies in the courts and law reviews around the nation.[29] It then noted that the source of the water problems in the driveway that ran alongside the building was not in an area controlled by the tenant and that she therefore had no duty to make repairs. The driveway was a common area under the control of the landlord. The court went on to note that, even if the water problems were in the area leased by Cooper, she still did not have to make repairs. State law, the court asserted, had long since placed the repair burden for such major defects on the landlord, especially when the defect was not discoverable or known by the tenant before moving in. In essence a repair warranty for latent defects was implied.

I must add that it is not at all clear that any of the statutes cited by the court as authority for placing the repair obligation on the landlord—generally housing and building codes—operated to impose tort duties of maintenance on commercial landlords for spaces inside rented areas. That, of course, seemed not to bother the court. In addition, all of this discussion about the first lease and, most importantly, the language about implied warranties, was totally unnecessary to the result. It involved Cooper's status under the first lease, which was not even in effect at the time Cooper left the premises. All the court had to do was decide that Cooper was constructively evicted. Everything else was dicta. The justices clearly went out of their way in this commercial case to write about issues they knew were percolating in residential landlord-tenant law—the area most disturbing to New Jersey's urban residents.[30]

Reste, therefore, was a wild opinion. The court threw everything at the problem it could. Property talk gave way to both contract and tort talk, intermingled in ways that are often impossible to untangle. Bargained-for duties of repair, like the landlord's oral promise, were treated as interchangeable with tortlike duties to repair. The court went out of its way to alter rules, create written contract clauses where none existed, enforce implied agreements that might not have been made, create tort duties where none were necessary to resolve the dispute, and pay attention to all that anger and disorder welling up outside the courthouse doors.

When all was said and done, the structure of suits for unpaid rent was dramatically altered. Combining the substantive legal changes enunciated in *Reste* with the sea change in civil procedure that had occurred in New Jersey since the nineteenth century, tenants became free to file defenses and counterclaims to actions for rent just as defendants raised such issues in other sorts of cases. But none of this touched summary dispossess court—the court dealing with actions for possession for nonpayment of rent rather than suits for unpaid rent against tenants who left before the end of their terms. The substantive rules of leases and suits for rent were changed, but the summary dispossess court statutes were not at issue in *Reste*. That, of course, was the much more difficult problem taken up in *Marini*.

Marini v. Ireland

As noted, the New Jersey summary dispossess statute at issue in *Marini* originally barred appeals from summary dispossess decisions. When New Jersey overhauled its civil procedure statutes and rules in 1951 to adopt many of the same reforms introduced by adoption of the Federal Rules of Civil Procedure in 1938, the summary dispossess statute was amended to allow appeal on issues of jurisdiction while continuing to bar all other higher court reviews. Anyone who has sat through Civil Procedure in the first year of law school knows that, if a plaintiff makes a colorable claim for relief, the court has jurisdiction to hear the matter. There may be defenses to the claim, but that does not disturb the right of the court to entertain the underlying dispute. The rule is that a complaint well pleaded by a plaintiff provides jurisdiction. It doesn't guarantee a victory, but it does guarantee a hearing. So, if appeal under the summary dispossess statute was available only on matters of "jurisdiction"—on the power of a court to hear a case—the traditional understanding of that term barred appellate courts from reviewing disputes over sufficiency of the evidence, the availability of various defenses, or the underlying structure of substantive law. In short, if the New Jersey Supreme Court was to hear the *Marini* dispute, it had to do a hatchet job on the well-pleaded complaint rule and the meaning of the word "jurisdiction." And that is exactly what the court did.

The case arose in a happenstance manner. Gordon Lewis, a legal services lawyer, was in landlord-tenant court in Camden one day with his usual load of cases. Alice Ireland was there, trying without much success to explain her problems with a toilet. Lewis went up to her and asked if he could help. She said yes, and the rest, as they say, is history. The fact that a lawyer working for tenants was even present represented a major shift in legal culture from a just a decade earlier.

Some form of legal services for the poor had been around for a while, usually in the form of volunteer services or offices funded with donations from lawyers and other generous souls. But these services and offices were usually small and overwhelmed. The Ford Foundation was the first major organization to display a deep interest in legal services for the poor. It funded some experimental programs in the early 1960s, including both offices with attorneys serving only the needy and law school clinical education programs. A major part of President Johnson's War on Poverty was the creation of the Office of Economic Opportunity (OEO) in 1964. It was an amazing agency, empowered to give grants for community organizing and other local projects to help the poor. The government actually gave out money to groups of people pursuing complaints against local, state, and federal agencies.

Funding legal services programs was one of the first, most important and (other than Head Start) only long-lasting effort of OEO. In the same year OEO was established, Jean and Edgar Cahn published a seminal law review article advocating the establishment of a nationally funded legal services program.[31] The Cahns were friends of Sargent Shriver, who had been appointed by President Johnson to run OEO. Their influence on Shriver's decision to begin funding legal services offices was critical. A large-scale grant program began in 1965. This infusion of funds allowed new legal services offices to open all over the country in the late 1960s, including the office where Gordon Lewis worked.[32]

Ireland gave Lewis a copy of the summons and complaint in her summary dispossess action, along with a plumber's bill and a cancelled check. Shortly after she moved into 503B Rand Street in Camden in the spring of 1969, she noticed that her toilet was leaking. After the landlord did not respond to repeated requests for repairs, Ireland hired a plumber and paid the $85.72 repair bill herself. When her July rent came due, she sent the landlord a copy of the bill, along with a check for $9.28 to cover the difference between her rent and the cost of the repair. Marini cashed the check but demanded that the remainder of the rent be paid in cash. Ireland refused and was sued for possession on July 23.

When the case was tried, the trial judge concluded that there was no authority for "giving the right to tenant to engage plumber and have repairs made, then deduct amt. from rent."[33] The tenant appealed and obtained a stay of the eviction from the appellate division of the superior court. Pending resolution of the appeal, Ireland was ordered to pay Marini her monthly rent, except for the month in question. The New Jersey Supreme Court took the unusual step of certifying the case to itself for resolution before the appellate division could hear the case. It also stayed, pending review, the judgment for possession entered against her.

Several arguments were made on behalf of Alice Ireland in the appeal.[34] First, the claim was made that N.J.S. §2A:18–59—the section of the summary dispossess statute limiting appeal to matters of jurisdiction—violated the Due Process and Equal Protection Clauses of the United States Constitution. The following section, N.J.S. §2A:18–60, allowed cases "of sufficient importance" to be transferred to the regular superior court, from which standard appeals were available. The contention was that this difference in treatment was arbitrary and made unfair distinctions between tenants.

Second, Ireland's side argued that, if the statute were valid, there was no difference between jurisdiction and the merits of a case. If the tenant had a defense that was denied, that decision on the merits raised jurisdictional issues. And, finally, Ireland's lawyers asserted that *Reste* and other developments required the court to allow tenants to raise repair-and-deduct defenses in actions brought for possession because of nonpayment of rent.

Gordon Lewis signed the brief for Ireland in the high court, but he was too busy to do much of the writing. Ken Meiser, a VISTA legal services attorney, and Joe Ippolito, then a third-year law student at Rutgers University School of Law in Camden, composed it.[35] Years later, Ippolito nostalgically recalled working on the case while he was a clinic student.[36] He was admitted to the bar just before the case was argued before the New Jersey Supreme Court. As a nice gesture, a motion was made at the beginning of the oral argument in *Marini* to add Ippolito's name to the brief as an author. The court granted the motion immediately.[37]

So what did the court do with the *Marini* case? N.J.S. §2A:18–53 provided that a landlord could obtain possession where a tenant "shall hold over after a default in the payment of rent, pursuant to the agreement under which the premises are held." As is quite clear from the *Marini* complaint, the landlord alleged all the necessary aspects of such a claim: ownership by the landlord, possession under a valid lease, and default in the payment of rent. There really was no question that, using standard meanings of legal terms, the Camden County District Court had jurisdiction over the dispute. Under the summary dispossess statute, appeal should have been barred.

But the court allowed the appeal. Whether rent was in default, Justice Haneman opined, raised questions about both jurisdiction and the merits. "Whatever," he wrote, "'jurisdiction' means in other settings, here it uniquely connotes the existence of one of the factual situations delineated in N.J.S. §2A:18–53. It follows that a finding, by the judge, that there is a default as alleged by the landlord, does not dispose of the meritorious issue alone. It as well disposes of the jurisdictional issue."[38] Since the merits and jurisdiction merged under this logic, the tenant could appeal the merits. Quick and nifty— but surely this was totally out of sync with both the original purposes of the summary dispossess proceeding and the standard well-pleaded complaint rule used to evaluate the sufficiency of complaints ever since the Federal Rules of Civil Procedure were promulgated in 1938 and largely adopted in New Jersey in the 1950s. The court, by merging jurisdictional allegations and proof of the merits, ignored the difference between the burden of pleading facts sufficient to provide a court with jurisdiction and the burden of proving facts sufficient to win a case once the court takes it. Presumably, the pressing social issues facing the court after the assassination of Martin Luther King Jr. and the dismal situation in New Jersey's urban areas led the court both to take the case away from the appellate division on its own motion and to render a result virtually unheard of in the annals of civil procedure courses everywhere.

After the court found it could entertain the appeal, it performed a second major reconstruction of the meaning of N.J.S. §2A:18–53 by holding that a default in the payment of rent occurred only if the rent was "owing." Under the old rules any unpaid rent was owing, period. Once the statute was construed this way, the court was free to rerun the reasoning of *Reste*, imply a warranty obligating the landlord to maintain the apartment according to the requirements of health and safety regulations, and find in favor of the tenant. By doing so, the court not only altered the old nineteenth-century notion that the conveyance of a period of possession in return for the payment of rent was a contract independent from the obligation to make repairs, it also took the critical step of moving the now interdependent covenants—including the implied warranty to maintain the premises—of a lease into summary dispossess court by allowing tenants to raise defenses to eviction actions.

Today we would ask whether such a major and arguably incoherent reconstruction of prior law was justified by the need for social reform. Why not wait for legislative action? In 1970, however, few doubted the wisdom of the court's actions. The justices felt compelled to act, and most of us attuned to the travails of landlord-tenant court at the time gave them a standing ovation for doing so.

Conclusion

The same extraordinary actions occurred elsewhere. As I noted in my *Javins* article, Judge Skelley Wright wrote an historically inaccurate but compelling opinion justifying the use of an implied warranty of habitability in Washington, D.C. And as I have written in another connection, the Illinois Supreme Court reconstructed the meaning of its summary dispossess statutes for the same reasons at almost the same moment. Other state courts behaved in a similar fashion. In short, the judicial creation of the implied warranty of habitability in landlord-tenant courts all over the country between 1968 and 1973 resulted from a widespread sense that elderly women in veils should no longer be seen struggling out of hearings bearing on their frail shoulders the weight of virtually uncontestable judgments of eviction for nonpayment of rent.

Did all of this legal reconstruction do any good? It certainly left most people with a sense that it was possible to obtain some justice in landlord-tenant courts. Landlords declining to repair apartments now run the risk of getting tied up in litigation and losing actions for possession for nonpayment of rent. Fairness actually does break out from time to time. That certainly is worth a significant round of applause. But, as a practical matter, little has changed for most impoverished residential tenants. The few tenants who manage to obtain legal assistance and happen to be living in substandard apartments may be better off. But the low budgets for legal services programs mean that the vast bulk of tenants still do not receive legal help. Many fail to show up for hearings, have no defenses to their evictions, or lack the ability to raise available issues pro se. Most judges do not actively assist in raising defenses on behalf of unrepresented tenants. Settlement agreements between landlords and tenants calling for the continued payment of the regular rent plus installments on the arrears are routinely approved in most places without much inquiry.

The grotesque unfairness of 1968 has been replaced by a less charged version of the same scenario. Despite the naïve hope of many in my generation that providing defenses in landlord-tenant court would help large numbers of tenants and improve the quality of low-cost housing, most studies find that has not happened.[39] The reasons, I think, are clear. The notion that private property owners can afford to provide good-quality housing for poor people is untenable. If we want to house all of our fellow citizens in acceptable quarters, we as a society must be willing to foot the bill. Historically, we have been unwilling to do it. Until we change that tune, all of us will continue to confront daily evidence of our culture's miserliness in the faces of the homeless and poor.

NOTES

1. *Rosewood v. Fisher*, 263 N.E.2d 833 (Ill. 1970), actually involved possession by a purchaser of residential real estate under an installment contract rather than possession by a tenant. In Illinois the same statute governed eviction of contract purchasers and tenants. The holding allowing defenses to be raised in possession actions was applicable to both kinds of disputes. For an exhaustive presentation of the history surrounding *Rosewood v. Fisher*, see "Discriminatory Housing Markets, Racial Unconscionability, and Section 1988: The Contract Buyers League Case," *Yale Law Journal* 80 (1971): 516. I have also added a bit to the historical record on *Rosewood*. Richard Chused, "The Roots of Jack Spring v. Little," *John Marshall Law Review* 40 (2007): 395. My article on *Javins v. First National Realty, Corp.*, 428 F.2d 1071 (D.C. Cir. 1970), is the most complete history of that case. See Richard Chused, "Javins (a.k.a. Saunders) v. First National Realty Corporation," *Georgetown Journal on Poverty Law and Policy* 11 (2004): 191–247. An abridged version of the piece is available in *Property Stories*, 2nd ed., ed. Gerald Korngold and Andrew P. Morriss, 123–170 (Eagan, MN: Foundation Press, 2009).

2. There are no major articles on the case and mine is the only teaching text to use it as a principal case. Richard Chused, *Cases, Materials and Problems in Property* (Dayton, OH: Lexis Nexis, 2010).

3. See, for example, Arthur M. Louis, "The Worst American City," *Harper's*, January 1975, 67 (rating Newark the worst of fifty cities by a large margin, with St. Louis next on the list).

4. For a brief summary of Camden's history see http://en.wikipedia.org/wiki/Camden ,_New_Jersey (last accessed June 18, 2010).

5. Camden, according to the 1950 Census, had a population of 124,555. That fell to 102,551 by 1970 and 84,910 in 1980. In thirty years Camden lost well over 30 percent of its population.

6. See Chused, "Javins," 191–247.

7. 53 N.J. 444 (1969).

8. Heckel served as dean between 1963 and 1970 and as acting dean in 1973–74. He also served as the moderator of the Presbyterian Church USA in 1972 and as an elder after his term as moderator ended. He died in 1988. "C. Willard Heckel, 74, Ex-Law Dean Dies," *New York Times*, April, 7 1988. As I wrote Dean Heckel a few years before his death, during my years at Rutgers, he was a gentle soul who served in the midst of tumult in both the law school and the state of New Jersey.

9. The *Newark Star-Ledger* maintains an excellent Web site on the city and the 1967 riot, which contains an interesting set of demographic tables. "1967 Newark Riots," *Star-Ledger*, accessed May 6, 2010, http://www.nj.com/newark1967/.

10. George Sternlieb, *The Tenement Landlord* (New Brunswick, NJ: Rutgers University Press, 1986), 228.

11. In addition to Newark, the commission investigated events in Northern New Jersey, Plainfield, and New Brunswick. *The 1968 Report of the National Advisory Commission on Civil Disorders*, 56–84.

12. Pub. L. 88–352, 78 Stat. 241, the major provisions dealt with employment; Pub. L. 89–110, 79 Stat. 437, commonly called the Voting Rights Act; Pub. L. 90–284, 82 Stat. 81, also known as the Fair Housing Act.

13. Economic Opportunity Act of 1964, Pub. L. 88–452, 78 Stat. 508.

14. Governor Richard J. Hughes, a Democrat, used such surprisingly strong language in describing the Newark riot. A "visibly haggard" governor, it was reported, "called Newark 'a city in open rebellion' after a day of touring the riot-torn area of the city." Donald Warshaw and James McHugh, "Hughes: 'A City in Open Rebellion,'" *Newark Star-Ledger*, July 15, 1967.

15. The modern era of the court began with the adoption of a new state constitution by New Jersey in 1947 and the appointment of Arthur Vanderbilt to run the reconstituted supreme court. During the years prior to the resolution of *Marini v. Ireland*, the court decided a number of important cases including *Michaels v. Brookchester*, 26 N.J. 379 (1958) (using building and housing codes as a basis for imposing tort duties on residential landlords); *Henningsen v. Bloomfield Motors*, 32 N.J. 358 (1960) (approving strict liability doctrine); and *Schipper v. Levitt & Sons, Inc.*, 44 N.J. 70 (1965) (imposing implied warranties on developers of new residential housing).

16. Some well-known personalities, including both Democrats and moderate Republicans, sat on the court. Chief Justice Joseph Weintraub was widely known as a leading independent-minded American jurist. Daniel J. O'Hern, "Some Reflections on the Roots of Differing Judicial Philosophies of William J. Brennan, Jr. and Joseph Weintraub," *Rutgers Law Review* 46 (1994): 1049; Dominick A. Mazzagetti, "Chief Justice Joseph Weintraub: The New Jersey Supreme Court 1957–1973," *Cornell Law Review* 59

(1974): 197; "Justice Joseph Weintraub Is Dead; Former New Jersey Court Head," *New York Times*, February 7, 1977; "A Humanist on the Bench: Joseph Weintraub," *New York Times*, August 8, 1957. Justice Haydn Proctor, a Republican, was a respected judge with a well-honed sense of fairness and empathy. Roger Lowenstein, "Remembering Haydn Proctor," in *Jersey Jurists: Profiles in the Law*, ed. Carol Vivian Bello and Arthur T. Vanderbilt, 97–99 (New Brunswick, NJ: New Jersey Institute for Continuing Legal Education, 1998); Robert McGill Thomas Jr., "Haydn Proctor, 93, a Judge and New Jersey Senator," *New York Times*, October 5, 1996; "Haydn Proctor, 93, Former N.J. Senator," *Miami Herald*, October 7, 1996. Justice John Francis, the author of the opinion in the *Henningsen* case, was one of the most well respected state court judges in the country. Thomas F. Lambert, "Changing the Law: Justice Francis and Products Liability Law," in Bello and Vanderbilt, *Jersey Jurists*, 63–67. Walter H. Waggoner, "John Francis Dies; Ex-Jersey Judge," *New York Times*, July 6, 1984. A few years after the *Marini* case was decided, Justice Frederick W. Hall authored the opinion in the famous zoning case of *Southern Burlington County NAACP v. Township of Mount Laurel*, 67 N.J. 151 (1975). The *Mount Laurel* result, which invalidated suburban zoning schemes that limited construction of multiple-family and other types of low-cost housing, reflected Hall's approach to civil law reform. Justice Vincent S. Haneman, another Republican and the author of the *Marini* opinion, worked his way up through the ranks of both the Republican Party and the New Jersey court system before being appointed to the supreme court in 1960. This was a common phenomenon through the middle of the twentieth century as powerful chief justices urged promotion of good judges through the lower courts and eventually to the high court.

17. 53 N.J. 444 (1969).
18. *Marini v. Ireland*, 56 N.J. 130 (1970).
19. Chused, "Jack Spring," 395–396.
20. See *Moore v. Townshend*, 33 N.J.L. 284, 300 (1869). The same rules that were applied to tenants were also used in other similar situations. The most common involved settings where one person had the right to possess land for his life and another had the right to own it after the life possessor died.
21. Act of March 17, 1795, Ch. DXLVII, 1795, N.J. Laws 1095 (preventing waste). Section two of this act provided: "[a]nd be it enacted by the authority aforesaid, That no tenant for life or years, or for any other term, shall, during the term, make or suffer any waste, sale or destruction of houses, gardens, orchards, lands or woods, or any thing belonging to the tenements demised, without special license in writing making mention that he may do it."
22. *Moore v. Townshend*, 33 N.J.L. 284 (1869).
23. 86 N.J.L. 648 (1914).
24. At common law, this sort of result applied even when the rented premises were destroyed by fire or other calamity. So long as the landlord was blameless the tenant still had to pay rent. *Coles v. Celluloid Manufacturing Co.*, 39 N.J.L. 326 (1877). This particular hardship was remedied in many places, including New Jersey, by statute in the nineteenth century. New Jersey's reform was adopted in 1874, and is now codified at N.J.S. §§ 46:8–6 and 46:8–7. This statute effectively requires the landlord, rather than the tenant, to maintain a hazard insurance policy on the premises.
25. Landlords, for example, had to reserve the right to retake possession in their leases in order to sue before the end of the term. They also had to prove that self-help remedies such as distraint or seizure of goods would not provide adequate financial relief.

26. Act of April 5, 1813, chapter 194, 1820 N.Y. Laws 176 (amending the "Act Concerning Distresses, Rents, and the Renewal of Leases"). Spurred by economic dislocations of the late 1830s and early 1840s, application of the statute later was limited to residential leases by excluding cases where tenants had more than five years of occupancy left under their leases. An Act to Amend the Revised Statutes, in Relation to Summary Proceedings to Recover Possession of Demised Premises, chapter 162, 1840 N.Y. Laws 119. The reasons for passage of this statute are set forth in Senate Report No. 65, *Documents of the Senate of the State of New York* (1840).

27. Act of March 4, 1847, 1847 N.J. Laws 142 (Supplement to "An Act Concerning Landlords and Tenants"). The New Jersey statute lacked the protections for long-term tenants found in New York.

28. Oral understandings modifying written contracts typically are barred both by the statute of frauds and the parole evidence rule. But a standard exception allows a court to review oral agreements if they are partially performed and relied upon by the tenant. Here, the landlord did make efforts to repair the problems and the tenant did rely on the promise in agreeing to the second lease.

29. The literature was indeed sparse. Only three articles of note existed. Hiram H. Lesar, "Landlord and Tenant Reform," *New York University Law Review* 35 (1960): 1279; Hiram H. Lesar, "The Landlord-Tenant Relation in Perspective: From Status to Contract and Back in 900 Years?" *Kansas Law Review* 9 (1961): 369; Robert Schoshinski, "Remedies of the Indigent Tenant: Proposal for Change," *Georgetown Law Journal* 54 (1966): 519. Only Schoshinski's piece discussed rent and summary dispossess actions—the arena of most importance for residential tenants.

30. Although less important for purposes of understanding the background to *Marini*, the *Reste* court also altered constructive eviction law and overruled *Stewart v. Childs Company*. Rather than requiring the tenant to show that the landlord intended to deprive the lessee of possession, the court ruled that effective dispossession was enough. Given the similarity in the facts of *Stewart* and *Reste*, the court elected to overrule the old case as it changed the rule.

31. Edgar S. Cahn and Jean Cahn, "The War on Poverty: A Civilian Perspective," *Yale Law Journal* 73 (1964): 1317.

32. For more on the early history of legal services, see Earl Johnson Jr., *Justice and Reform: The Formative Years of the American Legal Services Program* (New York: Russell Sage Foundation, 1973); Alan W. Houseman, "Civil Legal Assistance for Low-Income Persons: Looking Back and Looking Forward," *Fordham Urban Law Journal* 29 (2002): 1213; John Mahoney, "Green Forms and Legal Aid Offices: A History of Publicly Funded Legal Services in Britain and the United States," *St. Louis University Public Law Review* 17 (1998): 223.

33. Taken from judge's notes, Appendix of Brief of Appellant in *Marini v. Ireland*, p. 8a.

34. This summary is based on the briefs filed by the Defendant-Appellant in both the Appellate Division of the New Jersey Superior Court and the New Jersey Supreme Court.

35. VISTA (Volunteer in Service to America) was a federally funded program that placed him in the Camden Legal Services Office, where the case was handled. Interview with Fritz Mulhauser, February 1998.

36. Joseph V. Ippolito, "Marini v. Ireland: Recollections Thirty Years Later," *New Jersey Lawyer* 207 (2001): 38.

37. Joseph V. Ippolito, in an interview with Fritz Mulhauser, February 1998.

38. *Marini*, 56 N.J. at 138–39.

39. In general, litigation over housing conditions has had an impact on residential quality only in places with comprehensive, long-term code enforcement programs or similarly intensive efforts to use building receivership systems to control landlords who fail to repair their apartment buildings. Standard code enforcement programs or use of the implied warranty of habitability in landlord-tenant court has little impact. The literature is large. See Bruce Ackerman, "Regulating Slum Housing Markets on Behalf of the Poor: Of Housing Codes, Housing Subsidies and Income Redistribution Policy," *Yale Law Journal* 80 (1971): 1093; Neil Komesar, "Return to Slumville: A Critique of the Ackerman Analysis of Housing Code Enforcement and the Poor," *Yale Law Journal* 82 (1973): 1175; Bruce Ackerman, "More on Slum Housing and Redistribution Policy: A Reply to Professor Komesar," *Yale Law Journal* 82 (1973): 1194; Marilyn Mosier and Richard Soble, "Modern Legislation, Metropolitan Court, Miniscule Results: A Study of Detroit's Landlord-Tenant Court," *University of Michigan Journal of Law Reform* 7 (1973): 8; Werner Hirsch, Joel Hirsch, and Stephen Margolis, "Regression Analysis of the Effects of Habitability Laws Upon Rent: An Empirical Observation on the Ackerman-Komesar Debate," *California Law Review* 63 (1975): 1098; Note, "The Great Green Hope: The Implied Warranty of Habitability in Practice," *Stanford Law Review* 28 (1976): 729; Richard Markovits, "The Distributive Impact, Allocative Efficiency, and Overall Desirability of Ideal Housing Codes: Some Theoretical Clarifications," *Harvard Law Review* 89 (1976): 1815; Allan Heskin, "The Warranty of Habitability Debate: A California Case Study," *California Law Review* 66 (1978): 37; Duncan Kennedy, "The Effect of the Warranty of Habitability on Low Income Housing: 'Milking' and Class Violence," *Florida State University Law Review* 15 (1987): 485.

3

Southern Burlington County NAACP v. Township of Mount Laurel (1975)

Establishing a Right to Affordable Housing Throughout the State by Confronting the Inequality Demon

ROBERT C. HOLMES

This chapter tells the story of the landmark *Mount Laurel* case, primarily from the perspective of those who were plaintiffs.[1] Because of the plaintiffs' ethnic makeup, race theorists and civil rights advocates have argued that "at its core, the *Mount Laurel* doctrine targets residential segregation as a key factor in the perpetuation of racial inequality in New Jersey."[2] According to those commentators, *Mount Laurel* correctly recognized that exclusionary zoning exacerbates racial segregation and that full implementation of the law must include an ongoing attack on racial segregation anywhere it is found in the state.[3] Those who have interpreted the *Mount Laurel* doctrine differently insist that its focus is to cure economic, not racial or ethnic, discrimination.[4]

One of my main challenges in writing this chapter was to consider these competing views as I described and evaluated how the New Jersey Supreme Court approached *Mount Laurel*. More specifically, I had to try to understand and explain why the New Jersey Supreme Court, at least on the surface, appeared to focus only on economic discrimination and not on racial segregation and racial injustice in spite of the racial composition of the plaintiff group, the racially taut environment of the time, and the obvious relevance of race to the issues before the justices. My exploration of this puzzling aspect of the case led me to conclude that both sides of the debate have merit.

Whatever the court's intentions were regarding this central aspect of the litigation, it would be a mistake to ignore other important elements, such as regional planning, smart growth, and regional equity, that framed the court's consideration.

The Story Begins

In 1975, New Jersey was politically charged by the aftermath of the late 1960s civil uprisings in its deteriorating, racially segregated cities. There was growing impatience and frustration among both those who saw themselves as being forced to live in dysfunctional and dangerous urban ghettos and those who saw themselves as bankrolling the high cost of ineffective programs intended to improve conditions in America's cities.

Against this backdrop, the New Jersey Supreme Court made a passionate and bold attempt to provide a national model for resolving the most pressing societal problem of the time—America's failure to deliver on its promise of equal opportunity for a safe and decent quality of life for all of its citizens. Citing the critical importance of housing to this lofty American ideal, and the interrelationship of housing choices and other aspects of life such as education, employment, health, and happiness, the court seized an opportunity presented by the appeal of an exclusionary zoning case to advance a doctrine intended to level life's playing field for all New Jersey residents regardless of their financial status.

Court action was met by local resistance. After it became alarmingly clear that the state supreme court's 1975 rulings, popularly known as *Mount Laurel I*,[5] were not being followed by New Jersey municipalities, the court considered the matter again in 1983 in a case that came to be known as *Mount Laurel II*.[6] Chief Justice Robert Wilentz began the majority opinion in that case with the following words: "[We] believe that there is widespread non-compliance with the constitutional mandate of our original opinion in this case. . . . To the best of our ability we will not let it continue. This court is more firmly committed to the original *Mount Laurel* doctrine than ever, and we are determined to make it work."[7] Chief Justice Wilentz's passionate words embody the court's willingness to test the limits of judicial review and step deep into the breach between law and politics.

The justices' commitment to promoting the American ideal of economic integration, the boldness of their approach, and the national importance of the issue resulted in *Mount Laurel* receiving wide attention across the country. Beyond doubt, it deserves to be called a landmark case. Love it or hate it, *Mount Laurel* could not be ignored; it has been widely celebrated, studied, and emulated, and widely reviled. However, because the judiciary's ability to bring about social change is ultimately dependent upon the elected branches' cooperation and enforcement, the considerable promise of the court's bold rulings in *Mount Laurel* remains largely unfulfilled. In part, at least, that is the result of the court's unwillingness to remain engaged for the long haul in *Mount Laurel*'s implementation, a sharp departure from what the court did so courageously in *Abbott v. Burke* in the 1990s and beyond.[8]

The Genesis of the Case

The case of *Southern Burlington County NAACP v. Mount Laurel Township* began in a New Jersey trial court in 1971. It was inspired by Ethel Robinson Lawrence, an African American woman whose family had lived in rural Mount Laurel Township for more than six generations. In 1955, Mrs. Lawrence and her husband, Thomas Lawrence, purchased a home in the township where they raised nine children. It was the Lawrences' dream that their children and grandchildren would also have the opportunity to live and raise families in Mount Laurel. This was not to be.

Soon after Mr. and Mrs. Lawrence purchased their home, many rural areas in New Jersey, including Mount Laurel Township, began to change and take on the character of self-contained communities existing on the outskirts of cities. This change was aided and abetted by zoning policies that sought to limit "undesirable" forms of development, "undesirable" residents, and the costs of both. Restrictive zoning became the primary weapon. There were bans on mobile homes and apartment complexes, a requirement that homes only be built on large lots, minimum building size requirements, and restrictions on the number of bedrooms allowed to be included in a new home (the last measure intended to limit the number of school-age children moving into the municipality). These and other restrictive devices had the effect of driving up housing costs and effectively excluding people of limited financial means from purchasing new homes or finding affordable rental units. Ethel Lawrence's own daughter was able to remain in Mount Laurel Township only by living in a converted chicken coop.

Angered and frustrated by her community's changing character and the inability of her family, friends, and neighbors to move there or even to remain there, Mrs. Lawrence organized the Springville Community Action Committee. This multiracial nonprofit organization sought to develop low- and moderate-income housing in Mount Laurel. To do so, it followed normal development procedures for a nonprofit organization. It secured seed money from the New Jersey Department of Community Affairs, commissioned a design plan for a thirty-six-unit multifamily housing complex, and submitted the development plan to the municipal zoning board for approval. The proposed project required zoning board approval because it involved a zoning variance from the township's restrictive zoning ordinance to permit construction of the multifamily rental complex. The zoning board's denial led to the filing of a lawsuit in 1971.

From the outset, it was clear that the New Jersey courts were being asked to take on a critical societal problem with two interrelated components: inequality based on race and inequality based on economic status. Feelings about both ran deep in the African American community and beyond. The African American instigator of the case, Ethel Lawrence, became the subject of severe harassment, even death threats. She had to explain to her children why they were being harassed at school.

That racism and racial inequality were central to Mount Laurel's, New Jersey's, and the nation's most debilitating problems had been made clear by both a state and a federal commission charged with determining the root causes of racial disorders that erupted during the summer of 1967 in many American cities, including a number in New Jersey.[9]

The Lawsuit and the New Jersey Courts

The trial court in the *Mount Laurel* case bypassed the issue of inequality based on race. Instead, the court focused on inequality based on economic status, ruling that Mount Laurel Township's system of land use regulation was invalid because it unlawfully excluded low- and moderate-income families from the municipality. Thereafter, the case proceeded through the appeals process.

By the time *Mount Laurel* reached the New Jersey Supreme Court, the judicial approach to the challenge of ensuring equal access to the benefits of economic progress for all citizens had become complex and multifaceted. The court needed, for example, to determine the particular segment of the population to which its mandates would apply and in so doing describe the particular societal problem it intended to address. Other elements of the judicial approach included an attempt to understand and address the causes of the severe deterioration of urban areas where the state's poorest residents were forced to live, and a mandate that the cost of leveling the playing field between the rich and the poor must be shared by all of New Jersey's municipalities and residents on a regional basis. This mandate became the highlight and focus of the *Mount Laurel* story, a story that is still being written.

Attack the Inequality Demon's Most Inclusive Head

Early in its initial decision, the New Jersey Supreme Court made clear that it intended to broaden the scope of its ruling to include all persons who, like the minority poor, were excluded from living in Mount Laurel Township because of their limited income and resources or simply because of the paucity of housing choices. Justice Frederick W. Hall, writing for the court's majority, declared, "Plaintiffs represent the minority poor (black and Hispanic) seeking such quarters. But they are not the only category of persons barred from so many municipalities by reason of restrictive land use regulations." Justice Hall went on to say:

> We have reference to young and elderly couples, single persons and large, growing families not in the poverty class, but who still cannot afford the only kinds of housing realistically permitted in those places—relatively high-priced, single family detached dwellings on sizeable lots. . . . We will, therefore, consider the case from the wider viewpoint that the effect of

Mount Laurel's land use regulation has been to prevent various categories of persons from living in the township because of the limited extent of their income and resources.[10]

Directly on the issue of race, Justice Hall declared, "we accept the representation of the municipality's counsel at oral argument that the regulatory scheme was not adopted with any desire or intent to exclude prospective residents on the obviously illegal basis of race, origin or believed social incompatibility."[11]

The justices agreed with the trial court that Mount Laurel Township's zoning ordinance was invalid but, in far more sweeping terms, they established a doctrine under which exclusionary zoning practices would not be tolerated anywhere in the state where economic growth was occurring. This ruling was based on the justices' finding that governmental power can only be exercised for the general welfare of the people—that is, governmental power cannot be used to favor one group of citizens over another. The justices concluded that, because the state controls the use of all land in the state, neither the state nor local municipalities can enact land use laws effectively favoring the rich over the poor. Such discrimination was considered unconstitutional and, because exclusionary zoning favored the rich to the disadvantage of the poor, that land use practice was unconstitutional. The court said in part:

> A developing municipality, by its land use regulations, must make realistically possible the opportunity for an appropriate variety and choice of housing for all categories of people who may desire to live there, including those of low and moderate income; it must permit multifamily housing, without bedroom or other similar restrictions, as well as small dwellings on very small lots, low income housing of other types and, in general, high density zoning, without artificial and unjustifiable minimum requirements as to lot size, building size and the like, to meet the full panoply of these needs.[12]

While civil rights activists and others might have preferred a decision by the New Jersey Supreme Court dealing specifically with the issue of race, the justices believed they had identified a basis for broadening the population to be protected. They perceived that exclusionary zoning was inextricably linked to suburbanization and urban decline, and that the spectrum of New Jersey residents adversely affected by exclusionary zoning was far broader than the plaintiff class. Of course, this focus may have had a political or pragmatic basis as well as a principled basis since it enlarged those who might be expected to support the decision.

The court also expressed a strong view about the municipalities' motivation for adopting exclusionary zoning practices. In *Mount Laurel I*, the court declared emphatically "There cannot be the slightest doubt that the reason for this course of conduct has been to keep down local taxes on property . . . and that the policy was carried out without regard for non-fiscal considerations with respect to people, either within or without its boundaries."[13] The court referred to this basis for exclusionary zoning as "fiscal zoning." The court also noted that some municipalities used restrictive zoning devices to preserve a rural and eco- logically pleasing living environment, which the court referred to as "ecological zoning." In a sense, the court saw neither of these zoning motivations as being directed at people.

The court's expansion of the group to be protected did not, of course, exclude the racially defined plaintiff group who had brought the case. In the court's words, "[the minority poor] . . . are not the only category of persons barred from so many municipalities by reason of restrictive land use regula- tions."[14] Citing two significant empirical studies, Justice Pashman's concurring opinion in *Mount Laurel I* reminds his colleagues and others that exclusionary zoning not only has fiscal and ecological bases but also is "often motivated by fear of and prejudices against other social, economic, and racial groups."[15]

The New Jersey Supreme Court's decision to broaden the class of New Jersey residents to be protected by *Mount Laurel* should not be understood to reflect a judicial unwillingness to confront the issue of racial discrimina- tion. By 1975, the court had shown itself to be able and willing to deal with issues of race directly and boldly when that was necessary to vindicate con- stitutional rights. For example, ten years earlier the court had ruled in the *Booker* case that correctable racial imbalance in a district's public schools was unconstitutional even if it was de facto in character.[16] In 1971, in the *Jenkins* case, the court took the further step of ruling that school districts' borders could not prevent the achievement of racial balance in the schools, and that the commissioner of education could consolidate districts if, in his judgment, that was necessary.[17] In both cases, the New Jersey Supreme Court clearly went beyond the United States Supreme Court's jurisprudence under the federal constitution. Somewhat less directly, but even more boldly, the New Jersey Supreme Court's rulings since 1973 in *Robinson v. Cahill* and *Abbott v. Burke* have assured students in New Jersey's poorest urban districts, most of them black or Hispanic, that they would receive the funding necessary to achieve equal- ity of educational opportunity under the state constitution's "thorough and efficient" education clause.[18]

In *Mount Laurel II*, the court appears to agree with the position taken by Jus- tice Pashman in his concurring opinion in *Mount Laurel I*. In a much studied and debated footnote, the court illustrates the contribution exclusionary zoning makes to the destructive suburban-urban disparity by quoting from *The Report of the National Advisory Commission on Civil Disorders* that America is becoming "two societies, one black, one white—separate and unequal."[19]

Consistent with the *Mount Laurel* court's approach to the case and its description of the urgent societal problems the court sought to address, Justice Hall's summary of the manifestations of those problems in New Jersey's deteriorating cities focuses on the financial inability of those left behind to purchase or rent the kinds of housing permitted in the suburbs. For Justice Hall and his fellow justices, this protected class included all categories of residents who were financially unable to find housing in a developing municipality, not merely those in the poverty class.

The court was certainly correct in its finding that the outflow of industry, retail business, jobs, and workers from the cities occurred for many reasons other than just discrimination and racial bias. Both the Kerner and Lilley Commission reports found that modern technology, automation, and improved transportation were the main causes of suburbanization. On the other hand, by failing to take into account a principal finding of the Kerner Commission that "race prejudice has shaped our history decisively; [and] it now threatens to affect our future,"[20] the court risked an unintended consequence of its noble effort to begin to deliver on the promise of equal opportunity for all: ignoring racial prejudice, the court again risked leaving low-income black and Hispanic residents out of the court's plan to expand housing choices for all New Jersey citizens, including affordable choices in the suburbs. As *Mount Laurel* units were built and occupied, it became eminently clear that, while the court's mandate may have made the playing field more level as between rich and poor residents of the state, in the area of housing choices it had done very little to level the playing field between white and nonwhite residents.

In a 1984 article, I speculated that the court may have assumed low- and moderate-income black residents would be fully included in *Mount Laurel*'s benefits by virtue of the court's emphasis on the need to deconcentrate those living in urban poverty.[21] Although a large proportion of New Jersey's black residents lived in "poor" cities, they were far from a majority of those cities' residents. In addition to constituting a majority in the state's poorest cities, white urban residents also outnumbered black urban residents in terms of eligibility for access to low- and moderate-income housing as established by the U.S. Department of Housing and Urban Development (HUD).[22] Consequently, focusing on income and residency rather than race produced an eligible population of white applicants that could more than meet the supply of available *Mount Laurel* units. Nonetheless, if we look at the rate of black and white applicants compared to their respective levels of eligibility, we find that a far greater percentage of black eligible candidates became applicants than did their white counterparts.[23] This fact would tend to neutralize the impact and significance of any miscalculation of urban demographics by the court. On the other hand, selection criteria and other real-world factors that would tend to favor white applicants over black applicants, left unmonitored by the court, would tend to diminish black occupancy of *Mount Laurel* housing as well as the court's presumptive goal of including black urban poor in the benefits of its landmark ruling. Such has been the reality associated with *Mount Laurel* implementation.

Opening the Suburbs to the Poor as a Means to Improve Cities and Improve the Quality of Life for Those Forced to Live There

In *Mount Laurel I*, the New Jersey Supreme Court described the interrelationship among suburbanization, restrictive zoning, and the decline of cities. In *Mount Laurel II*, the justices more fully addressed the need to stem urban decline. It became an integral part of the court's effort to reduce the disparities between rich and poor in benefiting from the state's economic growth. According to the justices, deconcentrating urban poverty by expanding housing opportunities in emerging suburbs would advance a number of important goals simultaneously: including the urban poor in the benefits of the state's economic growth, which was occurring primarily in the suburbs; improving the condition of declining cities; and advancing the general welfare of all of the state's residents.[24]

In *Mount Laurel II*, the court further refined the *Mount Laurel* doctrine by limiting the protected class to households that could qualify for low- and moderate-income eligibility under the HUD standard and by replacing the "developing municipality" standard with a "growth area" designation, as determined by reference to the State Development Guide Plan[25] or by the facts and circumstances surrounding a particular case. In the latter instance, the court seemed to anticipate in *Mount Laurel II* a time when suburban growth would stall. The court intended, through its bold approach to the problem of economic inequality, to expand housing choices throughout the state—in suburbs and cities alike. The court offered the following observation: "The provision of lower income housing in the suburbs may help to relieve cities of what has become an overwhelming fiscal and social burden. It may also make jobs more accessible for the unemployed poor. Deconcentration of the urban poor will presumably make cities more attractive for businesses and upper income residents to return to."[26]

Having already established the legal principle that a municipality's exercise of the police power must promote the general welfare,[27] for example by adopting appropriate land use regulations, the supreme court then explicitly included improving the condition of the state's urban areas as part of promoting the general welfare. As the court said in *Mount Laurel II*:

> Cities, while most directly affected, are not the sole victims of exclusionary zoning. The damage done by urban blight and decay is in no way confined to those who must remain in our cities. It affects all of us. Violent crime and drug abuse spawned in urban slums do not remain within city limits; they spread out to the suburbs and infect those living there.

Efforts to combat these diseases require expenditures of public dollars that drain all taxpayers, urban and suburban alike. The continuing disintegration of our cities encourages business and industry to leave New Jersey altogether, resulting in a drain of jobs and dollars from our economy. In sum, the decline of our cities and the increasing economic segregation of our population are not isolated problems for those left behind in cities, but a disease threatening us all. Zoning ordinances that either encourage this process or ratify its results are not promoting our general welfare, they are destroying it.[28]

By the time of *Mount Laurel II*, the court's graphic description of the dreadful economic and social condition of New Jersey's cities was intended not only to expose the massive dimensions of the economic inequality problem but also to suggest that suburban growth areas presented an opportunity to improve both the quality of life for poor urban dwellers and the condition of New Jersey's failing cities. The court also was prescient in recognizing that responsibility for advancing its broad conception of promoting the general welfare, both promoting an economically integrated society and revitalizing failing cities, had to be widely distributed throughout the state. Hence, it advanced a regional approach to land use regulation and zoning that predates by decades the national focus on smart growth and regional equity. In *Mount Laurel II* the court declared: "[Z]oning in accordance with regional considerations is not only permissible, it is mandated. When [the] exercise of zoning power as [a] portion of police power by [a] municipality affects something as fundamental as housing, general welfare includes more than welfare of such municipality and its citizens; it also includes [the] general welfare of those residents outside [the] municipality but within the region that contributes to [the] housing demand within the municipality."[29]

Sharing the Cost of Economic Integration on a Regional Basis

The *Mount Laurel* court's focus on regional equity may have been influenced in part by comments found in the 1968 Lilley Commission Report to the Governor: "Suburban residents must understand that the future of their communities is inextricably linked to the fate of the city, instead of harboring the illusion that they can maintain invisible walls or continue to run away. Such change is only possible when the people in our more fortunate communities understand that what is required of them is not an act of generosity toward the people in the ghettos, but a decision of direct and deep self-interest."[30] In *Mount Laurel*, the New Jersey Supreme Court used its broad conception of the "general welfare" to convert the theme of economic integration from an expression of an American ideal reflecting direct and deep self interest to a constitutional mandate.

The idea of a regional approach to land use can be interpreted in two ways: first, as a mandate for a more managed approach to growth and planning, taking

into account considerations as varied as protection of environmentally sensitive areas and revitalization of deteriorating cities; second, as a cost-sharing
mechanism, taking into account the added burden low- and moderate-income
housing imposes on a municipal tax base and on municipal services.

While the *Mount Laurel* court raised many interrelated issues for consideration, the court remained consistent in its position that these issues were
more appropriately dealt with by the legislature. In remarks made following
the New Jersey Supreme Court's decision, for example, Justice Hall said in part,
"I was trying to promote the desirability of regional zoning, which . . . is not
forbidden by our constitution, but requires legislation. I was suggesting that
such legislation might come but it has not happened yet."[31] In recognizing the
necessity for legislative action, however, Justice Hall was not suggesting that
the judiciary merely encourage proper action by the legislature based on a
moral imperative. That, he said, would appear to be mere "wishful thinking"
by the court. Instead, his view of the relationship among the governmental
branches was that:

> The court does not live in a vacuum and it was fully realized that the
> decision would not immediately and in itself produce low and moderate
> income housing in outlying municipalities but was only a first step. It was
> apparent that nothing along this line would be accomplished until the
> court established the legal nature and extent of the municipal obligation
> to provide this opportunity through appropriate land use regulations.
> The court has fully appreciated that the bulk of lower income housing
> will remain in the cities and older suburbs, which cannot be abandoned,
> but must be rehabilitated and revitalized, with all inhabitants having the
> chance for suitable employment and to become imbued with an active
> spirit of civic and personal responsibility. The task is a huge and vital one
> and cannot be accomplished by the court alone.[32]

The Court's Bold Approach and the Separation
of Powers among the Branches of Government

At the same time that the New Jersey Supreme Court was boldly articulating
a new doctrine in the area of land use regulations, it was acknowledging that
the matter ultimately was best left to the legislative branch. Nonetheless, the
court has been widely criticized for going too far in its effort to press for resolution of the complex sociopolitical issues involved in *Mount Laurel.* The court's
action, according to its critics, amounted to an inappropriate encroachment on
the role of the elected branches of government that are supposed to be more
accountable to the will of the people. The court's rejoinder was that the *Mount
Laurel* doctrine did not represent new law, but rather constituted enforcement

of existing constitutional rights the legislature had failed to protect. In the words of Chief Justice Wilentz in *Mount Laurel II:*

> We act first and foremost because the Constitution of our State requires protection of the interests involved and because the Legislature has not protected them. We recognize the social and economic controversy (and its political consequences) that has resulted in relatively little legislative action in this field. We understand the enormous difficulty of achieving political consensus that might lead to significant legislation enforcing the constitutional mandate better than we can, legislation that might completely remove this Court from those controversies. But enforcement of constitutional rights cannot await a supporting political consensus. So while we have always preferred legislative to judicial action in this field, we shall continue—until the Legislature acts—to do our best to uphold the constitutional obligation that underlies the Mount Laurel doctrine. We may not build houses, but we do enforce the Constitution.[33]

The relevant state constitutional obligation, according to the court, included the right to substantive due process of law and to equal protection under the law. To satisfy these rights in the context of the constitutional power to zone, a municipality must exercise that power for the general welfare, not just for the welfare of that municipality and its current residents.

To reach this definition of the constitutional obligation, the New Jersey Supreme Court in the *Mount Laurel* cases had to overcome some stiff jurisprudential challenges. For example, in order to find a substantive due process right, the court had to identify a fundamental right. Typically, this requires a finding that the right was in, or derives from, the state or federal constitution. Thus, in *Mount Laurel*, the court had to, and did, find a right to housing embedded in New Jersey's constitution. Since that right, as compared to the right to a certain level of education, was not explicitly guaranteed by the constitution, the court had to take an expansive view of fundamental rights. But it went even further by determining that, to the extent poverty denies New Jersey citizens access to decent and affordable housing in the state's growth areas, poverty can be considered in determining which citizens can assert this constitutionally protected right.

The New Jersey Supreme Court's declaration of housing as a fundamental right and its imposition of an affirmative obligation on municipalities to provide for a fair share of housing needs for all income groups go beyond what any court, state or federal, had done by 1975 or has done since. Nor has any other court, state or federal, gone as far in recognizing poverty as a factor to be weighed in the constitutional inquiry. With its bold pronouncements in *Mount Laurel*, the New Jersey Supreme Court surely shook the nation.

In doing so, the justices appeared to invoke the spirit of United States Supreme Court Chief Justice John Marshall who, in the landmark case of *Marbury v. Madison*, declared, "It is emphatically the province and duty of the judicial department to say what the law is."[34]

Mount Laurel: Law or Politics?

The line between law and politics is often blurred. Whether a particular judicial decision is seen as legitimately grounded in sound legal principles and process or as primarily grounded in a court's view of what is appropriate policy is often the subject of heated debate. For those comfortable with the status quo, any judicial action to expand the liberty of certain people at the expense of others will be seen as judicial usurpation. For those who feel they are victims of the tyranny of the majority, expressed through the elected branches of government, the unelected judiciary will be viewed as the best and sometimes only hope for justice.

While constitutional interpretation is surely not always and inevitably political, it is fair to say that, because the judicial branch of government is not insulated from the prevailing political and social realities, some of its decisions undoubtedly are influenced by the judges' life experience and values. In that sense, courts render decisions that are "political."

The justices in the *Mount Laurel* case clearly interpreted the issues before them in accordance with their own views of the sociopolitical climate as well as of the particular facts of the case. In turn, they crafted a remedy consistent with what they perceived to be the political and social realities. The result was substantial deference to the elected branches, and a striking disparity between the boldness of their constitutional judgments and their approach to remedying the constitutional violations they found.

Choosing Tactics for Social Change

Ethel Lawrence could have responded in a number of ways to the exclusionary zoning practices she experienced in her community. She chose to challenge what she saw as an injustice within the strict confines of existing and prescribed political institutions. She sought relief from what she claimed was unfair land use legislation through an administrative process controlled by the executive branch. Only when that failed did she seek relief through the courts.

Social injustices of the kind Ethel Lawrence challenged may be violations of law, but, because such injustices almost always are the result of entrenched economic forces and institutions, social change and social justice seldom, if ever, can be achieved strictly through the courts. As powerful and significant as the outcomes associated with the *Mount Laurel* decisions may have been, with the benefit of hindsight they might have been even more powerful and achieved more had Mrs. Lawrence's effort been supported by a better organized social movement.

With her multiracial base of supporters, she might have addressed the exclusionary zoning challenge with a more multifaceted approach of the sort employed by other social activists. Ethel Lawrence might have looked for guidance to the methods employed by activists in the civil rights struggle, including marches, demonstrations, sit-ins, picketing, civil disobedience, and the like. Or she might have drawn on the efforts of Mahatma Gandhi and Nelson Mandela, whose work as community organizers and whose leadership in social struggle, not legal struggle, distinguishes them and their successes in the fight for social change (ironically, both Gandhi and Mandela were lawyers). This more multi-faceted self-help approach to social change does not preclude the use of litigation but does not solely rely on it.

Self-help approaches, on the other hand, would not have represented an easy course for Mrs. Lawrence and her supporters, nor would they have guaranteed a better outcome. Affordable housing activists might seek to enhance their power base by finding common ground between, on the one hand, low-income minority communities and the injustices visited upon them, and, on the other hand, low-income citizens in the majority community struggling to survive. But the common-ground strategy runs head-on into the tragically successful "divide and conquer" political strategy that seeks to engender the sometimes awkward bonding among disparate white interests while deterring more natural cross racial alliances.

Similarly, cooperation based on recognition of the link between the condition of deteriorating cities, with their increasing concentration of poor and minority citizens, and the general welfare of comfortable citizens in the majority community, runs head-on into promises that time and geography will continue to isolate one population from the other.

In addition, Ethel Lawrence and her self-help supporters would have been at the mercy of an ever-shifting judicial determination of what free speech and free association activities are protected under the First Amendment. In general, American courts have been slow to provide levels of protection for self-help efforts by minority groups.

Self-help efforts to secure equal rights also were discouraged by the Kerner Commission. Despite an eloquent minority view expressed by commission member Judge A. Leon Higginbotham, the commission's majority expressed the view that, if a law is challenged, "While the judicial test is in progress, all other dissenters should abide by the law involved until it is declared unconstitutional."[35] Judge Higginbotham, on the other hand, argued that "[r]ecent advances in the field of civil rights have not come about and would never have come about solely through judicial tests by one individual while all others in the silent black majority waited for the ultimate constitutional determination."[36]

Whether social movements can positively influence court actions has been the subject of vigorous debate. In connection with *Mount Laurel*, while there was no obvious economic equality movement accompanying the litigation, it is almost certain that the civil rights struggle of the 1960s and the violent upheavals in American cities, including those in New Jersey at the end of the 1960s, had to greatly influence the New Jersey Supreme Court's perception of the state's most critical societal problems, their intensity, and the action needed to begin to ameliorate them.

The courts, and in particular the nation's and states' highest courts, have traditionally been regarded as the last, best hope for the preservation of American-style democracy. After all, at least when judges are appointed rather than elected, there is a widely held belief that the judicial branch is free of partisan politics and can act to protect minority interests. To the extent that this belief is well grounded, Ethel Lawrence's pursuit of justice through the courts might have been both prudent and adequate. However, even if the judicial branch were willing to entertain litigation that reaches deeply into the political and legislative arenas by taking on cases at the intersection of law and policy, judicial rulings in such cases are almost never self-executing. Their implementation depends upon subsequent actions of the executive and legislative branches of government, both of which ultimately are dependent upon and responsive to the political will of the majority. Almost any court-inspired reform that lacks substantial community or political support is more likely to be reversed or to languish for years with little or no progress. Such has been the fate of *Mount Laurel*.

Had there been greater and more-organized support, efforts to assure that the *Mount Laurel* principles were fully and effectively implemented could have taken a number of forms. More sustained pressure could have been brought to bear on the courts to in turn pressure the other branches to carry out their functions. Coalitions might have been created to extend *Mount Laurel*'s reach and benefits, perhaps converting what had started as a minority interest into a majority interest. Or, even if those supporting *Mount Laurel*'s implementation remained a minority, they could have formed themselves into a more influential political force.

The reality, however, was that little if any effective direct pressure was brought to bear behind the enforcement of the *Mount Laurel* doctrine. Perhaps symptomatic was the state's dismantling of the Office of the Public Advocate in the 1990s after that office demanded that the state be more responsive to the supreme court's rulings.

While there was no substantial economic-equality or equal-access-to-housing movement responsible for, or even invested in, the success of the *Mount*

Laurel litigation, the landmark decision did not seem to spawn any such movement. As a result, the court left enforcement to a legislature largely uninfluenced by those who supported *Mount Laurel*'s principles. Effective enforcement inevitably became the victim of the entrenched social forces and prejudices that engendered the decision in the first place.

The Court Passes the Baton to the Legislature and a Rocky Road to Implementation Ensues

As a transitional step toward delegating *Mount Laurel*'s enforcement to the state legislature, the aforementioned State Development Guide then was adopted by the court. It served as the primary standard to determine the focus and extent of each municipality's fair share obligation to provide a realistic opportunity for the construction of low and moderate income housing. Transition from the judiciary to the elected branches of government was completed after the state supreme court's ruling in *Hills Development Co. v. Bernards Twp.*[37] In that case, the court upheld as fair and constitutional a statutory provision requiring all cases concerning the constitutional obligation embodied in the *Mount Laurel* doctrine to be transferred to an administrative body for review and appropriate action toward compliance. The *Hills* case is often referred to as *Mount Laurel III.*

To the extent the *Mount Laurel* court intended by its rulings to open the suburbs to all low- and moderate-income urban residents, if not because of their race at least regardless of their race, it invited a rocky road to implementation by the elected branches of government. Racism and racial inequality are an intractable part of American history and American culture that often create an otherwise inexplicable discrepancy between a society's stated ideals and the behavior of its people and those elected to represent them.

Scholars and others generally accept the presence of neutral principles on which the *Mount Laurel* decision can be based: principles that do not unfairly remove rights from one group in order to convey rights to another and principles that, if fairly and effectively enforced, would secure and advance, or at least not harm, societal interests and values deemed important by the majority of the people.

By contrast, there appears to be little or no agreement on remedies that, if adopted, would secure and advance the accepted principles. There seems little or no interest divergence between most white and minority citizens around advancing principles of fair share and regional equity and of preventing exclusionary and wasteful zoning and planning activities, as promoted by the court in *Mount Laurel I* and *Mount Laurel II*. On the other hand, implementing a remedy that distributes affordable housing to minorities and other less empowered groups at the arguable expense of more empowered groups, as promoted by more recent court cases and by the Council on Affordable Housing (COAH), does reflect interest divergence. This may explain why so little fair share housing has reached the original intended beneficiaries of the *Mount Laurel* doctrine.

Part of the remedial difficulty undoubtedly reflects the elected branches' desire to remain politically aligned with the majority view. Beyond that, however, ascribing motive or purpose to the elected branches' lukewarm response to *Mount Laurel*'s implementation is a matter of conjecture. One might speculate that the state was reluctant to disrupt its semiofficial policy of creating exclusive residential enclaves for corporate CEOs on the theory that, if they chose to live in New Jersey, they might locate corporate campuses and perhaps other facilities in the state. Or perhaps the elected branches intended to implement *Mount Laurel* just enough to minimize the prospects that a court seen as "activist" would remain directly involved in monitoring implementation.

A more direct attempt by the elected branches to blunt the impact of the *Mount Laurel* doctrine and gain greater control over the underlying political issues involved a proposal to amend the state constitution. The proposal, which attracted bipartisan support in the legislature and was embraced by the executive branch, was never adopted by the legislature or submitted to the people. It paved the way, however, for new legislation ostensibly intended to implement the *Mount Laurel* doctrine but regarded by *Mount Laurel* loyalists as a political compromise intended in part to delay implementation and minimize the law's impact on the state's suburban communities.

Any properly adopted constitutional amendment will take precedence over a judicial ruling. Chief Justice John Marshall may have been correct in his assertion that it is the duty of the judicial department to declare what the law is. Such declarations must conform to constitutional language, however, and changing that language would almost certainly change the judiciary's interpretation.

Whether the elected branches raised the constitutional amendment option as a threat upon which a bargaining position could be built, or because they planned to seriously consider it, is a matter of conjecture. More than likely, it was the former. It is unlikely that the governor or legislature wanted to be associated with a policy and strategy that could be interpreted as embracing exclusionary zoning.

A second obvious attempt by the state to exercise greater control over *Mount Laurel*'s implementation dealt with the focus and extent of fair share allocations. It was reflected in Governor Thomas Kean's 1982 decision to disband the Division of State and Regional Planning and relocate its function to the Office of the State Treasurer. In addition, by executive order Kean rescinded previous executive orders issued by Governor Brendan Byrne directing the Division of State and Regional Planning to calculate and project New Jersey's present and prospective housing needs. Ultimate control over implementation of *Mount Laurel*'s principal mandates by the elected branches was provided for by the adoption of two new laws: the Fair Housing Act in 1985 and the State Planning Act in 1986.

The Fair Housing Act

State Senator Wynona Lipman (D-Essex) was one of the original sponsors of the Fair Housing Act.[38] In devising the bill, she had worked with a broad-based committee that included planners, attorneys, builders, the League of Municipalities, the Public Advocate, and the governor's office. Lipman described her version of the bill by saying, "We believe [the bill] provides a straightforward planning mechanism which municipalities can use as an alternative to judicial determinations of housing obligations. It was designed to . . . provide clear direction to municipalities for complying with their constitutional obligation."[39]

Governor Kean's refusal to sign the bill as drafted by Lipman's committee caused her to charge the governor with deliberately attempting to "deflect the thrust of the legislation away from the constitutional issues involved . . . [and to] introduce[] procedural complications to the resolution of legal issues and greater confusion in the definition of key legal terms."[40] Lipman believed that Kean and those who supported his position were engaging in a strategy of delay. If resolution of fair share questions was substantially delayed, that would probably assure a continuing series of court challenges as interested parties attempted "to fathom the true meaning of the legislation."[41]

Lipman recognized the tension between the promise of a bold new law seeking to put "steel" in a lofty American ideal and the parochial interests of elected officials seeking to secure and maintain political favor and votes and willing, for those purposes, to resort to confrontation, delay, and demagoguery.

For a much different reason, builders joined attempts to forestall enactment of the Fair Housing Act. For them, passage would signal the judiciary's virtual removal from enforcement of the *Mount Laurel* rulings and the subsequent loss of the "builders' remedy" designed by the court to provide a site-specific right to rezoning in cases involving noncompliant municipalities.

Kean conditionally vetoed Lipman's version of the Fair Housing Act, recommending a number of changes that, if adopted by the legislature, would enable the governor to sign the revised bill into law. The governor and the senator agreed that the provisions of the Fair Housing Act would be carried out by a new administrative body, the Council on Affordable Housing (COAH), which would be responsible for establishing regulations under which municipalities would be required to demonstrate compliance with the court's rulings.

The governor's recommended changes included a twelve-month moratorium on enforcement of *Mount Laurel.* After the bill was revised in accordance with the governor's recommended changes, however, Lipman was so upset by what had emerged that she completely withdrew her support as a sponsor. By doing so, she communicated the message that the recommended changes would both undermine the constitutional basis for the *Mount Laurel* doctrine and invite bad-faith planning.

Lipman pointed out that, under the governor's version of the act, even after a municipality's fair share of the regional housing need was determined, the municipality could make fair share adjustments based upon a wide variety of considerations including historic preservation, environmental, agricultural, open space, recreation, and infrastructure. The criteria for invoking these adjustment factors were, in the Lipman's view, so vague as to be totally open-ended.

Senator Lipman also objected to a provision recommended by the governor that permitted a downward adjustment in a municipality's fair share allocation if the municipality lacked adequate public facilities and it would be prohibitively expensive to provide them. This provision, Lipman believed, was out of line with existing legal precedents to the effect that the existence or nonexistence of schools and other facilities cannot be used to deny a local development application.

Lipman was even more concerned about the governor's recommendation allowing adjustments in a municipality's fair share allocation if the "established pattern of development in a community would be drastically altered." With no criteria to guide COAH in this very subjective judgment, granting any such adjustment would, in her opinion, contribute to the perpetuation of exclusionary zoning wherever a municipality's established pattern of development was based on exclusionary practices.

In fact, the revised law permitted COAH to reduce or limit a municipality's fair share, even beyond the various downward adjustments, on the basis of any other criteria COAH might develop. In this regard, the revised law did not require that the criteria be general in application or be known to all—a certain recipe for additional litigation and delays in implementation.

One provision in the governor's conditional veto recommendations particularly troubled Senator Lipman, housing advocates, and others interested in seeing the *Mount Laurel* doctrine implemented. This provision allowed one municipality to enter into an agreement with another under which the "receiving" municipality could assume, for a price, up to 50 percent of the "sending" municipality's fair share housing allocation. These agreements, known as Regional Contribution Agreements (RCAs), were to be regulated by COAH, including the price to be paid to a receiving community, and were generally executed between a suburban sending municipality and an urban receiving municipality.

As has been noted, the *Mount Laurel* court believed that deconcentration of the urban poor would make cities more attractive for businesses and upper-income residents to return to, and there was no substantial racially or sociopolitically based disagreement on this principle. There was also substantial agreement across racial and socioeconomic lines on the fundamental principle that separate but equal housing facilities for black and white citizens are constitutionally unacceptable, by analogy to the landmark *Brown* case. Entrenched social customs and values have made agreement on racial integration of America's public schools far less feasible, however. This dichotomy has led race theorists like Derrick Bell to suggest that the interest of blacks in quality education might be better served by concentration on improving the quality of existing schools, whether desegregated or all black.[42]

Extending the analogy between schools and housing, if cities could offer housing choices as attractive and affordable as choices offered in the suburbs, the interest of blacks in quality housing might be better served by improving available urban housing stocks. Under that approach, there could be ancillary benefits, such as less disruption of social and familial networks, a more stable urban environment that could encourage employers to return, and an increased concentration of black voters that could assure political representation.[43]

Under this theory, if RCAs had been used to underwrite the cost of constructing housing units in New Jersey's cities on par with housing units constructed in the suburbs, the resulting parity might have contributed significantly to the court's principal goals. Unfortunately, COAH's implementation of RCAs actually worsened the preexisting situation. For example, COAH set the sale price of housing units transferred pursuant to RCAs so low (initially $20,000 per unit) that it only supported rehabilitation of existing substandard units, not the construction of new units. As a result, a suburban sending municipality would get credit for providing an affordable housing unit, reducing the statewide assessment of the need for such units, even though no additional affordable unit was actually added to the state's inventory.

The deleterious effects of RCAs were not reversed until 2008 when, amid widespread jubilation among the remaining *Mount Laurel* loyalists, legislation outlawing their use was adopted. Just one year later, however, COAH proposed new regulations that appeared to resurrect the RCA concept under a new name—Regional Affordable Housing Development Planning Programs (RAHDPPs). Under this new name, "regional planning entities" would be allowed to transfer a portion of one municipality's affordable housing obligation to another. For this purpose, regional planning entities include the New Jersey Meadowlands Commission, the Pinelands Commission, the Fort Monmouth Economic Revitalization Planning Authority, and the Highlands Water Protection and Planning Council.[44]

COAH's negative approach to implementing the *Mount Laurel* goals has gone well beyond its handling of RCAs, however. COAH recognized and awarded credits to municipalities to offset their fair share obligations that were clearly counterproductive to the court's intent. Credits were given, for example, for so-called alternative living arrangements that included group homes and other congregate living facilities. Under this policy, municipalities could count each bedroom of a group home as a separate unit, thereby greatly diluting the actual measure of prospective need for housing units. COAH inappropriately gave credits for rental units, for units built in a prior needs assessment cycle, and for units that did not correspond to any COAH assessment of housing need. It has been estimated that these and other actions taken by COAH resulted in dilution of the constitutional obligation by over 24,000 units, or 31 percent of the new construction obligation of 77,580 units set by COAH during the agency's second round of needs assessment for the period 1993–1999.[45]

COAH's failure to play a positive role in *Mount Laurel* implementation over the years makes some of the comments by Senator Lipman, as she withdrew her support for the Fair Housing Act in 1985, prophetic. She implored COAH to withstand pressure from elected officials and to exercise its powers in a manner that would not circumvent the spirit of the *Mount Laurel* doctrine, "in spite of an almost open invitation in portions of the Act to do otherwise."[46] COAH's decisions, since its inception in 1985, amount to an effort to both minimize and dilute the production of affordable housing in New Jersey. This may reflect both the revised Fair Housing Act's open invitation to do so and the will of the majority of the state's population. What it does not reflect is the New Jersey Supreme Court's original constitutional judgment about the need for affordable housing in every region of the state. Unfortunately, in upholding the Fair Housing Act in 1986 and transferring all pending litigation to COAH, the court's retreat from the affordable housing controversy, and the more fundamental matter of eradicating economic inequality in access to housing, was complete.

The State Planning Act

At about the same time that the legislature was enacting the Fair Housing Act, it was considering the State Planning Act, which it adopted in 1986.[47] The State Planning Act called for the creation of a seventeen-member State Planning Commission and an Office of State Planning. The act charged the commission and the office with the preparation and adoption of a comprehensive state development and redevelopment plan within eighteen months of the law's adoption.

In theory, there is a clear and positive relationship between the State Planning Act and implementation of the *Mount Laurel* doctrine. The State Planning Act included the following legislative finding: "An adequate response to judicial mandates respecting housing for low and moderate income persons requires sound planning to prevent sprawl and to promote suitable use of land."[48] As was the case with the Fair Housing Act, however, there is reason to question whether the State Planning Act was actually intended to advance the *Mount Laurel* doctrine or to provide yet another open invitation to circumvent its spirit.

Some things do seem clear. One is that in 1985 the executive branch, led by Governor Kean, sought to have greater control over the planning process that could ultimately determine whether municipalities were complying with

Mount Laurel's constitutional obligations. This was accomplished by replacing the existing planning process and development guide plan with an elaborate new planning apparatus. An inevitable effect of such a major adjustment was to delay implementing the *Mount Laurel* principles. It also was part of a shift in planning outcomes that reflected the mid-1980s shift in political alignment from urban and Democratic to suburban and Republican.

During the six years between the legislature's adoption of the State Planning Act and the State Planning Commission's adoption of a final plan, the commission administered a process referred to as cross-acceptance. This was intended to be a bottom-up inclusionary undertaking that would assure input from all levels of government and all sectors of the state. Predictably, a development plan that sought political cross-acceptance in mid-1980s New Jersey would take a very long time to complete and would not be a plan that zealously embraced the social policies embodied in the *Mount Laurel* doctrine.

The Implementation Story Is Not All Bad

To fairly assess whether available data describe the success, or failure, of *Mount Laurel*, it is necessary to enumerate the court's stated or presumed goals. They can be best summarized as follows:

- To increase housing opportunities for New Jersey's low- and moderate-income households throughout the state.
- To provide a realistic opportunity for poor urban residents generally and for racial minorities in particular to find housing opportunities in the suburbs, where restrictive zoning practices had excluded them in the past, and thereby begin the process of eradicating socially unacceptable ghettos of the urban poor and of racial and ethnic minorities, which in turn would make New Jersey's urban areas more attractive for all the state's residents to live or work in.

Despite what appeared to have been deliberate efforts by elected officials to blunt the impact of the *Mount Laurel* doctrine, some measurable gains have been made. Some of these gains go to the core of the court's objective; others appear to be more in the nature of incidental benefits.

In November 2000, the first tenants moved into the Ethel Lawrence Homes, thirty years after the *Mount Laurel* lawsuit was filed and six years after Mrs. Lawrence's death. These thirty-six symbolically important affordable housing units, located in Mount Laurel Township, contributed to a total of nearly 60,000 new units and nearly 15,000 rehabilitation units completed as of March 1, 2011 in compliance with COAH mandates.[49] Also, as of December 8, 2009, COAH-certified towns have proposed creating 129,999 affordable units to add to the nearly 75,000 that have already been completed.[50] Of the completed units, 10,400 were constructed or rehabilitated pursuant to a Regional Contribution Agreement. And of those, 6,881 (66 percent) are located in one of the municipalities designated by the Department of Community Affairs as an "urban aid" municipality. It is apparent from these data that over 68,000 new or rehabilitated housing units were created in areas of the state other than those designated by the DCA as the most urbanized, poor and racially concentrated.

On the other hand, according to a 2008 statewide assessment, the need for low- and moderate-income rehabilitated and new housing was calculated to be as high as 145,000 units.[51] Furthermore, many of the state's previously attractive and highly functional suburbs in near proximity to urban areas have, over time, taken on many of the unattractive and dysfunctional characteristics of the state's urban areas. To the extent, therefore, that the number of affordable housing units reportedly produced to date outside of the state's urban areas include a substantial number located in these urban ring suburbs, the gross number loses much of its luster.

Legal Services of New Jersey (LSNJ) describes in a number of interesting and compelling ways both the state's critical need for affordable housing and the human consequences of the absence of affordable housing.[52] LSNJ notes, for example, that more than 80 percent of the state's low-income households (those below 50 percent of median income) have housing problems, including overcrowding, cost burden (paying more than 30 percent of their incomes for housing), and living in substandard units lacking complete kitchen or plumbing facilities. New Jersey, according to LSNJ, is the fifth least affordable state in the country for tenants.

As part of the housing crisis, LSNJ describes the "spatial mismatch of jobs and housing." LSNJ points out that half of all the affordable housing in the state is concentrated in a handful of municipalities, while those municipalities with a growing number of jobs do not have a corresponding supply of affordable housing units. LSNJ also describes the affordable housing crisis in terms of "continued racial and economic segregation" as well as the alarming number of homeless people in the state.

It seems clear that the court's wholesale validation of the political response to *Mount Laurel* implementation was far too optimistic.[53] For much of the case's history, critics have charged the political response with minimizing and diluting *Mount Laurel*'s potential for leveling the playing field between the rich and poor in the search for decent and affordable housing. At least partly as a result, *Mount Laurel* has recently returned to the courts.

In October 2010, the Appellate Division of the Superior Court rejected COAH's methodology for determining growth share among New Jersey municipalities. That decision was appealed to the New Jersey Supreme Court by the

League of Municipalities. In March 2011, the court granted the petition for certi-fication. As a result, the court has before it once again many of the critical issues raised by *Mount Laurel*, including the determinations of the state's current and projected need for affordable housing and of the most appropriate method for deriving a municipality's fair share obligation to satisfy that need.

Overhanging these questions is the extent to which *Mount Laurel*'s imple-mentation has met the goal of enabling the urban poor and racial minorities to leave New Jersey's cities if they wish and to relocate elsewhere in the state. To shed light on that question it is necessary to review who actually lives in *Mount Laurel* housing.

Who Lives in Mount Laurel Housing

Aside from a few attempts to create profiles of occupants in *Mount Laurel* hous-ing related to particular projects, the most extensive data are within the broader database maintained by the New Jersey Affordable Housing Management Ser-vice (AHMS). AHMS is a state agency created by the Fair Housing Act to assist municipalities and developers in identifying eligible households for low- and moderate-income housing. AHMS databases include both applicants for and occupants of affordable housing built pursuant to a number of housing subsidy programs, including *Mount Laurel.*

Beyond the difficulty of identifying precisely which families in the AHMS database applied for or live in *Mount Laurel* affordable housing units, as opposed to units built pursuant to other housing programs, there is the broader ques-tion of whether everyone who applied for or lives in a *Mount Laurel* housing unit necessarily advances the doctrine. For example, should someone who lives in a unit in an urban area that was rehabilitated pursuant to an RCA be counted? Should a family that was already living in a suburban community and happened to satisfy selection criteria that placed an emphasis on proximity of the current residence to the workplace be counted? Must the unit have been constructed to directly meet a fair share housing obligation?

AHMS data do not attempt to address these issues and are, therefore, an imperfect guide to understanding who lives in *Mount Laurel* housing. Despite their limitations, however, AHMS data can be and have been used to create a relevant profile of *Mount Laurel* applicants and occupants, especially as related to units constructed in suburban communities. The most extensive among these efforts was underwritten by the Ford Foundation and is usually referred to as the Wish and Eisdorfer Report (the Report) after its primary authors.[54]

As to *Mount Laurel*'s dispersal goals, the Report reveals that implementa-tion has resulted in very few urban residents moving to suburban areas, and even fewer black or Latino urban residents doing so. It points out that, among households in the AMHS database for which previous residence and race and ethnicity are known, only 7 percent moved from urban areas to suburban areas. And of that 7 percent, 66 percent were white, 23 percent were black, and 2 percent were Latino. Among those households that moved from suburban communities to urban communities, none were white, 90 percent were black, and 3 percent were Latino. The net effect of this pattern of movement, according to the Report, is that, while 81 percent of all suburban AHMS-administered units are occupied by white households, 85 percent of all urban AHMS-administered units are occupied by black or Latino households.

While the causes of these outcomes cannot be identified with certainty, a number of likely factors can be. Selection criteria for occupancy in *Mount Laurel* housing, when left to the discretion of suburban municipalities and builders, for example, seemed inevitably to result in outcomes that were counterproductive to *Mount Laurel* goals. With its reference to the importance of reducing commuting distances from home to the workplace, the court paved the way for suburban municipalities to comply with its mandate in a perverse way by providing preferences for residents who worked in close proximity to the suburban project site.

With its concern for commuting distances, the court certainly did not intend to render life easier for those who had already escaped the grip of New Jersey's deteriorating cities. Rather, it intended to enhance job opportunities that it saw as flowing from an expansion of housing opportunities. In other words, the court intended for the *Mount Laurel* remedies to expose low-income workers to greater job markets by reducing the financial and practical limitations associated with commuting.

The reality, however, has proven to be that placing emphasis on the proximity of the workplace to the project site only perpetuates the vicious cycle that the *Mount Laurel* doctrine sought to eliminate. Moreover, it has produced a constitutionally indefensible Catch 22: a person's home should be in reasonable proximity to his or her workplace, but he or she first needs the job to qualify for access to such a home. In creating this unintended outcome, the court likely misunderstood the relationship between housing and employment. It is more likely that employment opportunity, not housing opportunity, dictates migration patterns.

In addition to selection criteria, access to mortgage financing emerges as a critical factor in determining the profile of occupants of *Mount Laurel* units that were sold rather than rented. An overwhelming majority of applicants who failed to make it through the purchase process failed at the mortgage-financing stage. It would appear that being poor enough to qualify for a *Mount Laurel* home often also meant one was too poor to obtain a mortgage loan to buy it. If, therefore, developers priced units at or near mortgage-qualifying levels, they would include only a very narrow pool of potential buyers. The pool would include only those low- and moderate-income households at the very top of their respective income eligibility categories. Slightly higher unit prices would tend to render the relationship between *Mount Laurel* income tests and mortgage-qualifying tests an insurmountable problem. Lower prices could render the market-rate unit component of the project unmarketable because of the stigma associated with very low income neighborhoods.

It has also been suggested that often black residents didn't move from cities to *Mount Laurel* housing in the suburbs as a matter of voluntary choice. However, although smaller in total numbers, a larger percentage of low- and moderate-income urban black families entered the applicant pool for *Mount Laurel* housing than did their white counterparts. This would suggest that low- and moderate-income black families were willing to test the suburban waters.

It appears from available data that limiting *Mount Laurel* housing eligibility to low- and moderate-income families and placing an emphasis on relocating eligible families out of deteriorating cities and into growing suburbs did not constitute sufficient guidance or enforcement by the court to engender meaningful dispersal. Within the predominantly white pool of successful applicants for *Mount Laurel* housing built in the suburbs, 39 percent are sixty-two years of age or older; 15 percent are white females over the age of sixty-two living alone; 64 percent are female-headed households; 17 percent are single-parent households; and 20 percent are households with residents ranging in age from eighteen to thirty-five. Suburban municipalities and builders appear to have taken care of their own.

The Mount Laurel Legacy

Bold and passionate actions that take the judiciary into the breach between law and politics often result in both intended and unintended consequences or interpretations. This may result from failures on the court's part—by not making its intentions clear; by misunderstanding the facts and circumstances surrounding the case; by not putting sufficient "steel" in its rulings (to use Chief Justice Wilentz's word) to prevent the elected branches from diluting and minimizing the court's intentions; or by not retaining a presence to monitor implementation of the law.

In formulating the *Mount Laurel* doctrine, the New Jersey Supreme Court intended for there to be a substantial increase in the production of affordable housing in the state. And a significant number of affordable housing units were constructed in the state as a direct result of the court's rulings.

The court also intended, at least in the early stages of implementation, that affordable housing constructed pursuant to the *Mount Laurel* doctrine be located in the state's developing suburbs where such housing had previously been discouraged. Other than units created as a result of Regional Contribution Agreements, a majority of the affordable housing units created in response to the mandates of the new law were in fact constructed in the state's growing suburbs.

The court intended that the newly constructed affordable housing units be occupied by low- and moderate-income families who had previously lived in the state's economically and socially declining cities. The court's intention in this regard was, for the most part, not accomplished.

Moreover, by not directly addressing the racial element of America's unfulfilled promise of equal justice for all, the court may have unintentionally omitted significant segments of the population from the reach of *Mount Laurel.* And by providing an avenue of escape from the grip of declining cities to low- and moderate-income households of the majority community, the court may have unintentionally fueled both white flight and suburbanization, the very symptoms and causes of social inequality the court sought to eradicate.

While Justice Hall expressly disavowed any intention for *Mount Laurel* to serve as a planning decision addressing the needs of the state's cities, it is largely in the area of state planning that the landmark case has earned its national reputation. In Justice Hall's words, "This is a housing opinion, a rights opinion, put practically on a moral basis." He said as well that "[the case] also does not deal with the red hot issue of timed growth or managed growth."[55]

Scholars, having defined "smart growth" as patterns of development that are environmentally and economically sustainable and socially equitable, have described the *Mount Laurel* court as being prescient in its understanding of this planning principle, which would not be widely embraced until more than a decade later. That *Mount Laurel* positioned New Jersey as a pioneer in the area of state growth management is attested to by the fact that, as of 1983, only six other states had adopted laws creating statewide agencies and planning regulatory systems to address land use growth management issues. Of these six, only Oregon included housing needs explicitly as part of a statewide growth management program.[56]

Mount Laurel has been duly credited with positioning New Jersey as a national pioneer in the area of statewide housing needs assessment and allocation. This view is supported by the fact that, as of 1983, only California regularly assessed and allocated housing needs to local governments albeit in a much less direct manner than provided for under the *Mount Laurel* doctrine.[57]

The courageous and persistent efforts of Ethel Lawrence to challenge the exclusionary zoning practices that forced her daughter to live in a converted chicken coop and many of her neighbors to leave their homes have been compared to the courage exhibited by Rosa Parks when she refused in 1955 to give up her seat to a white passenger on a bus in Montgomery, Alabama. The arrest and prosecution of the quiet and dignified Mrs. Parks for her seemingly harmless act shook the state of Alabama and the nation and triggered the earliest elements of the civil rights movement, which in turn changed the nation's view of African Americans and ended legal segregation in this country. Initial reports of the invidious effects of exclusionary zoning on the life of a quiet and dignified lady named Ethel Lawrence likewise shook the state of New Jersey and the nation and triggered a refocusing on fundamental American values and principles.

The difference between the two events is that the former mobilized great numbers of outraged black Americans and launched a movement for social change and social justice that found sympathy and cooperation from similarly large numbers of white Americans. The latter launched a long and tedious series of lawsuits. A nation that had again been awakened to the failure of America to keep its promise of equality and equal access to life, liberty, and property for all of its citizens was allowed to dissociate itself from these injustices while lawyers fought the battle in the courts. Outrage among both black and white citizens dissolved into apathy, and what might have been another serious social movement became a spectator sport.

Gandhi and Mandela understood that social change and the eradication of social injustice are far more likely to occur as a result of social struggle and political empowerment than through legal struggle. Even for those who believe that racism and racial injustice are a permanent part of American culture, the struggle is itself liberating and, therefore, important. The struggle can, and should, include involvement of the courts. And the struggle should continue whether the gains are meager or substantial, permanent or temporary. In the words of Derrick Bell on the matter of the effects of the civil rights movement: "[T]angible progress has been made and the pull of unfinished business is sufficient to strengthen and spur determination."[58]

For a brief moment, though, the nation shook as word spread of Ethel Lawrence's defiant act against rules intended to obstruct America's promise of equality for all, and of the New Jersey Supreme Court's bold reaction to her claim. The tremors quickly subsided, however, and they will not be felt again until the injustices uncovered and attacked by Mrs. Lawrence and the court become part of a broad-based political strategy to organize and unify urban and suburban interests into an empowered coalition—that is, until a legitimate movement for social change in the area of affordable housing choices has been launched by activists, strengthened and determined by the pull of unfinished business.

NOTES

1. Like many landmark cases, *Mount Laurel* is actually a series of cases generally referred to as *Mount Laurel I, Mount Laurel II,* and *Mount Laurel III.* As of this writing the case is before the New Jersey Supreme Court for what will ultimately be *Mount Laurel IV.*

2. See, for example, Brief for New Jersey State Conference of the National Association for the Advancement of Colored People and Latino Network as Amici Curiae Supporting Appellants, In the Matter of the Adoption of N.J.A.C. 5:96 and 5:97 by the New Jersey Council on Affordable Housing, 416 N.J. Super 462 (App. Div. 2010) (Docket No. A-5382–07t3).

3. Ibid. at i.

4. See, for example, Brief for New Jersey Coalition on Affordable Housing as Amici Curiae Supporting Appellants, In The Matter of the Adoption of N.J.A.C. 5:96 and 5:97 by the New Jersey Council on Affordable Housing, 416 N.J. Super 462 (App. Div. 2010) (Docket No. A-5382–07t3).

5. *Southern Burlington County NAACP v. Township of Mount Laurel,* 67 N.J. 151 (1975) (hereafter *Mount Laurel I*).

6. *Southern Burlington County NAACP v. Township of Mount Laurel,* 92 N.J. 158 (1983) (hereafter *Mount Laurel II*).

7. Ibid. at 199.

8. *Abbott v. Burke,* 119 N.J. 287 (1990). This case has been before the New Jersey Supreme Court twenty-one times; the decisions are referred to as *Abbott v. Burke I* through *Abbott v. Burke XXI.* Some commentators describe the court's retreat in *Mount Laurel* as being both appropriate and predictable. See, for example, Paula A. Franzese, "Mount Laurel III: The New Jersey Supreme Court's Judicious Retreat," *Seton Hall Law Review* 18 (1988): 30. Such commentators contend that the court's attempt to implement the constitutional obligation was never intended to usurp the responsibilities of the political branches and that creation of legislation purporting to implement the new law represented a presumptively meaningful response from the political branches that deserved deference from the court. I fully agree with the first point and equally disagree with the second. In my view, the political response to implementing the mandates and goals of *Mount Laurel* goes far beyond normal and acceptable political compromise and represents instead a deliberate attempt to blunt the intent and promise of the ruling. This reality, in my view, provides a more than adequate justification for the court to have remained more deeply engaged in *Mount Laurel's* implementation.

9. The National Advisory Commission on Civil Disorders was established by President Lyndon B. Johnson on July 28, 1967, to investigate the causes of the 1967 race riots in the United States and to provide recommendations for the future. The eleven-member commission was chaired by Otto Kerner, then governor of Illinois. The commission is often referred to as the Kerner Commission and its report as the Kerner Commission Report.

   The Governor's Select Commission on Civil Disorder was established by Governor Richard J. Hughes on August 8, 1967, to examine the causes, incidents, and remedies for the civil disorders that occurred in New Jersey in that year. The ten-member commission was chaired by Robert D. Lilley of New Jersey Bell. The commission is often referred as the Lilley Commission and its report as the Lilley Report.

10. *Mount Laurel I,* 67 N.J. at 159.

11. Ibid.

12. Ibid. at 174.

13. Ibid. at 170.

14. Ibid. at 160.

15. Ibid. at 196 (Pashman, J., concurring).

16. *Booker v. Bd. of Ed of Plainfield*, 45 N.J. 161 (1965).

17. *Jenkins v. Twp. of Morris School District*, 58 N.J. 483 (1971).

18. See, for example, *Robinson v. Cahill*, 62 N.J. 473 (1973).

19. *Mount Laurel II*, 92 N.J. at 210, n.5 (1983).

20. National Advisory Commission on Civil Disorders, *Report of the National Advisory Commission on Civil Disorders*, 5 (1968).

21. Robert C. Holmes, "A Black Perspective on Mount Laurel II: Toward a Black 'Fair Share,'" *Seton Hall Law Review* 14 (1984): 944.

22. Poor cities were designated by the New Jersey Department of Community Affairs as "urban aid" municipalities. Criteria for this designation included the number of children in the Aid to Dependent Children Program, the extent of publicly assisted housing, and the relative stability of the municipal tax base. According to the 1980 U.S. Census, 75 percent of the state's black residents lived in the forty-two urban aid municipalities, but black residents still only accounted for 31 percent of the overall population of those municipalities, a clear majority being white. Similarly, while 18,183 black families qualified as low income and 20,907 as moderate income in the forty urban aid communities, 37,803 white families qualified as low income and 59,934 as moderate income in these same municipalities.

23. Naomi Bailin Wish and Stephen Eisdorfer, "The Impact of Mt. Laurel Initiatives: An Analysis of the Characteristics of Applicants and Occupants," *Seton Hall Law Review* 27 (1997): 1268.

24. Deconcentration of the urban poor (often particularly focused on minority poor) has been described as sometimes being used as "a smokescreen to conceal what amounted to the cleansing of cities." See, for example, Stephen Steinberg, "The Myth of Concentrated Poverty," in *The Integration Debate: Competing Futures for American Cities*, ed. Chester A. Hartman and Gregory D. Squires (New York: Routledge, 2010), 214. According to this theory, the "cleansing" was done to make increasingly desirable (and, therefore, valuable) urban real estate available for gentrification.

25. New Jersey Department of Community Affairs, Division of State and Regional Planning, State Development Guide Plan (SDGP) (May 1980). The SDGP, promulgated pursuant to *New Jersey Statues Annotated*, sec. 13:113–115.52, serves as a master plan for the state's future development.

26. *Mount Laurel II*, 92 N.J. at 210, n.5 (1983).

27. In this context, "police power" refers to the fundamental power vested in states to govern, including making and enforcing laws. Controlled by state constitutions and other limitations, such as due process, this power must be exercised for the protection and preservation of public health, morals, order, safety, and the general welfare of the state's inhabitants and can be delegated to local units of government.

28. Ibid. at 211.

29. Ibid. at 238.

30. *Report for Action of the New Jersey Governor's Select Commission on Civil Disorder* xi (State of New Jersey ed., 1968).

31. Jerome Rose and Robert E. Rothman, *After Mount Laurel: The New Suburban Zoning* (New Brunswick, NJ: Center for Urban Policy Research Press, 1977), 11.

32. Ibid., 44.

33. *Mount Laurel II*, 92 N.J. at 212.

34. *Marbury v. Madison*, 5 U.S. 137, 177 (1803).

35. Derrick A. Bell Jr., *Race, Racism and American Law* (New York: Aspen Publishers, 2008), 597.

36. Ibid., quoting Additional Statement of Judge Higginbotham, Commission of Civil Disobedience, National Commission on the Causes & Prevention of Violence at 16 (December 1969).

37. *Hills Development Company v. Bernards Twp.*, 103 N.J. 1 (1986).

38. Senator Lipman was first elected in 1971 and continued to be the only black woman elected to the state senate through five successive terms.

39. Wynona Lipman, "The 'Fair' Housing Act?" *Seton Hall Legislative Journal* 9 (1986): 569.

40. Ibid., 570.

41. Ibid.

42. Derrick A. Bell Jr., "Brown v. Board of Education and the Interest-Convergence Dilemma," *Harvard Law Review* 93 (1980): 518.

43. See John O. Calmore, "Spatial Equality and the Kerner Commission Report: A Back-to-the-Future Essay," *North Carolina Law Review* 71 (1993): 1487. Calmore reminds us that decades ago the Kerner Report concluded that the future of American cities would be enhanced only through the combination of enrichment programs designed to improve the quality of life in black communities and programs designed to encourage integration of substantial numbers of blacks into American society beyond the ghetto. The Kerner Report, according to Calmore, warned that integration would not occur quickly and that enrichment ("spatial equity") therefore had to be an important adjunct to any program of integration. The *Mount Laurel* court's focus on deconcentration of the urban poor as a way to improve cities, as opposed to improving cities as part of a plan to improve the quality of life for the urban poor, opens the door for a challenge to the court's motive.

44. Steven Oroho, "Another COAH Surprise: RCAs Outlawed by Corzine to Be Reincarnated Under New Name," *New Jersey Senate* (2009), http://www.senatenj.com/index.php/oroho/another-coah-surprise-rcas-outlawed-by-corzine-to-be-reincarnated-under-new-name/4074 (last accessed October 24, 2012).

45. See David Kinsey, "Smart Growth, Housing Needs, and the Future of the *Mount Laurel* Doctrine," in *Mount Laurel II at 25: The Unfinished Agenda of Fair Share Housing*, ed. Timothy N. Castano and Dale Sattin (Princeton, NJ: Public Institute for the Region, 2008). This is an excellent discussion of COAH's shortcomings and the effect of those shortcomings on *Mount Laurel* outcomes.

46. Lipman, "Fair Housing," 573.

47. New Jersey Statutes Annotated, sec. 52:18A-196 (West 2012).

48. Ibid.

49. "Proposed and Completed Affordable Units," *New Jersey Department of Community Affairs—Local Planning Services* (March 1, 2011), http://www.nj.gov/dca/services/lps/hss/transinfo/reports/units.pdf (last accessed October 25, 2012).

50. New Jersey Department of Community Affairs, *State of New Jersey 2010–2014 State of New Jersey 2010—2014 Consolidated Plan*, 58 (State of New Jersey, 2010).

51. Statewide housing needs assessment is difficult to state precisely because different sources offer conflicting estimates, and the numbers continuously change based upon unit counts as they are completed.

52. Brief for the Legal Services of New Jersey as Amici Curiae Supporting Appellants, In the Matter of the Adoption of N.J.A.C. 5:96 and 5:97 by the New Jersey Council on Affordable Housing, 416 N.J. Super 462 (App. Div. 2010) (Docket No. A-5382–07t3).

53. Franzese makes this point in her article but concludes that the proper relationship among the branches of government justified the court's retreat. Franzese, "Mount Laurel III," 50.

54. See Wish and Eisdorfer, "The Impact of Mt. Laurel Initiatives."

55. Rose and Rothman, *After Mount Laurel*, 11 and 12.

56. Kinsey, "Smart Growth," 5.

57. Ibid., 6.

58. Derrick A. Bell Jr., *And We Are Not Saved: The Elusive Quest for Racial Justice* (New York: Basic Books, 1987), 5.

4

In Re Karen Ann Quinlan (1976)

Establishing a Patient's Right to Die in Dignity

ROBERT S. OLICK AND PAUL W. ARMSTRONG

On September 10, 1975, Joseph and Julia Quinlan petitioned the Morris County, New Jersey, court for legal guardianship of their twenty-one-year-old daughter Karen Ann, who was in a persistent vegetative state (PVS). They sought permission to direct removal of the respirator sustaining her life. Approximately six months earlier, Karen had been rushed to the emergency room of Newton Memorial Hospital after suffering a cardiac arrest, being deprived of oxygen to the brain, and falling into a coma. Soon thereafter, Karen's care was transferred to Saint Clare's Hospital in Denville, a larger and better-equipped facility known to the Quinlans, where she was being cared for at the time of the petition.

PVS is a condition in which all cognitive functions of the brain have been lost, resulting in complete unawareness of self and the environment. At the same time, PVS patients retain some of the brain stem functions that regulate autonomic activities of the body such as breathing. There is virtually no hope of recovery from an accurately diagnosed PVS to a cognitive sapient state. With medical interventions, hospital and nursing home patients have been known to survive in PVS for as long as thirty-seven years.

Karen had been adopted as a baby after Julia suffered several miscarriages and a stillbirth. Julia would later give birth to two children who would grow to look up to Karen as their big sister. Her siblings, parents, and many friends knew her as smart, funny, warm, and vibrant—a young girl with a marked streak of independence and a joy for living. The Quinlans were a hardworking, private, middle-class, and devoutly Catholic family, well liked in their community. As they confronted Karen's dilemma, and theirs, with both profound sadness and extraordinary dignity, they would look often to their faith for guidance.

After much private and public agonizing, and many consultations with their parish priest, Father Thomas Trapasso, the Quinlans resolved that Karen would not want to have her biological life sustained indefinitely in this unblessed condition and that it was in her best interests to be set free from the tyranny of the machine that forced her to breathe. In keeping with the treating physician's initial suggestion, they requested that the respirator be removed, allowing her to die. Initially, the hospital agreed to honor their request and asked the Quinlans to sign a consent and release form directing the physician to "discontinue all extraordinary measures, including the use of a respirator" and releasing the physician and the hospital from liability.[1] However, the physician and hospital quickly changed their positions. They refused to comply with the parents' request, setting the stage for the landmark litigation to follow.

This was a time when high-technology medicine's capacity to deploy respirators, feeding tubes, dialysis, and other tools to prolong life and forestall death was growing rapidly, but the nascent field of bioethics had just begun to sprout roots, and the voice of the law was largely silent. In another societal sphere, the civil rights movement was expressing a broad cultural commitment to the rights of the individual.

In health care these forces converged in profound questions that to this day reverberate throughout society: How do we die? Is there a right to refuse treatment? Who should decide for incompetent patients? And on what basis—the patient's wishes or best interests?

Questions surrounding decisions near the end of life quickly became the core of bioethical discourse, and Karen Ann Quinlan's plight the polestar of the debate. The New Jersey Supreme Court's seminal opinion remains the most frequently cited case in the annals of American bioethics.

The Right to Refuse Treatment on Trial

The Quinlans' petition asserted that Karen had a right to refuse life-sustaining treatment, and sought to have the power to exercise that right reposed in her father with express authority to direct discontinuance of "all extraordinary means" sustaining her life. Karen's right to refuse treatment was premised on a number of grounds, most significantly the constitutional right of privacy to be free from unwanted medical interventions.

Opposing the petition were her physicians, the hospital, the county prosecutor, the state of New Jersey, and the guardian *ad litem* appointed by the court to represent Karen's best interests. In essence, these parties collectively maintained that there is no constitutional "right to die;" there is a compelling state interest in favor of preserving human life, and to remove the respirator would be homicide and an act of euthanasia. Protective of decisions once the exclusive province of their profession, the physicians argued that whether to continue the respirator was for the medical profession to decide, and that accepted norms of medical practice required aggressive efforts to sustain life. It was further contended that removing the respirator demanded that others assess the quality of Karen's life, a morally objectionable precedent for future cases.

After six days of trial, and testimony from medical experts, theologians, and, most importantly, Karen's father, mother, sister, and a good friend, the trial judge rejected the Quinlans' position and adopted instead that of the medical profession and the state. Siding with the medical profession, he ruled that "[t]here *is* a duty to continue the life-assisting apparatus if, within the treating physician's opinion, it should be done."[2] Striking an extra blow at the family, the judge kept the court-appointed attorney as guardian of Karen's person and refused to appoint Joseph Quinlan as his daughter's guardian. The Quinlans' reaction to the trial court's ruling is chronicled in their book *Karen Ann.*[3] The decision was clearly disheartening, but from a legal standpoint it was not surprising. Asking a trial court to find a "new" constitutional right was a legal long shot. But the argument artfully set forth precisely the sort of questions that typically come before appellate courts. The ruling was soon followed by an expedited appeal to the New Jersey Supreme Court.

The New Jersey Supreme Court's Landmark Decision

A Constitutional Right to Refuse Treatment

In the first judicial ruling of its kind, the New Jersey Supreme Court held that Karen Quinlan, an incompetent patient in a persistent vegetative state, had the right to refuse the respirator which artificially sustained her life, and appointed her father the legal guardian with authority to exercise this right on his daughter's behalf. Reversing the lower court's decision, the New Jersey Supreme Court ruled that a patient has a fundamental constitutional right to refuse life-sustaining treatment, grounded in the right of privacy under the federal and state constitutions. Finding the legal underpinnings for the right of privacy in the U.S. Supreme Court's decisions in the area of procreation, *Quinlan* held that "this right is broad enough to encompass a patient's decision to decline medical treatment under certain circumstances, in much the same way as it is broad enough to encompass a woman's decision to terminate pregnancy under certain conditions."[4] The court also ruled that the right of privacy under the New Jersey state constitution encompasses the right to refuse life-sustaining treatment.

Like other constitutional rights, the constitutional right to refuse treatment is not absolute and must be balanced against certain countervailing state (societal) interests. At issue here were the state's interests in preserving life, in preventing suicide, and in safeguarding the integrity of the medical profession. In an often-quoted passage, the court said in *Quinlan* that "the State's interest *contra* weakens and the individual's right to privacy grows as the degree of bodily invasion increases and the prognosis dims."[5]

Society's interest in preserving the life of a vegetative patient with no hope of recovery must be subordinated to the contrary assertion of the patient's right to refuse unwanted life support. Further, rejection of life support in these circumstances is an exercise of self-determination, not an act of purposeful self-destruction, which defines suicide. Nor is removal of life support in compliance with the patient's and family's request homicide or euthanasia (sometimes known as mercy killing). Finally, removal of the respirator in accordance with the family's request did not offend principles of medical ethics. The court's strongly worded conclusion was that "no external compelling interest of the State could compel Karen to endure the unendurable, only to vegetate a few measurable months with no realistic possibility of returning to any semblance of cognitive or sapient life."[6]

Just five years earlier in, *John F. Kennedy Memorial Hospital v. Heston*, the New Jersey Supreme Court had held that a hospital could overrule a mother's refusal of a life-saving blood transfusion on behalf of her now-incompetent adult daughter that was based on their shared commitment to the Jehovah's Witness faith.[7] In *Quinlan*, the court distinguished this precedent on the ground that the state's interest was far weightier in *Heston* where the intervention was lifesaving and would likely serve to restore the patient's health and well-being. But the court's commitment in *Quinlan* to putting the patient's voice first also meant that *Heston* would later be seen as wrongly decided.

Two further constitutional arguments were presented in *Quinlan*. First, if the refusal of life-sustaining treatment is firmly based on Karen's and her family's religious beliefs, then the constitution's free exercise of religion clause compels the state to honor these beliefs, not overrule them as in *Heston*. Second, mandating continued life support for a PVS patient violated the constitutional prohibition against cruel and unusual punishment. In the court's view, neither argument presented a constitutional issue, nor have these constitutional provisions played a meaningful role in the development of jurisprudence since that time.

But framing the issues in terms of Judeo-Christian traditions and teachings with respect to forgoing extraordinary medical interventions was part of a multifaceted strategy and would play a critical role in the case. Emphasis on the family's Catholic faith established that removal of the respirator was consistent with Karen's and her family's values and wishes, was ethically permissible and morally licit. It also placed Joseph Quinlan's character beyond reproach in bearing this extraordinary burden.

Was Karen Alive?

Before reaching the constitutional question, the court had to first determine that Karen was alive: that there was a living individual to whom such significant rights would attach. As a general matter, there is no duty to treat a dead patient; if Karen were legally dead, the controversy would be moot.

This aspect of the case is often overlooked because it is now a relatively easy and straightforward matter. All fifty states and the District of Columbia recognize, as a legal standard of death, the irreversible loss of all functions of the entire brain, including the brain stem (often called "whole brain death"). Because the PVS patient retains some brain stem (lower brain) functions that regulate autonomic functions of the body (not to mention that PVS patients show involuntary movements), the patient does not meet this standard. PVS patients are living human beings for whom treatment decisions must be made. The court easily reached this same conclusion, agreeing with the lower court's finding.

At the time, however, the law had only begun to establish whole brain death as a legal standard for determining death. The opinion's extensive discussion of this question presaged the court's explicit recognition of whole brain death in *Strachan v. J.F.K. Memorial Hospital*.[8] It was influential in development of the New Jersey Bioethics Commission's proposed legislation recognizing the whole brain death standard, enacted into law in 1991.[9] That the issue is rarely even mentioned in later cases addressing treatment refusal attests to the infancy of bioethical jurisprudence at the time of *Quinlan*.

Putting Patients and Families in Charge

Chief Justice Hughes's opinion for a unanimous court signaled a radical transformation of the way we understand the patient-family-physician relationship and the place of societal values in shaping that relationship. The court sent the clear message that ultimate decisional authority rests with the patient and family, not with the physician. In the words of the chief justice, "the interests of the patient, as seen by her surrogate, the guardian, must be evaluated by the court as predominant, even in the face of an opinion *contra* by the present attending physicians."[10]

The opinion turns on its head the lower court's view that law and society had ceded responsibility for medical ethical decisions to physicians. To the contrary, the authority of medicine ultimately derives from the society it serves. The consensus of members of a professional organization, such as positions of the American Medical Association (AMA) regarding forgoing medical treatment, are critically important, but must yield to more foundational principles of medical ethics embodied in the legal and moral rules of our society. Patients, families, physicians, and societal values are all moral players in decisions near the end of life; ultimately the voice of the patient trumps.

Having established the patient's central place in decisions about his or her own body, the court remained bound to respect (if not embrace) established medical standards and the integrity of the medical profession, and it went to some length to reconcile those standards with the family's refusal of the respirator. At the time, no consensus within medicine could be articulated. Many physicians felt compelled to continue life support for a dying patient, but many others had refused to prolong an undesired dying process for a patient whose condition was irreversible with no hope of cure or recovery. Thus, there was no conflict between the Quinlans' request and medical ethics. By the mid-1980s, the AMA Council on Ethical and Judicial Affairs would issue a series of statements and opinions officially embracing the position that it is ethically permissible to honor the request of an irreversibly dying patient to forgo life-sustaining treatment and to look to appropriate surrogates to make these decisions on the incompetent patient's behalf.

In order to grant the requested relief, the New Jersey Supreme Court had to find that Karen's constitutional right to privacy could be exercised on her behalf even after she became unable to speak for herself. Reversing the lower court's ruling, Karen's father was appointed legal guardian with authority, in consultation with the family, to make decisions on Karen's behalf. This straightforward procedural mechanism answered the question of who should make the decision for Karen in the exercise of her right of privacy.

How this decision should be made, that is, by what substantive standard, was a more challenging question. The Quinlans were authorized to use their "best judgment" to effectuate Karen's interests and wishes. This standard has come to be known as the "substituted judgment" test. Substituted judgment literally means that a decision maker is substituted for the patient who is incapable of making her own decision, and the substituted decision maker is responsible for making the decision the patient would make for herself if competent to do so.

A surrogate's (here the guardian's) primary task is to ascertain and effectuate what the patient would want. In practice, however, the decision to forgo life support also involves assessment of the patient's objective best interests. Families commonly consider a mix of subjective (patient's wishes) and objective (best interests) factors in making substituted judgments. Karen's family and friends knew that she had made prior statements disapproving the use of extraordinary medical procedures to sustain life in circumstances like hers. And they knew that "living" indefinitely in a vegetative state offended her personal values. But, to the court, a handful of previous conversations recounted by friends offered scant evidence to conclude that Karen would refuse the ventilator.

In exercising their best judgment, the Quinlans also used their own judgment of what would be best for Karen. This approach to decision making on behalf of formerly competent patients has long been part of the legal doctrine of substituted judgment developed in other contexts. Since *Quinlan* it has become a core concept in decisions near the end of life. The New Jersey Supreme Court's subsequent end-of-life opinions, in *Conroy* (1985) and in *Farrell, Peter*, and *Jobes* (the 1987 trilogy), provide a more extensive articulation of the continuum of standards and evidence at work in surrogate decisions.[11] The standard for surrogate decisions, examined further below, has been among the most difficult and controversial legal issues in end-of-life jurisprudence.

The petition for authority to direct discontinuance of "all extraordinary medical procedures" sustaining Karen's life was carefully crafted in conformity with the family's values. As devout Catholics, the Quinlans could not in good conscience choose to withdraw the ventilator unless they could place this decision squarely within the teachings and tenets of their faith.

Traditional Judeo-Christian teaching holds that extraordinary medical treatment may be withheld or withdrawn based on the patient's wishes. A widely accepted definition of "extraordinary" treatment holds that an intervention is extraordinary when it would impose excessive pain, suffering, expense or inconvenience and offers no reasonable prospect of benefit for the patient. By contrast, "ordinary" treatment offers a reasonable hope of patient benefit and does not impose excessive pain, suffering, expense or inconvenience.

Applying these concepts to particular cases involves asking whether the benefits of the treatment are proportional to its risks and burdens for the patient. On this view of Catholic teaching, interventions considered ordinary are often deemed obligatory; those considered extraordinary are deemed optional and may be withheld or withdrawn. In consultation with Father Trapasso, who testified at trial, and aided by scholarly commentary, official Church pronouncements and other experts, the Quinlans concluded that the ventilator sustaining Karen's biological life was an extraordinary intervention that imposed an extraordinary burden with no meaningful benefit, and that it was permissible to withdraw it to allow a natural dying process to take its course.

This framing of the argument placed a doctrinal dialogue before an American court of law in a manner that was both unusual and remarkable. The court allowed an amicus curiae (friend of the court) brief to be filed by the New Jersey Catholic Conference, reviewed the "allocutio" (address) of Pope Pius XII, and reviewed testimony at trial from a number of theologians. After a fashion, the teachings of the Church and the testimony of theologians played the part of moral and spiritual advisor.

Yet, in the final analysis, the court's decision was decidedly secular. The stated purpose of the court's doctrinal exploration was to examine and confirm Joseph Quinlan's character, conscience, motivation, and commitment as guardian. The opinion makes clear that no precedent concerning the role of religion in the civil law was intended, nor has the case been interpreted in this way. This aspect of the case has received comparatively little attention over the years. But inquiry into and respect for patients' religious values and beliefs have become standard guideposts in the process of asking what the patient would choose and constructing a substituted judgment in keeping with the patient's wishes and values.

Process and Safeguards: Institutional Ethics Committees

Quinlan is also notable for its introduction of institutional ethics committees as participants in end-of-life decisions. It had been some time since Karen's medical condition had been confirmed. Her parents were free to choose different physicians for Karen, and the treating physicians might harbor concerns about legal liability even after the New Jersey Supreme Court's ruling. To address these concerns, the court designed a process and safeguards to facilitate implementation of its decision. In sum, if the treating physicians concluded, based on a current medical evaluation of Karen, that her condition was irreversible with no reasonable prospect of recovery to a cognitive, sapient state, and the family maintained its request for withdrawal of the ventilator, an "ethics committee" of the hospital should be established and consulted. If that consultative body agreed that there was no reasonable possibility of Karen's ever emerging from her comatose condition, the ventilator could be withdrawn. The family, physicians, hospital, and others involved in implementing this decision would be immune from civil or criminal liability.

The court also prescribed that this process be followed in future cases in which termination of life support for permanently unconscious patients is considered. In doing so, it understood ethics committees as a mechanism to free physicians from concerns about legal entanglements (such as charges of homicide or civil suits) that might otherwise impair their ability to exercise independent medical judgment in the best interests of dying patients. Going a step further, *Quinlan* extended a grant of judicial immunity from civil and criminal liability for future cases in which the so-called Quinlan procedures are followed. This novel approach was primarily intended to foster private, institutionally based resolution of treatment decisions for dying patients without need to seek judicial intervention. The concept of ethics committees emerged from the justices themselves (*sua sponte*) drawn from a 1974 law review article authored by a pediatrician; the idea was not advanced by any of the parties to the case.

The ethics committee directive has drawn criticism on at least two noteworthy grounds. Although the court used the term "ethics committee," it assigned to the committee the narrow medical task of confirming Karen's prognosis. Having itself resolved the legal and ethical issues, the opinion crafted a process for ensuring that the decision to remove the ventilator was based on a current and accurate medical diagnosis and prognosis. This made sense as a way to bring closure to the family's dilemma. Arguably, however, it ceded back to the medical profession some of the family's decisional authority. And in the aftermath of *Quinlan*, with the proliferation of ethics committees, there has also been confusion about their functions and those of prognosis committees. As later interpreted by New Jersey hospitals, other courts, and the New Jersey Supreme Court itself, the *Quinlan* procedure mandates prognosis confirmation for PVS patients by a "prognosis committee" comprised of physicians (or by qualified physicians in the absence of a committee), not review of the ethical issues by a multidisciplinary ethics committee.

Nonetheless, multidisciplinary ethics committees would emerge as an important vehicle for shielding the privacy of end-of-life decisions and would come to embrace a patient-centered ethic that serves to empower patients and families facing conflicts with physicians or other health care professionals. By the early 1990s, the Joint Commission on Accreditation of Healthcare Organizations that accredits hospitals would require that all hospitals establish a mechanism for addressing ethical issues in patient care, typically an ethics committee. *Quinlan*'s salutary and lasting contribution, therefore, has been to lay the foundation for evolution of a local institutional process that allows private decisions to be made privately, away from the public glare of the courtroom, in the vast majority of instances.

With the New Jersey Supreme Court's March 31, 1976, decision, the Quinlan family experienced a flood of emotions. Profound gratitude for the courage and compassion of Chief Justice Hughes and the entire court stood beside the somber expectation of transition to rites of passage. The decision should have marked release from their tragedy, a final chapter in their long journey. Shortly after the opinion was rendered, the Quinlans again asked that the respirator be removed, and a while later that Saint Clare's hospital convene an ethics committee pursuant to the court order.

Unfortunately, the attending physician in charge of Karen's care did not fully accept the decision and continued to maintain that he could not in good conscience simply remove the respirator. Instead, the physicians chose to wean her from the respirator, removing it and then reattaching it on a number of occasions when she failed to breathe on her own. Remarkably, after a time Karen did have the strength to breathe on her own. Not long after, she was transferred to Morris View Nursing Home, where she lived for another nine years until her death from pneumonia on June 11, 1985.

During these years, she received daily artificial nutrition and hydration through a nasogastric tube and from time to time antibiotics for infections. Believing that the feeding tube and antibiotics were ordinary care and an expression of basic human caring, the Quinlans never requested that they be stopped.

Rules for Dying: Emergence of a National Consensus

Of the approximately 1.5 million people who die in a hospital setting each year (more than half of all U.S. deaths annually), nearly 70 percent die after a decision to forgo life-sustaining treatment has been made. Most often it is a decision made by family and other surrogates who are called upon to bear the burdens of decision because life-threatening illness and disease have deprived their loved one of the ability to make his or her own decision.

Families struggle daily, in consultation with physicians, nurses, palliative care specialists, and others, to answer the questions: What would my spouse, parent, sibling, or child choose in the face of this irreversible dying process? What is in his or her best interests? What ethical and legal principles and rules should guide us in deciding for others? In the more than thirty years since *Quinlan*'s clarion call, an ethical, legal, and societal consensus has been established about the rules and principles to follow when forgoing life-sustaining treatment.

The Judicial Consensus

As a matter of law, *Quinlan* was binding precedent only in the state of New Jersey. But its reasoning soon began to take hold as persuasive authority across the country. State after state has witnessed an intractable end-of-life controversy involving its own citizens, subjected to the glare of its own courtrooms, vigorously covered and debated before the local and national media. As with Karen Ann Quinlan, we have come to know the names and legal battles of Joseph Saikewicz, William Bartling, Nancy Cruzan, and others for the way they died and for their families' courageous love, much more than for the way they lived.

State courts have consistently embraced the core principles of *Quinlan* to establish rights, processes, and boundaries for decisions near the end of life. Some courts ground the right to refuse treatment in the constitutional right of privacy, others in the common law doctrine of self- determination. The common law has long recognized our right to control our own bodies and to be free from bodily invasions without our consent. In matters of medical treatment, this right is protected by the doctrine of informed consent, which requires physicians to provide patients with information about their medical condition and the risks, benefits, and burdens of treatment options, and to obtain the patient's consent prior to performing a treatment or procedure. The right of self-determination means that patients, and families acting on an incompetent patient's behalf, can choose to accept or to refuse medical treatment, including life-sustaining treatment.

Whether grounded in common law or constitutional law, courts have uniformly recognized a patient's right to refuse life-sustaining treatment as a fundamental tenet of respect for patient autonomy and self-determination, and have consistently held that the incompetent patient's rights may be exercised by an appropriate surrogate on the patient's behalf. In the case of Nancy Cruzan, a young woman from Missouri who, like Karen, was in a persistent vegetative state, the U.S. Supreme Court, in 1990, looked to the liberty interest in the U.S. Constitution to affirm the constitutional basis for the right to refuse treatment.

Courts nationally have uniformly maintained that the right to refuse life support must be balanced against the potentially countervailing state interests: preserving the patient's life and protecting life generally, including the prevention of suicide; safeguarding the integrity of the medical profession; and protecting innocent third parties. But recitation of these societal interests has become pro forma. The consistent message is that society's indirect and abstract interest in preserving life must yield to the individual's much stronger, direct, and personal claim to control the course of his or her own life. Further, refusal of life support is not suicide or attempted suicide, because the patient's intention is not to inflict self-harm directly by ending his or her own life, it is to be free from unwanted medical interventions and dependence on the full array of medical techniques to prolong the dying process. It is the underlying disease or condition that is the cause of the patient's death.

Respecting the patient's refusal honors the patient's intent to allow the dying process to take its course. In rare instances protecting innocent third parties from harm has been found to justify providing medical procedures over the objection of a surrogate (as in the *Heston* case), most often when the patient is a child and the intervention is potentially lifesaving. But the interests of others have not been found sufficient to override an incompetent dying patient's refusal of treatment.

The judiciary has had no difficulty finding that well-established medical authorities, including official policy statements from the AMA and state-level professional and regulatory bodies (such as state medical societies and professional licensing boards), strongly support the physician's professional obligation to respect a patient's right to refuse life-sustaining treatment, whether exercised by the patient or by a family member, health care proxy, or legally appointed guardian. The contention that decisions to terminate life support belong exclusively to the medical profession, which so occupied the *Quinlan* court, has hardly received serious consideration since. Only in rare cases, such as when the patient or surrogate requests active assistance in dying (assisted suicide, which is illegal in nearly all states except Oregon, Washington, and Montana) or insists on medically futile interventions that physicians believe would provide no meaningful benefit, has honoring the patient's wishes presented serious concerns about the boundaries of professional norms.

An especially controversial question has been whether artificially provided fluids and nutrition constitute medical treatment that the patient may refuse on the same basis as other forms of treatment, such as a respirator, dialysis, or surgery. This issue was first addressed by the New Jersey Supreme Court in 1985 in the case of Claire Conroy, an eighty-four-year-old woman with serious and irreversible physical and mental impairments; she was terminally ill (defined as having a life expectancy of one year or less) and her nephew requested withdrawal of a nasogastric feeding tube.

In *Conroy*, the court ruled that the insertion of a feeding tube is a medical procedure like any other intervention upon the body. All life-sustaining interventions are designed to prolong life through artificial means when the body's vital functions are impaired and failing, and all may be refused by the patient or by an appropriate surrogate on the patient's behalf. Again following New Jersey's lead, courts nationally have reached the same conclusion and have drawn no distinction between artificially provided fluids and nutrition and other forms of life-sustaining treatment.

In *Cruzan v. Director, Missouri Dept. of Health*, the U.S. Supreme Court put any lingering controversy about the law to rest. As forcefully stated in Justice Sandra Day O'Connor's concurring opinion, "The liberty guaranteed by the Due Process Clause must protect, if it protects anything, an individual's deeply personal decision to reject medical treatment, including the artificial delivery of food and water."[12] It is important to note, however, that some, like the Quinlans, take a different view of feeding tubes on ethical or religious grounds. Some health care professionals may believe that providing artificial fluids and nutrition (predigested amino acid formula) is very much like food and water and is, therefore, basic human care and an obligatory treatment. The law generally respects such claims of professional conscience and allows health care professionals to transfer care to another provider and withdraw from the case.

How Much Do Surrogate Decision Makers Need to Know?

Families and other surrogates making decisions on behalf of incompetent patients must recall the patient's prior statements, values, and beliefs and construct a narrative of what their loved one would want in the current circumstances. This can often be a difficult task. The challenges inherent in substituted judgment have been among the most controverted and persistent in law, ethics, and practice.

The central legal issue concerns the appropriate standard and burden of proof that must be met before forgoing of life support can be authorized. Couched against the law's time-honored presumption in favor of life, the burden of proof that the patient would refuse life support rests with the surrogate. As in *Quinlan*, courts nationally have received testimony from family, friends, and sometimes religious advisors, attesting to the patient's prior statements, preferences, and values; the same process that occurs informally when such decisions are contemplated in hospitals and within the private confines of the physician-patient-family relationship. Courts have repeatedly struggled with the "probative value" (reliability) of the evidence presented, weighing such factors as specificity, consistency, remoteness in time, and thoughtfulness of prior statements and actions.

Several New Jersey Supreme Court cases after *Quinlan* make plain what was implicit in the *Quinlan* decision. The appropriate legal standard is that families must show by a preponderance of the evidence or by some trustworthy evidence that this is the choice their loved one would make if able to do so. This low evidentiary standard recognizes that families are typically best situated to make decisions faithful to the patient's own wishes and values, but that patients often have not made lengthy and specific statements about the end of life nor put their wishes in writing. It is a family-friendly approach that expresses trust in families and other close surrogates. Adopting a similar approach, sometimes without expressly stating the governing evidentiary rule, most courts across the country have been deferential to the family's role in making these difficult decisions.

A small but significant number of courts have adopted the higher, more burdensome requirement that families show by clear and convincing evidence that the patient would refuse life support under the circumstances. This test demands that proof be sufficiently clear to convince the court that the patient would refuse life support and choose death under the circumstances. A rigorous formulation, set forth by the New York Court of Appeals in 1988, required proof that the patient held a firm and settled commitment to refuse life support under circumstances like the patient's current condition.

The case of Nancy Beth Cruzan ultimately reached the U.S. Supreme Court because the Missouri Supreme Court ruled that her family did not present clear and convincing evidence that she would refuse life support rather than be sustained indefinitely in a persistent vegetative state. The U.S. Supreme Court affirmed the patient's constitutional rights to refuse life support, but it also held that states may (but are not required to) adopt procedural rules to govern how these decisions are made, including to require clear and convincing evidence of the patient's refusal of life support. This more demanding standard expresses skepticism, if not distrust, of the family's ability to make substituted judgments and creates significant obstacles to family authority in the handful of states to adopt this standard.

A state's legal standard has a significant impact on patient-care decisions. The more stringent clear and convincing evidence rule in force in a handful of states may influence health care providers to be unduly cautious and to reject the family's account of the patient's wishes, fearing that compliance with the family's decision would contravene the law. This risk-averse posture can have a chilling effect on respect for patients' previously expressed wishes and on the authority of families to decide. Holding families to a less rigorous standard, such as having some trustworthy evidence, proof by a preponderance of the evidence, or a similar formulation—the rule in New Jersey and a majority of states—induces greater deference to the special role of loving family members at the bedside.

In practice, however, attaching a legal label to the degree of certainty needed to warrant termination of life support does little to help family and physician decide when to take comfort in the belief that this is what the patient would want. The clear and convincing standard suggests that family and physician must believe the patient would refuse life support with a bit more certainty, but it offers little guidance to those who must daily weigh and balance what is known of the patient's prior expressions.

Ethics Committees

Overall, the judicial response to *Quinlan*'s deployment of ethics committees has been far less uniform. A number of states mirror the *Quinlan* procedure for PVS patients. Other courts encourage, but do not require, resort to ethics committees in their broader, more familiar role. There is nonetheless broad acceptance of *Quinlan*'s underlying objective. Decisions near the end of life should be made privately, with resort to a local review process to resolve disagreements where necessary. Courts should not be involved in life-sustaining treatment decisions except in unusual circumstances.

Against this legal backdrop, ethics committees have emerged to play an important dispute resolution role in hospitals across the country. The ethics committee movement received a major shot in the arm in the early 1990s when the Joint Commission mandated that all facilities it accredits establish and maintain a mechanism for addressing ethical issues in patient care, a quasi-legal mandate widely interpreted to mean an ethics committee. Though hospitals have rarely been legally required to establish an ethics committee, most hospitals in the United States have done so; those that have not typically rely on one or more ethics consultants.

Legislatures Respond: The Proliferation of Advance Directive Laws

Concurrent with the judiciary's involvement in resolving refusal-of-treatment cases, state legislatures began to grapple with end-of-life decisions. In many cases, the issues first played out in a poignant and public courtroom drama, contributing to heightened public demand for the right to control one's own dying process and stimulating otherwise reticent state legislatures to act.

Legislative activity focused on the root problem of substituted judgment—how can we know what the patient would choose? The answer has been to authorize, permit, and encourage individuals to put their wishes for future care in writing, in order to guide and control decisions at a later time when competence is lost and one is unable to decide for oneself. All fifty states and the District of Columbia now have laws recognizing the right of citizens to author an advance directive for health care, that is, a health care proxy (durable power of attorney for health care), a living will, or both. New Jersey's Advance Directives for Health Care Act, written by the state Bioethics Commission and enacted into law in 1991, recognizes all three approaches to advance care planning.[13]

The health care proxy appoints a trusted family member or friend to engage in the informed consent process in the patient's place and to make decisions on the patient's behalf. First and foremost, the proxy's fiduciary responsibility is to respect and implement the patient's wishes and values; secondarily it is to decide in accord with the patient's best interests. The living will sets forth with some specificity instructions to family, physicians and others, perhaps stating the sorts of conditions (dependence on a ventilator, inability to meaningfully communicate with others) that are unwanted, where one would choose to allow a natural dying process to take its course.

The first advance directive law, California's Natural Death Act," was enacted in 1976, several months after the *Quinlan* decision.[14] Mirroring the judicial consensus, every state now expressly authorizes use of advance directives to refuse life support when a person is terminally ill or permanently unconscious.

In many parts of the country, the symbolic and cultural significance of providing basic sustenance, together with the mistaken belief that discontinuing artificial fluids and nutrition for PVS patients causes death by starvation and dehydration, made the feeding tube issue the most contentious one in the advance-directives debate. The vast majority of states follow the judicial consensus, making no distinction between feeding tubes and other forms of medical treatment. Some state laws establish special rules, however, such as requiring that refusal of artificially provided fluids and nutrition be reasonably and specifically known or proved by clear and convincing evidence.

Like most bioethical issues, decisions near the end of life have historically been seen as state law matters, to be addressed in the "laboratory of the states." Departing from this convention, in 1990 Congress passed the Patient Self-Determination Act (PSDA).[15] Under the PSDA, upon admission to the hospital all patients are to be given information about their rights to make decisions near the end of life and to write an advance directive, are to be asked whether they have an advance directive, and the patient's "advance directive status" is to be documented in the medical chart. Collectively, this body of state and federal statutory law builds upon and expands the end-of-life consensus that began with the judiciary.

The quest for responses to the evidentiary dilemma and to the value we attach to dying on our own terms has led to widespread acceptance of advance directives in the medical, legal, and academic communities and throughout society. Advance directives have come to be regarded as the preferred and legally recognized mechanism for assuring that it is one's own wishes and values that count when treatment decisions must be made. It is most often recommended that one designate a health care proxy and also give that person some specific written guidance, combining the health care proxy and living will approaches. But some prefer the ease and flexibility of the short proxy form, especially in those few states (New York is one) that recognize by statute only the proxy document. By far the most common use of advance directives is to refuse unwanted life-sustaining treatments and to choose a more natural dying process, but these documents can also be used to request treatment near the end of life.

Despite their featured place in approaches to deciding on behalf of incompetent patients, advance directives refusing treatment have fallen far short of widely shared expectations, largely because most of us do not write advance directives. National studies have consistently found that only approximately 20 percent of people have done so. Patients with diagnosed chronic illnesses and the elderly tend to put their wishes in writing more often than the national average.

Even when patients do have advance directives, if they were made years earlier they must be interpreted to see how closely they fit the current circumstances. While substantial deference is due the health care proxy's view, family members and physicians sometimes disagree about the meaning and interpretation of the document, together with other evidence of the patient's wishes. Advance directives offer substantial assurance that the patient's wishes will control, and they also ease the burdens of decision for those responsible for the patient's care, but they do not always answer with sufficient clarity the central question—what would the patient choose?

Summary of the End-of-Life Consensus

The *Quinlan* legacy is aptly summarized by the following principles that form the pillars of the widely accepted framework for deciding to forgo life-sustaining treatment on behalf of incompetent patients. Many can be found in the *Quinlan* decision itself; others represent later developments in the law governing end-of-life decisions.

1) Competent patients have a constitutional and common law right to refuse treatment, including life-sustaining treatment.
2) No right is absolute, and countervailing interests in preserving life, preventing suicide, safeguarding the integrity of the medical profession, and

protecting innocent third parties from harm must be considered. But instances in which these societal interests outweigh a patient's right to refuse life support when terminally ill or permanently unconscious are rare.

3) The right to refuse treatment encompasses all life-sustaining treatments, including artificially provided nutrition and hydration.

4) These rights are not lost with loss of decisional capacity and may be exercised by families, health care proxies, and other appropriate surrogates on behalf of incompetent patients.

5) Surrogate decision makers should seek first and foremost to follow the patient's wishes. In the exercise of this fiduciary responsibility, the proxy, family, and physician should rely on a patient's advance directive if one has been written, and should look to the patient's past statements, values, and beliefs.

6) When this subjective assessment proves inadequate, the decision may also be based on the patient's best interests, but decisions to terminate life support usually find some basis in the patient's prior expressions.

7) Withholding or withdrawing treatment from a terminally ill or permanently unconscious patient allows a natural dying process to take its course. It does not constitute killing, suicide, assisted suicide, or euthanasia.

8) A local process of review in the clinical setting, such as a hospital ethics committee or ethics consultation service, should be employed to facilitate resolution of misunderstandings and disagreements. Recourse to the courts should be pursued only in exceptional or intractable cases.

9) The right to refuse treatment applies in hospitals, nursing homes, and other care settings.

One critical set of issues regarding the scope of the right to refuse treatment remains largely unaddressed three decades after *Quinlan*. Few cases have squarely reached the issue of forgoing life support for an incompetent patient suffering from a nonterminal, progressive, and irreversible illness, such as early stages of Alzheimer's dementia or those who are substantially cognitively impaired with extremely limited capacity for interaction ("minimally conscious") but are not clinically in PVS. It is clear that the patient's right of refusal is not expressly bounded by the nature of his or her medical condition and prognosis. And a handful of state laws have expressly recognized that advance directives can be used to refuse life-sustaining interventions when a patient is facing a progressive, debilitating, but not yet terminal illness or disease. However, these are issues at the edges of the consensus that await further development. As our population ages and medical science advances, we will need to revisit and come to grips with the full scope of the right to refuse treatment.

Reflections on the Quinlan Legacy

Speaking of the nature of the judicial process, Justice Benjamin Cardozo eloquently wrote, "The sordid controversies of litigants are the stuff out of which great and shining truths will ultimately be shaped. The accidental and the transitory will yield the essential and the permanent."[16] This chapter has discussed how the *Quinlan* case laid the foundation for a legal and ethical consensus about decisions near the end of life.

The Quinlan story extends far beyond the courtroom, the statehouse, and the bedside. Unprecedented national and international media coverage captured the headlines in newspapers large and small across the country, and as far away as France, Germany, Japan, and elsewhere around the world. In a prescient passage, Chief Justice Hughes wrote that the opinion "should be accepted by society, the overwhelming majority of whose members would, we think, in similar circumstances, exercise such a choice in the same way for themselves or for those closest to them."[17] Indeed, the decision would quickly become a symbol and guiding light of a patients' rights movement and a "right to die" (right to refuse treatment) movement that have radically influenced the delivery of health care and have transformed the rights of patients and their families to control medical treatment decisions and the dying process. What was once a cultural phenomenon is now woven into the fabric of society.

NOTES

1. *In re Quinlan*, 137 N.J. Super. 227, 250 (Ch.Div. 1975).
2. Ibid. at 259.
3. Joseph and Julia Quinlan, with Phyllis Battelle, *Karen Ann: The Quinlans Tell Their Story* (New York: Doubleday, 1977).
4. *In re Quinlan*, 70 N.J. 10, 40, *cert. denied sub nom. Garger v. New Jersey*, 429 U.S. 922 (1976).
5. Ibid. at 41.
6. Ibid. at 39.
7. 58 N.J. 576 (1971).
8. 109 N.J. 523 (1988).
9. New Jersey Statutes Annotated, sec. 26:6A-1–8 (West 2012).
10. *In re Quinlan*, 70 N.J. at 40.
11. *In re Conroy*, 98 N.J. 321 (1985); *In re Farrell*, 108 N.J. 335 (1987); *In re Peter*, 108 N.J. 365 (1987); *In re Jobes*, 108 N.J. 394 (1987).
12. *Cruzan v. Director, Missouri Dept. of Health*, 497 U.S. 261, 289 (1990) (O'Connor, concurring).
13. New Jersey Statutes Annotated, sec. 26:2H-53.
14. California Health and Safety Code, sec. 7185.5 (West 2012) superseded by California Probate Code, sec. 4600 (West 2012).
15. Patient Self-Determination Act of 1990, Pub.L. No. 101–508, sec. 4206, 104 Stat. 1388–115 (codified at 42 United States Code Annotated, sec. 1395cc(f) (West 2012)).
16. Benjamin N. Cardozo, *The Nature of the Judicial Process* (New Haven, CT: Yale University Press, 1921), 35.
17. *In re Quinlan*, 70 N.J. at 41–42.

5

Right to Choose v. Byrne (1982)

Establishing a State Constitutional Right to Publicly Funded Abortions

LOUIS RAVESON

Of all the constitutional issues that have come before our courts, few have been as intractable, as divisive, or as impassioned as that of a woman's right to terminate a pregnancy by abortion. The issue pits personal rights against public policy and invariably evokes the most intense and deeply held personal feelings and beliefs about health, family, religion, privacy, the nature of life, and a woman's control over her own body.

Advocates of reproductive freedom have called for recognition of a woman's fundamental constitutional right to control her own body, including the freedom to abort a pregnancy. By contrast, the antiabortion movement has argued that abortions kill babies and therefore should never be legal. Antiabortion zealots have gone so far as to murder abortion providers in the name of protecting unborn children. Although pro-choice advocates have presented, and courts have considered, evidence of the terrible harm to women's physical and psychological health inflicted by the criminalization of abortion, the juxtaposition of the two interests—a woman's right to choose versus protection of the potential life of the unborn fetus—has largely continued to frame the conflict.

A Woman's Constitutional Right to Choose an Abortion and Legislative Efforts to Restrict It

In 1973, the United States Supreme Court issued its historic opinion in *Roe v. Wade*, ruling that the Texas criminal abortion statutes prohibiting abortions at any stage of pregnancy except to save the life of the mother were unconstitutional.[1] Before *Roe v. Wade*, circumstances were grim for pregnant women, and particularly for poor pregnant women, who sought to terminate unwanted pregnancies. Abortion was legal in only four states, and many women died every year

from illegal "back alley" and self-induced abortions using nightmarish methods such as wire coat hangers, fertilizer, drain cleaner, and worse. Many more
women suffered severe infections, crippling disabilities, and infertility from
these "kitchen table" procedures, and every year, many thousands of women
were compelled to give birth to children they did not want, were ill equipped to
protect and nurture, and could not afford to raise.

When the Supreme Court struck down the laws criminalizing abortion in
Roe v. Wade, it balanced the competing interests concerned—a woman's right to
terminate a pregnancy inherent in her constitutional right to personal privacy,
against the state's interest in protecting the fetus as potential human life—by
fashioning the now familiar construct of viewing the nine months of a woman's
pregnancy as three trimesters. The Court held that, in the first trimester, the
abortion decision must be left to the woman and the medical judgment of her
attending physician. In the second trimester, the state, in promoting its interest
in the health of the pregnant woman, could regulate the abortion procedure in
ways that are reasonably related to maternal health. Finally, in the third trimester, or the stage subsequent to fetal viability, the state could promote its interest
in the potentiality of human life by regulating, or even prohibiting, abortion.
The only limitation on the state's power to do so was when, in the appropriate
exercise of medical judgment, abortion was deemed necessary for the preservation of the pregnant woman's life or health. Thus, as a woman's pregnancy
progresses, the state's interest in the potential life of the fetus grows, justifying
greater regulation by the state.[2]

Roe v. Wade changed everything. And it didn't. Finally, the Supreme Court
had recognized that a woman's right to obtain an abortion was protected by the
Constitution, and, as a result, women throughout the country could begin to
obtain safe and legal abortions. On the other hand, the Court in *Roe* held that
the state could regulate abortion procedures in the second trimester of pregnancy, and even proscribe abortions in the third trimester. The Court, therefore, left the door open to inroads upon a woman's right to have an abortion
and, almost immediately following the decision in *Roe*, states began to impose
restrictions upon a woman's ability to terminate a pregnancy.

States and municipalities enacted legislation and promulgated a variety of
regulations: prohibiting abortions in public facilities; requiring doctors to use
particular abortion procedures designed to maximize the chance of fetal survival in post-viability abortions; prohibiting public personnel from performing
abortions; requiring ultrasound tests in pregnancies of twenty weeks or more to
determine fetal viability; requiring that only licensed physicians perform abortions; banning abortion counseling; imposing mandatory waiting periods and
parental consent requirements and other limitations on a woman's ability to
obtain an abortion. The United States Supreme Court has upheld virtually all

of these restrictions as appropriate measures to protect the state's interest in potential life, so long as the laws preserved the ability of the pregnant woman to obtain an abortion when necessary to preserve her life or health.[3]

The Ban on Public Funding for Abortion

One of the most insidious ways in which numerous states and Congress sought to curtail women's ability to obtain abortions was to prohibit the use of public funds to pay for them.[4] Under these laws, the poorest women in the country— women who qualified for government-funded health care under the federal Medicaid program—could no longer procure medical treatment to terminate a pregnancy. In 1975, just two years after the Court decided *Roe v. Wade*, the Connecticut Welfare Department promulgated a regulation that prohibited state Medicaid payments for first trimester abortions except for those the state deemed medically necessary. The U.S. Supreme Court upheld the regulation in *Maher v. Roe*.[5] It ruled that the regulation did not violate a woman's constitutional right of privacy recognized in *Roe v. Wade* because a state may make a value judgment favoring childbirth over abortion and may implement that judgment through the allocation of public funds.[6]

In 1976, Congress, too, passed its own more severe prohibition on the use of public funds for abortion, the Hyde Amendment, which prohibited the use of Medicaid funding for any abortion.[7] The original version of the measure enacted by Congress did not exempt pregnancies resulting from rape or incest, or even those that were necessary to save the life of the pregnant woman. In subsequent years, powerful protests from the women's rights movement persuaded Congress to add exceptions for these three circumstances. Even with the few exceptions, however, the Hyde Amendment made it extremely difficult, if not effectively impossible, for indigent women to obtain a safe abortion from a qualified physician.

New Jersey also was quick to ban public funding for abortions in the wake of *Roe v. Wade;* in 1975, before Congress enacted the Hyde Amendment, Governor Brendan Byrne signed into law a statute that prohibited payments for termination of a woman's pregnancy for any reason except where it was medically necessary to save her life.[8] Pursuant to the statute, Medicaid would no longer pay for an abortion unless a physician determined that there was a near certainty of death for a pregnant woman if she did not terminate her pregnancy. Prior to this enactment, the New Jersey Medicaid Program, established by the state legislature in 1968 to provide medical assistance to people whose resources were inadequate to enable them to secure medical care at their own expense, covered all abortion services for eligible recipients. Shortly after the law went into effect, a federal district court in New Jersey enjoined the enforcement of the statute but then vacated its own injunction after the Supreme Court handed down its decision upholding the Connecticut funding restrictions in *Maher v. Roe*.[9]

The passage of New Jersey's ban on public funding for abortions resulted in the virtual elimination of abortion services for Medicaid recipients in the state. The number of abortions in the state funded by Medicaid plummeted from an average of 1,150 per month to 19, a reduction of 98.4 percent. Charitable sources, which used to provide some health care services for the poor, had diminished significantly since the inception of Medicaid and did not step in to provide funds for these indigent women to obtain abortions.

In the late spring of 1978, Fran Avallone, the director of New Jersey Right to Choose, a reproductive rights advocacy organization, approached Nadine Taub, a professor at Rutgers Law School in Newark, to ask for legal representation to mount another challenge to the New Jersey abortion funding restriction. Rutgers Law School already had a rich tradition of feminist scholarship and legal activism. Supreme Court Justice Ruth Bader Ginsburg had served on the faculty from 1963 to 1972; through scholarship and advocacy she pioneered cutting-edge theories in support of women's rights and against gender discrimination. The law school also created the first law journal—the *Women's Rights Law Reporter*— and the first law school clinical advocacy program in the country devoted to women's rights issues. Taub was the founder and director of that program, the Women's Rights Litigation Clinic.

Because it was clear to Taub that the case was going to demand an enormous effort and require greater resources than she and her students could manage themselves, she approached the Law Reform Unit of Essex-Newark Legal Services to ask if it would join the effort as co-counsel, and its lawyers jumped at the opportunity. Harris David, the director of the Law Reform Unit and a brilliant litigator, had assembled a group of young lawyers who, like him, had all gone to law school to fight inequality and injustice, particularly on behalf of those who were poor and underrepresented in the political process and whose crushing poverty infected every aspect of their lives.

I was privileged to be among those lawyers. My involvement in the case had a profound and continuing effect on my professional and personal life. It also made writing this chapter an opportunity to relive the whole experience.

The Women's Stories

The New Jersey Welfare Rights Organization, the New Jersey Religious Coalition for Abortion Rights, and Edward Milner Jr., a physician who performed abortions in New Jersey, joined Right to Choose as plaintiffs. At the heart of the litigation, though, were the individual women plaintiffs, impoverished pregnant women who desperately sought abortions. These women were divided into two representative classes tracking the emerging legal classifications: one consisted of women for whom abortions were medically necessary and the other of women for whom abortions were deemed elective. Whichever grouping they fell within, these individual plaintiffs represented, both legally and emotionally, the women directly affected by the case. It was their case and their story.

There was E.R., who joined the litigation on behalf of her daughter, E., a twelve-year-old child who was pregnant as a result of having been raped. When she learned of her daughter's pregnancy, E.R. contacted two physicians and her county welfare board and was informed by all three that Medicaid would not pay for her daughter's abortion. E. was examined by a specialist in obstetrics and gynecology who concluded that an abortion was medically necessary to preserve her health. A psychiatrist also examined E. and she, too, determined that an abortion was medically indicated to prevent further deterioration of E.'s emotional and psychological well-being. However, E.'s family did not have the money to pay for an abortion.

D.T. was a forty-two-year-old pregnant woman with an extensive history of nervous breakdowns and hospitalization in mental institutions. A physician who examined her advised that an abortion was medically necessary to preserve D.T.'s health, but D.T. could not afford to have the procedure.

D.T. and E. were representatives of the class of poor pregnant women for whom abortions were a medically necessary or therapeutic procedure. Abortions for them constituted essential medical care to preserve their physical or psychological well-being, which was threatened by the pregnancy or would be endangered by giving birth. For many pregnant women, like D.T. and E., especially those who are poor, abortion is not simply an alternative to carrying a pregnancy to term. It is a form of medical treatment understood, by accepted standards of medical practice, to be necessary for the protection of their health.

To exercise their best medical judgment, physicians must take into account a number of variables that pertain to the patient's health, including physical, emotional, psychological, and familial factors, as well as the person's age. By contrast, for those patients seeking Medicaid abortions in New Jersey, one factor alone determined what treatment they would receive—the near certainty of death. In this way, the funding restriction compromised the well-being of the patient and interfered with the judgment of her physician in rendering essential medical services to her.

Many medical experts view all abortions, in a sense, as medically necessary. That is, they understand pregnancy to be a medical condition that requires one of two modes of medical treatment—either termination of the pregnancy or medical care attendant to the course of pregnancy and eventually childbirth. However, in *Maher v. Roe*, the case that had challenged funding restrictions with exceptions for medically necessary abortions, the U.S. Supreme Court had already drawn a medical and legal distinction between medically necessary abortions and elective abortions in its constitutional analysis. *Maher* had ruled that states could, consistent with the Constitution, cut off Medicaid funding for elective abortions—those that women chose to have for reasons of personal circumstances and choice. The question of whether a state could restrict funding for medically necessary abortions was proceeding from the federal district courts to the federal circuit courts, but it hadn't yet reached the U.S. Supreme Court. When the Supreme Court finally decided those cases, its decisions had a profound effect on New Jersey's Right to Choose litigation.

It has to be said that for the "elective abortion" class, "elective" certainly did not mean that the decision to seek an abortion was casually or frivolously made, and the stories these women presented also were compelling. P.B. was thirty years old and the mother of three children, aged six, two, and six and a half months. At the time she joined the case as a plaintiff, her income was $356 per month, which she received from welfare. Her youngest child had been born prematurely at seven months with hydrocephalus and a heart murmur. The child had already had major surgery and was scheduled to undergo a second major operation at age two. There was a 50 percent chance that she would not survive that surgery, and she presently needed intensive care. P.B. decided prior to the birth of her third child that she would undergo sterilization after the birth and arranged with her physician to have the procedure. However, because of the premature delivery and P.B.'s weakened condition, this was not possible at that time. Six months after her third child was born, P.B. learned that she was approximately ten weeks pregnant.

P.B. was examined by a specialist in obstetrics and gynecology, who indicated that her substantially weakened physical condition since the recent birth of her youngest child made her pregnancy undesirable. Taking into account her family situation, it was his opinion that an additional child could create further emotional strain on her and her family. He concluded that, while an abortion was not medically necessary at that time, the situation could change during the course of the pregnancy, based on the potentially deteriorating condition of her health.

Cases such as P.B.'s are at the interface between elective and medically necessary abortions. Physical and emotional stress during the course of the pregnancy may result in the need for a medically necessary or therapeutic abortion later in the pregnancy. To the extent that P.B. and other women like her do not wish to carry the pregnancy to term, medical opinion is that they will fare far worse in terms of physical health than will a woman in the same situation who desires to continue the pregnancy.

A.C. was a twenty-one-year-old woman when she joined the case as a named plaintiff and class representative. She was the mother of two children, aged fourteen months and three months. Her total income was $310 per month from welfare. At the time when her second child was born, she asked to have an intrauterine device inserted as a method of birth control. She was told that she would have to wait until her six-week checkup to have the procedure. At that checkup, she was told that she would have to wait until her next menstrual period. Two and a half months after the birth of her second child, A.C. learned that she was approximately four weeks pregnant. She sought to terminate her pregnancy, she said, because she had enough trouble raising her two children and she did not want a third child.

New Jersey's prohibition on Medicaid funding for these elective abortions denied A.C., P.B., and others like them the ability to obtain the procedure and subjected them and their children to increased stress, severe social and economic circumstances, and despair. The prohibition denied them control over their own reproductive capacities and their very lives, a denial that was intentionally inflicted by the state solely because the women's poverty made them dependent on the Medicaid program for their care.

The Trial Court Litigation

From the moment my colleagues and I became involved in the case, there was enormous pressure to seek an injunction against New Jersey's funding prohibition as soon as possible. Any delay in securing an abortion increased the health risks posed by the procedure, particularly for those women for whom an abortion was medically necessary. Moreover, the health of many women who needed a therapeutic abortion because of serious medical conditions that were caused or exacerbated by their pregnancy, such as diabetes, sickle cell anemia, heart disease, certain cancers, hypertension, and preeclampsia, continued to deteriorate, sometimes drastically, while they waited and hoped that some court would invalidate the statute. Health-threatening conditions frequently became life-threatening conditions. Finally, unless a woman could obtain an abortion before her twenty-fourth week of pregnancy, it would be too late to perform the procedure legally in New Jersey. Faced with those realities, we had to conduct the litigation on an emergent basis.

We quickly divided up responsibility for the various aspects of the case. At the time, in another politicized effort to limit indigent women's ability to obtain abortions, a federal regulation prohibited Legal Services attorneys from representing a woman in any effort to procure an elective abortion. Nadine Taub took responsibility for developing the argument that women were entitled to Medicaid funding for nontherapeutic abortions. The Legal Services attorneys began preparing the case for medically necessary abortions. One of them, Joan Vermeulen, began working on a legal argument that the federal statutory framework for Medicaid required New Jersey to fund therapeutic abortions. Ed Tetelman started working on the factual bases for the arguments, preparing affidavits from medical experts and our clients. I took on the argument that New Jersey's refusal to pay for medically necessary abortions was unconstitutional under the federal and state constitutions.

On June 14, 1978, we filed suit to invalidate the statute in the state's Superior Court Chancery Division for Middlesex County in New Brunswick. Our complaint challenged the New Jersey statute on the grounds that it failed to provide coverage for medically necessary abortions, violated the Social Security Act, the First and Fourteenth amendments to the United States Constitution, and the New Jersey constitution. The complaint also alleged that, by failing to cover elective abortions, the statute violated the equal protection provisions of the New Jersey constitution.

We chose to file our case there because the chancery judge we knew would be assigned the case, David Furman, was an extremely intelligent and fair-minded jurist. We were able to file in that county because our plaintiff reproductive rights organization, Right to Choose, was located there.

On the same day we filed the complaint, we also filed a motion with Judge Furman for emergency relief ordering the state to provide Medicaid reimbursement for a medically necessary abortion for one of our plaintiffs, E.M., whose fetus had been damaged as a result of medication and x-rays she had undertaken in treatment of back injuries and asthma. E.M. had experienced severe depression upon learning of the deformity and, in the opinion of her physician, the likelihood of her continued mental and physical deterioration warranted a therapeutic abortion. The court ruled in our favor, and E.M. was able to obtain the abortion she needed to stop further deterioration of her health.

Over the next few weeks, we continually added new plaintiffs who sought either an elective or a medically necessary abortion, and we moved for temporary restraining orders allowing each one of them to obtain a Medicaid-funded abortion. One of our plaintiffs, introduced earlier in this chapter, was E., the twelve-year-old girl who was pregnant as a result of having been raped. Although several of her own physicians had concluded that an abortion was necessary to protect E.'s physical and mental health, none of them believed that E.'s life was even remotely threatened by the pregnancy.

Because E. was an exceptionally sympathetic plaintiff, a plaintiff who so starkly exposed the terrible harm caused by the Medicaid ban's rejection of medical necessity as the appropriate standard for this single category of state-funded medical care, the state's attorneys sought to exclude her as a plaintiff. To do so, they requested the court's permission, which was granted, to have a doctor employed by the state Medicaid Program examine E. to determine whether she was eligible for Medicaid reimbursement for an abortion under the New

Jersey statute. Although E.'s life was not in any way threatened by her pregnancy, the state quickly informed the court, after its physician examined her,
that she was eligible for Medicaid coverage under the challenged statute. The
state utilized the same tactic to eliminate other plaintiffs whose circumstances
were especially compelling.

As to all the other individual pregnant women for whom we sought funding
to terminate their pregnancies on an emergency basis, the judge ordered the
state to fund all medically necessary abortions, but denied that relief for plaintiffs seeking purely "elective abortions."[10] Shortly thereafter, the court ordered
that all the women in New Jersey who sought medically necessary abortions
were entitled to state funding to procure the procedures.[11]

At about the same time, the court granted the requests of a number of
antiabortion groups, and several physicians, to intervene in the case in support
of the state's abortion funding ban.[12] That decision led to a difficult moment in
the case for plaintiffs' attorneys. One of the individual interveners represented
to the court that, if any of the women who were our named plaintiffs were to
carry her fetus to term, he would adopt the baby. The judge asked if we would
communicate that offer to our plaintiffs, and we refused. We felt that our clients
already knew that adoption was an option if they chose not to terminate their
pregnancies. Moreover, the state, through its Medicaid program, which paid
for childbirth but not abortion, had already placed our clients who needed a
medically necessary abortion in circumstances that tended to coerce them into
giving birth even though doing so was dangerous or damaging to their health.
We did not want to make the women's choice to terminate their pregnancies
and protect their health even more difficult.

The judge, however, wouldn't take our no as the answer; he ordered plaintiffs' attorneys to communicate the intervener's offer of adoption to our clients.
This ratcheted up the difficulty of our decision. We understood that our legal
responsibility was to obey the court's order or attempt to have it reversed in an
emergency appeal. On the other hand, we firmly believed that it was in the best
interest of our clients not to convey the adoption offer, which we believed would
add to the emotional and psychological trauma they were already suffering and
might further pressure them to do something that would also cause them physical injury.[13]

The intervener's offer to adopt and the court's order that we convey the
offer to our clients inappropriately treated the women's decision whether to
have an abortion as though the two options were fungible—as though the experience of terminating a pregnancy was equivalent to going through nine months
of pregnancy, giving birth, and then giving the baby away to the very interloper
who was opposing their right to have an abortion. Moreover, for these women,
all of whom needed medically necessary abortions, continued pregnancy and

childbirth meant that they would be damaging their health and endangering their lives. The offer and court order also felt offensive because many women of various religious faiths did not consider the fetus to be a human life until the moment of birth, further differentiating the options of abortion versus childbirth and adoption.

Although the judge surely believed that he was providing the women with information that might assist them in their decision, the offer and order felt to us like further coercion in the guise of assisting the women's choice—like placing an additional and unreasonable burden on the decision the women had already made not to give birth. The whole point of a woman's constitutional right to choose whether to terminate a pregnancy was that it should be the woman's choice, not the state's, not the court's, and certainly not the "right to life" intervener's in offering to adopt. All of them needed to respect the women's right to be left alone with this deeply private decision, and not be bombarded by those who believed that they had an even stronger stake in the outcome of that decision than the pregnant women themselves.

Plaintiffs' attorneys spent considerable time talking among ourselves about whether we would defy the court's order, either openly by informing the judge that we would not comply or covertly by disingenuously claiming to the judge that we had conveyed the offer and none of our clients were interested. Of course, as officers of the court, we couldn't do either. The discussions we had with our clients pursuant to the court's order are protected by attorney-client privilege. But I can say that not a single one of our pregnant plaintiffs chose to give birth to a child and give that child up for adoption.

Plaintiffs' Arguments before the Trial Court

Several of the plaintiffs' constitutional arguments required a hearing to provide the court with the basis for making critical findings of fact concerning freedom of religion. We were arguing that the state's funding restriction was rooted in the religious beliefs of the Roman Catholic Church, which we alleged had intervened in the legislative process with undue pressure for the enactment of the challenged statute, thereby violating the Establishment of Religion Clauses of the First Amendment to the United States Constitution and the religion clauses of the New Jersey constitution. We also claimed that the funding ban conflicted with the religious obligations of some women to have an abortion in circumstances where their pregnancies threatened their life or health, violating the Free Exercise Clauses of the federal and state constitutions. Neither of these constitutional issues had been raised before the U.S. Supreme Court in *Maher*, the case upholding governmental restrictions on public funding for elective abortions.

The parties conducted a weeklong trial on these religious issues, present-ing experts from numerous religious faiths who testified about the views of their respective religions on abortion. Religious leaders from various denomi-nations, including several Protestant sects, the Unitarian Church, and Juda-ism, testified about their respective religions' views of when, in the process of gestation and childbirth, life begins. These witnesses informed the court that, although the Roman Catholic Church maintains the belief that human life begins at the moment of conception, other mainstream religions believe, for example, that life does not begin until the baby's head emerges from its mother's body during childbirth. They also testified that some religions impose an affirmative obligation on a pregnant woman to place her own life and health above that of her fetus and to terminate a pregnancy where either it or the act of giving birth would threaten the woman's well-being. Indeed, one Protestant clergyman, a Presbyterian theologian, testified that, pursuant to his faith, a pregnant woman has a religious duty to submit to an abortion under many cir-cumstances, such as the woman's inability to care for an infant, abnormality of the fetus, conception out of wedlock, and impoverishment if the family already had several children.

Throughout the proceedings before the trial court, press coverage was extensive, and journalists and television news sketch artists packed the court-room. Outside the courthouse, right-to-life activists confronted pro-choice advocates every day as both groups demonstrated in support of their positions. My colleagues and I were accosted on several occasions as we made our way into the courthouse.

After the evidentiary hearing, it was time for the attorneys to make their final arguments in the case. The U.S. Supreme Court decision in *Maher* already foreclosed us from arguing as a matter of federal constitutional law that the withholding of Medicaid funding for elective nontherapeutic abortions was a denial of a woman's constitutional rights to privacy, due process, or equal pro-tection. *Maher* did not and could not dispose of any state constitutional claims, however. Therefore, Taub argued that Article I of the New Jersey constitution provided a right to women of moral initiative and ethical choice that was vio-lated by the state's action in refusing to pay the medical expenses of indigent women who made one procreative choice while agreeing to pay the medical expenses of those making a different choice favored by the state.

Just the year before plaintiffs filed suit in this case, U.S. Supreme Court Jus-tice William Brennan published what was to become an extremely influential article in the *Harvard Law Review* encouraging state courts to recognize the inde-pendence and integrity of their state constitutions, in order to better "protect the people of our nation from governmental intrusions on their freedoms."[14] Actually, the New Jersey Supreme Court had begun years earlier to recognize that the state constitution provided an independent source of individual rights and freedoms, and that state constitutional guarantees of these rights may provide greater protection than the federal Constitution. In *Robinson v. Cahill*,[15] a case discussed by Paul L. Tractenberg in chapter 10, the court said explicitly in 1973 that state constitutions could be more demanding than the federal constitution in the area of equal protection because the principle of federalism, which cautions against too expansive a view of federal constitutional limitations upon state power, is absent when states seek to cope with their own problems in the light of their own circumstances.

The *Maher* decision made clear that the federal Constitution merely restrains the government from imposing substantial barriers to obtaining an abortion. In essence, the *Maher* court ruled that the state, by paying the medical expenses for childbirth but not for abortion, was not imposing any obstacle in the path of the pregnant woman that was not already there as a result of her poverty. In focusing single-mindedly on state-created barriers to access—once the woman has arrived at her decision—the Court was dismissing any notion that the federal Constitution sheltered the woman's moral choice itself from governmental intervention. Rather, the Court concluded that the federal Constitution "implies no limitation on the authority of a State to make a value judgment favoring childbirth over abortion, and to implement that judgment by the allocation of public funds."[16]

In contrast, Taub argued, the language and history of Article I, paragraph 1 of the New Jersey constitution makes clear that that provision bars public attempts to deprive individuals of the opportunity to make meaningful moral choices free from governmental efforts to coerce their decision. Echoing the Declaration of Independence, Article I, paragraph 1 provides: "All persons are by nature free and independent, and have certain unalienable rights, among which are those of enjoying and defending life and protecting property, and of pursuing and obtaining safety and happiness." This provision differs from the Fourteenth Amendment both in the greater sweep of its scope and its affirmative recognition of rights, including the right to "pursue and obtain safety and happiness," retained by the people.[17]

New Jersey's guarantee of "unalienable rights" derives from the philosophical works of John Locke, who conceived of government as a social contract that individuals enter into to better secure and promote their life, liberty, and property.[18] Locke developed his theory of happiness as an individual matter inextricably linked to the freedom to act according to one's own best judgment following due consideration.[19] Applying these concepts embodied in the state constitution, New Jersey courts have protected the right to confront fundamental decisions and choose one's own course free from external value judgments, whether imposed by state or private agencies.

For example, in *In re Quinlan*, the focus of chapter 4, the New Jersey Supreme Court held that the father of a woman in a persistent vegetative state could decide, together with her family, whether the woman would have wanted to terminate her life support systems.[20] The court referred repeatedly to Karen Quinlan's "right of choice," and a subsequent state supreme court case stressed that *In re Quinlan*'s "underlying concern was with the protection of personal decisions."[21]

In our case, the extent of the state's intrusion on women's intensely personal choices emerged with painful clarity when one considered the circumstances of our plaintiffs who sought nontherapeutic abortions. P.B., for example, was a woman who sought desperately to avoid subjecting her children to the neglect she herself suffered as a child. As a welfare mother, there were tremendous obstacles in the way of her being able to give adequate care to the three children she already had, particularly as one child was hydrocephalic. She looked forward to "getting off welfare" and "making something of herself." But, despite attempts to secure birth control, she found herself pregnant and unable to obtain Medicaid assistance for an abortion, simply because the state did not wish to permit her to decide how she could best fulfill her responsibilities.

A.C. also feared that she could not adequately care for another child. At twenty-one, she had given birth to two babies only eleven months apart and was the victim of physical abuse by her husband. Unable to obtain birth control, she became pregnant again while her husband was in prison. She, too, was denied funds for an abortion because the state had determined for her that she should carry the pregnancy to term.

Once the U.S. Supreme Court had decided in *Roe v. Wade* that women cannot be required, in the name of the public good, to surrender their liberty to choose not to bear children, New Jersey's constitutional right to pursue happiness should preclude state interference with that right so that women can determine their own course according to their own moral judgment and deeply held beliefs.

In comparison to the complex case we presented for elective abortions, Joan Vermeulen's statutory argument that federal legislation implementing the Medicaid program required the state to fund therapeutic abortions, like all other necessary medical care, was relatively straightforward. The federal Medicaid statute's statement of purpose provided that the legislation was enacted "[to enable] each State . . . to furnish . . . medical assistance on behalf of families . . . whose income and resources are insufficient to meet the costs of necessary medical services."[22] Vermeulen, who for a time was associated with Rutgers Law School's Constitutional Litigation Clinic, argued that, in limiting Medicaid funding for abortions to life-threatening circumstances, New Jersey's statute was more restrictive than the federal act, which imposed an obligation on New Jersey as a participating state to provide Medicaid funding for all medically necessary care, including abortions.

Finally, I argued that New Jersey's prohibition on funding medically necessary abortions violated the due process and equal protection guarantees of the federal and New Jersey constitutions, as well as the freedom of religion clauses of the First Amendment. The equal protection argument—that the funding ban was unconstitutional because, unlike all other Medicaid-eligible persons with a medical necessity for treatment, Medicaid-eligible women with a medical necessity for an abortion are denied Medicaid benefits and thus effectively denied the abortion because they lacked the financial means to pay for it—had never before been adjudicated in abortion litigation.

The Trial Court's Rulings

The trial court held, with regard to women denied public funding for elective abortions, that New Jersey's constitutional rulings were consistent with the United States Supreme Court's reading of federal constitutional law in *Maher*.[23] Therefore, the trial court upheld New Jersey's ban on Medicaid funding for nontherapeutic abortions.

As to therapeutic abortions, the court accepted our argument that, under the federal legislation establishing the Medicaid program, participating states were obligated to provide Medicaid funding for all necessary medical services, including abortions to protect a pregnant woman's health. Accordingly, the court ordered that New Jersey's Medicaid Program had to pay for all medically necessary abortions.

Subsequent to the court's decision, two federal circuit courts of appeals held that the federal Hyde Amendment impliedly repealed the general provisions of the Medicaid Act and limited a state's obligation to provide its share of Medicaid funding for abortions to the Hyde Amendment standards. Thereafter, the trial court reversed itself on the statutory argument under which we had just prevailed. And because the Hyde Amendment standards were more restrictive than the standard we urged was constitutionally mandated for abortion funding under Medicaid—medical necessity—the court now had to reach the constitutional issues it had refrained from deciding in its earlier decision.

The Constitutional Arguments

An equal protection challenge to the constitutionality of a statute is based on a claim that two classes of similarly situated people are being treated differently in some impermissible manner. In *Right to Choose*, we were arguing that one class of women—those Medicaid-eligible women whose doctors recommended an abortion as medically necessary, but were barred from Medicaid funding—were discriminated against in comparison to all the other Medicaid-eligible individuals with a medical necessity for any other treatment, who were granted funding.

Where the victims of such discrimination are members of a suspect class— groups that have suffered historically from discrimination because of their race, ethnicity, or national origin—the state can only justify the difference in treatment by establishing that the statutory classification furthers a compelling governmental interest and that no less restrictive alternative is available—so-called "strict scrutiny."[24] Similarly, if a discriminatory statute infringes a fundamental constitutional right, the statute is unconstitutional unless the state can demonstrate a compelling interest for the disparate treatment. When the state's action neither discriminates against a suspect class nor impinges upon a fundamental right, the state need only show that the law is rationally related to a legitimate state interest—a lower tier of scrutiny and, in practice, an exceedingly easy standard for the state to meet.

In our case, the state could meet that lower tier of scrutiny because *Roe v. Wade* had already ruled that the state had a legitimate interest in protecting the potential life of a fetus. But the state could not demonstrate a compelling interest to uphold its Medicaid funding restriction, because *Roe* had also concluded that the state's interest in protecting the fetus did not become compelling until the fetus reached viability at approximately the end of the second trimester of pregnancy.

The U.S. Supreme Court also had already concluded that women are not a suspect class and, in *Maher*, had held that Medicaid-eligible women were not a suspect class because of their poverty. Therefore, there were two possible approaches for prevailing on our equal protection challenge, and I argued both of them.

The first was to try to persuade the court to reject the federal two-tier test for equal protection, which resulted either in strict scrutiny or the rational relationship standard, in favor of a balancing test, which would more precisely weigh the harm caused by the state's funding restriction against the state's asserted justification.

The second approach was to convince the court that New Jersey's funding ban infringed a fundamental constitutional right. *Maher* had held that a funding restriction on elective abortions did not infringe a woman's fundamental constitutional privacy right to choose to have an abortion announced in *Roe v. Wade*, because it was the woman's poverty in the first instance that prevented her from obtaining an abortion, not the state's refusal to pay for it. The question of whether a state's funding ban on medically necessary abortions infringed a woman's right to have an abortion was almost certainly going to be addressed shortly by the U.S. Supreme Court. But, although we hoped that the high court would find such an infringement, we certainly couldn't count on that, especially after *Maher*.

It was imperative, then, to persuade the state court in our case that New Jersey's statute infringed a fundamental right guaranteed by the New Jersey Constitution. This would serve two critical purposes. First, it would allow us to prevail even if the U.S. Supreme Court were to rule, in accord with *Maher*, that barring funding for therapeutic abortions did not place an obstacle in the path of indigent women seeking an abortion additional to their poverty. Second, because state courts are the final arbiters of their own constitutions, by basing their decision on the violation of a state constitutional right, the trial court, and ultimately the New Jersey Supreme Court, could insulate their decisions from review by the U.S. Supreme Court.

The top candidate for a fundamental state constitutional right that was violated by the Medicaid funding restriction seemed obvious to me—a woman's right to protect her own health. The problem was that such a constitutional right had never explicitly been identified before—not in New Jersey, not in any other state, and not in any federal court in the country. Nevertheless, it seemed to me that Article I, paragraph 1 of the New Jersey constitution, guaranteeing that all persons have the unalienable right of "defending life" and of "pursuing safety and happiness," spoke directly to one's right to protect her health. Moreover, the seeds of a compelling argument for recognition of a constitutional right to protect one's health had already been planted in other cases where an individual's health interests were pitted against conflicting rights and interests.

The record we had established in the trial court demonstrated that, in withholding public funding for virtually all medically necessary abortions, the state's restriction exacted appalling suffering and health damage upon poor women seeking a therapeutic abortion. In imposing this solitary exclusion from New Jersey's Medicaid coverage of women who, by definition, were confronted with a choice between two serious courses—serious health damage or death to themselves on the one hand and abortion on the other—the state forced these indigent women to bear the substantially increased risks of disability and death associated with delivery, or the substantially increased risks associated with late abortions obtained after a difficult search for charitable care, or the grave risks of death and disability associated with "back alley" abortions. In arguing for recognition of a woman's fundamental right to preserve her own health, the central issue in our case became whether the state can implement a moral judgment that a poor pregnant woman must sacrifice her health and sometimes her life to preserve the potentiality of life in a fetus.

In arguing that the funding ban violated a woman's right to choose an elective abortion free from governmental efforts to manipulate her choice, we had already traced the derivation of Article I, paragraph 1 of the New Jersey constitution from the philosophy of John Locke. As Locke developed in his social theory of government, under natural law, an individual has the power to harm neither another nor herself. And in ceding her power to government, "[n]obody can give more power than he has himself; and he that cannot take away his own life cannot give another power over it."[25]

We argued that the government's interest in the health of the people derived from the people's inherent and constitutional right to protect their own health. Therefore, there is an inherent limitation on the power of the state: government cannot, in the context of a publicly funded medical care program, deliberately harm poor women who need a medically necessary abortion by offering them money to carry a fetus to term, while withholding the funding needed to avert such damage to their health or even save their lives.

The courts' solicitude for an individual's right to preserve her health had been voiced in what appeared to be an antithetical set of cases where an individual's interest in health had been pitted against other fundamental rights (antithetical because the courts seemed to be saying that the state's interests overcame the rights of the individuals).

Those cases suggested that the right to health is overcome only on rare occasions, and then only by an individual's fundamental rights to privacy and religious freedom. There, courts compelled individuals to undergo medical treatments that they or, in the case of children, their parents, objected to on religious or privacy grounds.[26] Acknowledging that freedom of religion and the right of parents to determine the proper care for their children, and the right of privacy of an adult to choose whether to undergo particular medical procedures, are fundamental rights to be accorded the highest possible respect, the courts nevertheless overrode the individuals' beliefs and wishes, grounding their decisions on the more compelling necessity to protect the individuals' health.[27]

If the state has such a compelling interest in protecting an individual's health, I argued, then the person herself must have the same fundamental right; indeed, the state's interest necessarily springs from the individual's. It would be perverse for a court to recognize that the state's interest in an individual's health trumps the individual's own religious beliefs, privacy interests, and moral judgments, but that the individual's own interest in health does not outweigh the moral judgment of the state that would necessarily damage that person's health.

Thus, even in cases where the right to preserve one's health (or the state's derivative interest in preserving health and life) is weighed against the most fundamental constitutional rights, such as freedom of religion and privacy, the interest in protecting health overcomes all others. In the case of the Medicaid funding ban, however, the woman's interest in health is not in opposition to her constitutional rights of privacy and religious freedom; to the contrary, all the woman's rights are aligned against the state's moral judgment to protect the potentiality of human life in the fetus—an interest that *Roe v. Wade* had already determined is subordinate to the right of a pregnant woman to have an abortion.

Our formulation of this argument proved to be persuasive and the trial court ruled in plaintiffs' favor, holding that "[e]njoyment of one's health is a fundamental liberty which is shielded by the Fourteenth Amendment to the Federal Constitution and by Article I, paragraph 1 of the State Constitution against unreasonable and discriminatory restriction," and that the state's funding ban unconstitutionally infringed upon that right.[28] The court explicitly recognized, for the first time in the country, a fundamental constitutional right to protect one's health.[29] Moreover, the court's decision was the first in the country striking down a statute restricting Medicaid funding for medically necessary abortions, and the opinion and plaintiffs' briefs became models for similar litigation throughout the country.

The New Jersey Supreme Court Reaches Out for the Case

We weren't finished yet; this was the trial court. The state appealed the court's decision on medically necessary abortions, and we cross-appealed the court's ruling on elective abortions. Before we briefed the case in New Jersey's intermediate-level appellate court, the New Jersey Supreme Court reached down and, because of the importance of the case, bypassed the intermediate appellate court and took the appeal directly. Just as we were beginning to prepare our briefs to the state supreme court, the U.S. Supreme Court, in *Harris v. McRae*, upheld, in a five-to-four decision, a version of the Hyde Amendment that prohibited the use of Medicaid funds for abortions except where the life of the mother was endangered.[30] In effect, *McRae* overruled the declaration of the trial court in our case that funding Medicaid abortions to protect the life, but not the health, of pregnant women violated the equal protection clause of the federal Constitution. *McRae* also held that the denial of Medicaid funds for abortion did not violate the First Amendment provision against the establishment of religion.[31] Now our plaintiffs could only prevail on state constitutional grounds or on our First Amendment claim that the New Jersey statute violated the free exercise of plaintiffs' religion.

At about this time, I had begun teaching at Rutgers Law School alongside my litigation partner, Nadine Taub, and we both worked on our respective points in the brief to the New Jersey Supreme Court, assisted by a number of our students, as well as by Joan Vermeulen, and another attorney, Claudia Davidson. Amicus curiae, or friend of the court, briefs flooded into the New Jersey Supreme Court attesting to the national significance of *Right to Choose v. Byrne.* They came from Planned Parenthood, the National Association of Social Workers, the League of Women Voters, the National Conference of Black Lawyers, and more than twenty other national organizations.

When it came time to argue the appeal before the state supreme court, Nadine Taub continued to present the case for elective abortions and I argued the constitutional issues with respect to medically necessary abortions. The argument was the first for me in the New Jersey Supreme Court and was perhaps the most meaningful of my career.

It was difficult to gauge the justices' sentiments during the argument. Rhonda Copelon, who had argued *McRae* in the U.S. Supreme Court, sat in the courtroom and took verbatim notes of the justices' questions and the attorneys' answers, but even going over her notes after the argument gave us little insight into how the court was likely to decide.

The New Jersey Supreme Court Decision

Three months later, the court issued its opinion. With one impassioned dissent in each direction, the five-justice majority opinion, written by Justice Stuart Pollock, affirmed the trial court's decision as to all aspects of the case:

> By granting funds when life is at risk, but withholding them when health is endangered, the statute denies equal protection to those women entitled to necessary medical services under Medicaid.
>
> Thus, the statute impinges upon the fundamental right of a woman to control her body and destiny. That right encompasses one of the most intimate decisions in human experience, the choice to terminate a pregnancy or bear a child. This intensely personal decision is one that should be made by a woman in consultation with trusted advisors, such as her doctor, but without undue governmental interference. . . . Once it undertakes to fund medically necessary care attendant upon pregnancy . . . , government must proceed in a neutral manner. Given the high priority accorded in this State to the rights of privacy and health, it is not neutral to fund services medically necessary for childbirth while refusing to fund medically necessary abortions. Nor is it neutral to provide one woman with the means to protect her life at the expense of a fetus and to force another woman to sacrifice her health to protect a potential life.[32]

Despite having achieved an important victory on behalf of women seeking therapeutic abortions, we were terribly disappointed that the New Jersey Supreme Court had agreed with the trial court that the state could constitutionally deny Medicaid funding for elective abortions. Justice Morris Pashman, one of the most brilliant and progressive justices in the history of the state's high court, wrote a separate and powerful opinion concurring in the majority's decision to invalidate the statute's restriction on Medicaid funding for therapeutic abortions and dissenting from the court's ruling on elective abortions. His dissent presaged a controversy that continues to be fought in courtrooms throughout the country—whether federal or state constitutions that grant certain affirmative rights to individuals impose correlative obligations on government to help individuals exercise those rights, at least when they relate to basic needs of survival, or whether those constitutions merely serve as limitations on governmental power. Justice Pashman championed the more expansive understanding of constitutional rights: "The freedom to choose whether or not to bear a child is of such fundamental importance that I believe our [state] Constitution affirmatively requires funding for abortions for women who choose them and cannot afford them. The freedom to act is meaningless if it is not coupled with the ability to effectively enjoy that freedom."[33]

He went on to make one of the most far-reaching statements in the history of American jurisprudence about the complicity of government in creating conditions of poverty and the state's concomitant responsibility to help the poor exercise constitutional rights denied them solely as a function of their impoverishment. Beginning with a quote from Justice Blackmun's dissent in *Beal v. Doe*, he stated, "The [majority] concedes the existence of a constitutional right but denies the realization and enjoyment of that right on the ground that existence and realization are separate and distinct. For the individual woman concerned, indigent and financially helpless . . . , the result is punitive and tragic. Implicit in the Court's holdings is the condescension that she may go elsewhere for her abortion. I find that disingenuous and alarming, almost reminiscent of: 'Let them eat cake.'"[34] Justice Pashman added, "Further, it is simply not true that the actions of the state have played no role in creating the poverty in which one-seventh of our citizens are now mired. The state defines and enforces property rights, creates the economic climate in which private enterprise operates, and in myriads of ways [a]ffects the economy of the state and the wealth or poverty of its citizens."[35]

The New Jersey Supreme Court's decision that New Jersey's ban on Medicaid funding for medically necessary abortions was unconstitutional, however, was an important victory for the poor women who sought to exercise their constitutional right to have an abortion and whose health the state of New Jersey was so quick to sacrifice in order to promote its own moral judgment that the potential life of the fetus was more deserving.[36] The genuine humanity of Justice Pollock and the majority and their overriding concern for the actual damage to the lives and health of poor women inflicted by the abortion funding ban were apparent throughout the opinion and stood in stark contrast with *McRae*'s callous pronouncement that "although government may not place obstacles in the path of a woman's exercise of her freedom of choice, it need not remove those not of its own creation. Indigency falls in the latter category."[37]

In determining that the appropriate construction of the challenged statute was that it limited Medicaid funds to abortions medically necessary to preserve the life or health of the woman,[38] the court broadly defined "medical necessity" as the proper province of physicians consistent with competent medical treatment, which, the court suggested, might well encompass abortions to terminate pregnancies where the woman was the victim of rape or incest.[39]

The Legacy of *Right to Choose v. Byrne*

The New Jersey Supreme Court's opinion in *Right to Choose v. Byrne* has had a significant influence on the development of the law of reproductive freedom, poverty law, economic rights, and a number of other constitutional issues, both in New Jersey and in courts around the nation.[40] In no small part because the court that decided the case was widely regarded as one of the finest in the country, the case continues, decades later, to help shape the evolution of these facets of constitutional law. There are other reasons as well.

First, the court's opinion was one of the early and prominent decisions in a burgeoning movement of state courts turning to their own constitutions as a separate source of individual freedoms that may mandate more expansive protection of individual rights and liberties than the United States Constitution. In holding that the state's Medicaid funding ban impinged upon a woman's interests in privacy and health, the court concluded that these interests were both more forceful and more sensitive to governmental intrusion, including indirect interference, than the federal right to privacy guaranteed by the United States Constitution.[41]

Second, although the New Jersey Supreme Court declined to go as far as the trial court had in explicitly declaring that the United States and New Jersey constitutions guaranteed a fundamental right to health, it did recognize a right to health and the high priority accorded that right by the State of New Jersey.[42] It treated that priority as though it were a fundamental right in the court's constitutional calculus.[43] In other words, the court found that the Medicaid proscription infringed on women's right to health, in addition to privacy, and therefore required the state to justify such interference by demonstrating a compelling state interest, which could not be satisfied by the state's proffered concern for potential life prior to the time of fetal viability. Furthermore, the court concluded, contrary to the U.S. Supreme Court's holding in *McRae*, that "the State may not use its treasury to persuade a poor woman to sacrifice her health by remaining pregnant."[44] This conception of an individual's right to protect her own health is being asserted by legal scholars as a better basis than privacy for protecting a woman's reproductive freedom,[45] and in support of such diverse claims as the right to receive aggressive palliative care,[46] medical marijuana,[47] experimental medical treatments, and the right to purchase human organs from willing sellers for life-saving transplants.[48]

Third, the court's opinion has broad implications, generally, for the doctrine of unconstitutional conditions and, more specifically, in the context of social welfare programs. In ruling that the state cannot use its largesse to encourage its citizens to harm themselves, the court was saying that the government may not make the exercise of one right (here, the right to receive funds for medical care under the Medicaid program) contingent upon the forbearance of another right (here, the right to protect one's health, as well as the right to choose to have an abortion). As the court concluded, "Statutes such as [New Jersey's Medicaid funding ban] 'can be understood only as an attempt to achieve with carrots what government is forbidden to achieve with sticks.'"[49]

Fourth, the court rejected the conventional two-tier test for determining whether a governmental action violates an individual's constitutional right to equal protection. That mechanical test virtually guaranteed that, where a statute or other state action did not directly infringe on a fundamental right or discriminate against a suspect class, the governmental action would be upheld because the state could almost always demonstrate that the discrimination bore a rational relationship to a legitimate state interest.[50] Instead, the court embraced the more protective balancing test that we urged in our briefs.[51] It ruled that "[u]ltimately, a court must weigh the nature of the restraint or the denial against the apparent public justification, and decide whether the State action is arbitrary. . . . Where an important personal right is affected by governmental action, the Court often requires the public authority to demonstrate a greater public need than is traditionally required in construing the federal constitution."[52] Here, too, the court was in the vanguard of a trend that continues around the country.

Moreover, the court concluded that even indirect interference with an important personal right triggers this balancing test, requiring the government to justify its action by demonstrating a public need weightier than a mere rational relationship to a legitimate state interest. This divergence from federal constitutional analysis was a striking acknowledgment that the government may unconstitutionally infringe upon an individual's rights in subtler and less tangible ways than by imposing obstacles to their exercise, as the Supreme Court had insisted in *McRae*.

Finally, as public interest lawyers engaged in law reform litigation, we were, to a great extent, focused upon how to construct novel arguments to persuade the New Jersey Supreme Court to protect the constitutional rights of poor women to a greater degree than the U.S. Supreme Court. We had the luxury of thinking about and advocating for the long-term evolution of various constitutional principles of law not just as they applied to Medicaid funding for abortion but as they would apply to the diverse array of constitutional cases that the New Jersey Supreme Court and other courts around the country would confront in the future. Of course, we had real clients in the case; however, we also viewed the public interest as our client—the people.

But, clearly, the most significant impact of *Right to Choose* was upon the lives of the women who were our clients at the time we litigated the case, and the hundreds of thousands of women in the future who would be able to obtain abortions to protect their lives and health. For these women and their families, the litigation will never be a debate about abstract constitutional questions, but the realization of their fundamental right to control their own bodies and destinies, and a lifeline to the critical health care they so desperately needed. No longer can New Jersey and the other states, whose high courts have followed in the footsteps of *Right to Choose*, force poor pregnant women to sacrifice their health to pay for the state's moral judgment that abortion is wrong.

NOTES

1. 410 U.S. 113 (1973).
2. In *Doe v. Bolton*, 410 U.S. 179 (1973), a companion case to *Roe* decided the same day, the Court also struck down state regulations requiring that abortions be performed only at accredited hospitals and only after approval by two consulting physicians and a hospital committee.
3. States have also enacted legislation directly contrary to *Roe v. Wade* in an effort to bring the holding in *Roe* back before the Supreme Court in the hope that different personnel on the court might reverse the decision. So far, however, the Court has remained steadfast in reaffirming the core holding of *Roe v. Wade* that women have a constitutional right to choose an abortion before fetal viability. See, for example, *Casey v. Planned Parenthood of Southeastern Pennsylvania*, 505 U.S. 833 (1992).
4. As William Faulkner said, "The past is never dead. It's not even past." William Faulkner, *Requiem for a Nun* (New York: Random House, 1950). Thus, it is distressing, if not surprising, that in 2010, President Obama, in order to garner enough votes to enact the Patient Protection and Affordable Care Act, issued an executive order barring the use of public funds for abortions except in cases of rape, incest, or where necessary to save the life of the pregnant woman, consistent with the then existing Congressional restriction on Medicaid funding for abortion. Today, forty years after the Court decided *Roe v. Wade*, Congress and many states regularly propose and enact new restrictions on women's right to obtain an abortion.
5. 432 U.S. 464 (1977).
6. Similarly, the Supreme Court in *Beal v. Doe*, 432 U.S. 438 (1977), upheld a Pennsylvania statute prohibiting Medicaid funding for "elective" nontherapeutic abortions. There, Justice Powell commented for the Court: "Although serious statutory questions might be presented if a State Medicaid plan excluded necessary medical treatment from its

coverage, it is hardly inconsistent with the objectives of the Act for a state to refuse to fund unnecessary—though perhaps desirable—medical services." Ibid. at 444.

7. The original Hyde Amendment was enacted as a rider to the Departments of Labor and Health, Education, and Welfare Appropriations Act, Pub. L. No. 94–206, § 210, 90 Stat. 20, (1976).

8. New Jersey Statutes Annotated, sec. 30:4D-6.1 (West 2012).

9. *Doe v. Mathews*, 420 F.Supp 865, 874 (D.N.J. 1976).

10. *Right to Choose v. Byrne*, 165 N.J. Super. 443, 455, 463 (Ch. Div. 1979).

11. *Right to Choose v. Byrne*, 169 N.J. Super. 543, 552 (Ch. Div. 1979).

12. The New Jersey Right to Life Committee, the Student Ad Hoc Committee Against the War in Vietnam, and the New Jersey Concerned Taxpayers.

13. Even where a woman who has no choice but to carry a fetus to term chooses to give the baby up for adoption, her life will have been significantly changed by the pregnancy and birth. Women who give children up for adoption often suffer terrible guilt for having abdicated parental responsibility, even if they would not have been able to fulfill that responsibility had they kept the child. See, for example, Arthur D. Sorosky, Annette Baran, and Reuben Pannor, *The Adoption Triangle* (Westminster, CA: Triadoption Publications, 1978), 72. Moreover, giving the child up for adoption is frequently perceived by others as abandonment, resulting in ostracization of the mother by family and friends. See, for example, Betty J. Lifton, *Lost and Found: The Adoption Experience* (Ann Arbor: University of Michigan Press, 1979), 207–227.

14. William Brennan, "State Constitutions and the Protection of Individual Rights," *Harvard Law Review* 90 (1977): 503.

15. 62 N.J. 473 (1973).

16. *Maher v. Roe*, 432 U.S. 464, 474 (1977).

17. New Jersey's Bill of Rights, which includes that provision, has been described as expressing "the social, political, and economic ideals of the present day in a broader way than ever before in American constitutional history." Leon S. Milmed, "The New Jersey Constitution of 1947," in New Jersey Statutes Annotated, commentary at 110 (West 1997).

18. J. Locke, "Second Treatise on Government," also known as "Of Civil Government." See *The Works of John Locke* (1823; reprinted 1963), vol. 5, book 2.

19. J. Locke, "Essay on Human Understanding," *The Works of John Locke*, vol. 1, book 2, chapter 21, especially §47, §48, §51.

20. 70 N.J. 10 (1976).

21. *State v. Saunders*, 75 N.J. 200, 213 (1977). Similarly, in *Saunders*, the court's concern for personal autonomy and individual decision making led it to reject as unconstitutional the state's proffered justification for a statute proscribing nonmarital sexual activities as a means of encouraging marriage. Ibid. at 219. The court stated: "We do not doubt the beneficent qualities of marriage, both for individuals and society as a whole. Yet we can only reiterate that decisions such as whether to marry are of a highly personal nature; they neither lend themselves to official coercion or sanction, nor fall within the regulatory power of those who are elected to govern."

22. 42 U.S.C. § 1396–1 (2012).

23. *Right to Choose v. Byrne*, 165 N.J. Super. 443, 463 (Ch. Div. 1979).

24. The United States Supreme Court currently recognizes lawful resident aliens as the only other suspect class.

25. Locke, "Second Treatise on Government," 23.

26. See, for example, *State v. Perricone*, 37 N.J. 463 (1962) (ordering blood transfusion for infant whose parents objected to procedure on religious grounds); *John F. Kennedy*

Memorial Hospital v. Heston, 58 N.J. 576 (1971) (stating that an adult may be compelled to submit to lifesaving medical procedures despite her religious objections); *Young v. Bd. of Health of Somerville*, 61 N.J. 76 (1972) (permitting state-ordered medical treatment that transgressed religious beliefs in order to promote physical well-being of community).

27. *In re Quinlan*, 70 N.J. 10 (1976) may seem to contradict this line of cases, but it does not. In *Quinlan*, Karen Quinlan's individual interest in health was overcome by her fundamental rights to privacy and religious freedom. There the court struck a balance between the woman's fundamental constitutional right of privacy and the state's compelling interest in her health. However, the court concluded that the state's interest in her health weakens and her right of privacy grows as the prognosis dims and the degree of bodily invasion increases, until the point where the individual's rights overcome the state's interest. *Quinlan* concluded that the right of privacy prevailed essentially because the state's countervailing interest in health had significantly diminished and the degree of bodily invasion was high.

28. *Right to Choose v. Byrne*, 169 N.J. Super 543, 551 (Ch. Div. 1979).

29. "In order to prevail in their challenge to the proposed guidelines, plaintiffs must establish an infringement of a fundamental right and the lack of a compelling state interest to justify the infringement of the fundamental right.That [infringement of a] fundamental right is established in the view of this court. Enjoyment of one's health is a fundamental liberty which is shielded by the Fourteenth Amendment to the Federal Constitution and by Article I, paragraph I of the State Constitution against unreasonable and discriminatory restriction." Ibid.

30. 448 U.S. 297 (1980). On the day the Supreme Court decided *McRae*, it applied the same analysis to sustain an Illinois statute that, like New Jersey's funding restriction, prohibited Medicaid funds for all abortions except those to preserve the life of the pregnant woman. See *Williams v. Zbaraz*, 448 U.S. 358 (1980).

31. Because the plaintiffs in *McRae* lacked standing to assert the issue, the United States Supreme Court declined to reach the claim that the Hyde Amendment violated the free exercise of their religion.

32. *Right to Choose v. Byrne*, 91 N.J. 287, 305–06 (1982).

33. Ibid. at 325 (Pashman, J., dissenting). Justice Pashman also agreed with us that the distinction between medically necessary and elective abortions was specious: "There is no medically valid distinction between therapeutic abortions and so-called elective abortions. When a woman is forced to bear a child against her will, a wide variety of physical and psychological injuries can result. I know of no definition of health which does not take these into account. Further, the pregnancy itself is a medical condition which impairs women in a wide variety of ways; moreover, childbirth always carries a risk to a woman's health or even life. There is no basis for concluding that any abortion performed after consultation with a physician is not medically necessary." Ibid. at 320.

34. Ibid. at 327, 328 (quoting *Beal v. Doe*, 432 U.S. 454, 462 [1977] [Blackmun, J., dissenting]). *Beal v. Doe* was a companion case to *Maher* in which the United States Supreme Court upheld a Pennsylvania statute prohibiting Medicaid funding for "elective" abortions.

35. Ibid. at 328.

36. Justice Daniel O'Hern was the sole dissent from the court's holding that the statute's proscription of Medicaid funds for therapeutic abortions was unconstitutional. Justice O'Hern essentially agreed with the holding of the U.S. Supreme Court in *Harris v. McRae* that the statute did not unconstitutionally obstruct Medicaid-eligible women

from procuring abortions. Perhaps more fundamentally, Justice O'Hern espoused the view that, absent exceptional circumstances, once the U.S. Supreme Court has decided a constitutional question, a state court's inconsistent interpretation of its own constitution undermines the authority of the Supreme Court.

37. *McRae*, 448 U.S. at 316.

38. Rather than striking down the challenged statute altogether as unconstitutional, Justice Pollock allowed the law to survive with coverage extended to medically necessary abortions. *Right to Choose*, 91 N.J. at 311–12. This "judicial surgery" to preserve and interpret a law consistent with the constitution is a theme that Justice Pollock returned to repeatedly after *Right to Choose*.

39. Ibid. at 312. The court also suggested that physicians may be guided by New Jersey Department of Human Services regulations, which at the time included physiological, psychological, emotional, and familial factors, as well as age, as the criteria for defining medical necessity. Compare ibid. at 320 (Pashman, J., dissenting) (arguing that "[t]here is no basis for concluding that any abortion performed after consultation with a physician is not medically necessary").

40. One small measure of the case's influence is the fact that it has been cited nearly six hundred times by courts, legal commentators, and scholars in various fields, both in the United States and abroad.

41. The court found that the right to privacy was protected by Article I, paragraph I of the New Jersey constitution.

42. *Right to Choose v. Byrne*, 91 N.J. 287, 305–06 (1982).

43. The court stated that "[a]mong the most [important] of personal rights, without which man could not live in a state of society, is the right of personal security, including 'the preservation of a man's health from such practices as may prejudice or annoy it,' a right recognized, needless to say, in almost the first words of our written Constitution." *Right to Choose*, 91 N.J. at 303 (quoting *Tomlinson v. Armour & Co*, 75 N.J.L. 748, 757 (1908) (citations omitted)).

44. Ibid. at 308.

45. See, for example, Jessie Hill, "The Constitutional Right to Make Medical Treatment Decisions: A Tale of Two Doctrines," *Texas Law Review* 86 (2008): 277. Many commentators on both sides of the abortion debate have criticized the Supreme Court's conceptual analysis of the right to privacy in *Roe v. Wade* as the constitutional guarantee of a woman's right to obtain an abortion. See, for example, Anita Allen, "Tribe's Judicious Feminism," *Stanford Law Review* 44 (1991): 179; Wendy Kaminer, *A Fearful Freedom: Women's Flight from Equality* (Boston: Addison-Wesley, 1990).

46. *Right to Choose*, 91 N.J. at 312.

47. Ibid. at 330.

48. See Eugene Volokh, "Medical Self-Defense, Prohibited Experimental Therapies, and Payment for Organs," *Harvard Law Review* 120 (2007): 1813.

49. *Right to Choose*, 91 N.J. at 308 (quoting Laurence Tribe, *American Constitutional Law* (Eagan, MI: Foundation Press, 1978), 933n. 77). Unfortunately, the majority in *Right to Choose* failed to see, as Justice Pashman did in his dissent, that providing Medicaid funds for poor women to give birth but prohibiting funds for elective abortions created the very same unconstitutional condition—coercing women to forego their constitutional right to choose to terminate a pregnancy in exchange for receiving the medical treatment attendant to childbirth.

50. Interestingly, the court concluded in a footnote that the statute's distinction between funding lifesaving abortions but not all medically necessary abortions was

not even minimally rational under the traditional two-tier equal protection test. The court stated: "Although the State has a legitimate interest in protecting potential life, that interest ceases to be legitimate when the result is to deprive a woman of her right to choose to protect her life and health." Ibid. at 307n. 6. Thus, the court went further than it needed to in rejecting the two-tier equal protection analysis in the body of its opinion.

51. Of course, utilizing a balancing test does not guarantee that the court will find that an individual's rights outweigh the state's asserted interest. Thus, for example, in *Sojourner A. v. N.J. Dep't of Human Services*, 177 N.J. 318 (2003), the court employed the *Right to Choose* balancing test in holding that a family cap on welfare benefits, which denied an increase in the cash benefit upon the birth of an additional child, did not violate the equal protection or due process guarantees of the state constitution. The disparate outcomes in the two decisions are almost certainly attributable, at least in part, to the differing political realities presented by the cases and the role that such realities play, whether consciously or unconsciously, in any balancing of interests. In *Right to Choose*, funding medically necessary abortions would save New Jersey money because medical care for childbirth costs substantially more than paying for an abortion. In contrast, invalidating the family cap in *Sojourner A* would have been far more expensive for the State.

52. *Right to Choose*, 91 N.J. at 308. The court further noted that this balancing test is particularly appropriate when, as here, "the statutory classification indirectly infringes on a fundamental right." Ibid. at 310. Weighing the respective interests in this case, the court concluded: "In balancing the protection of a woman's health and her fundamental right to privacy against the asserted state interest in protecting potential life, we conclude that the governmental interference is unreasonable." Ibid.

6

State v. Hunt (1982)

Protecting Privacy from Unwarranted Searches amid a National Road Map to Independent State Constitutional Rights Cases

ROBERT F. WILLIAMS

Our country was still fairly early in the development of what we now call the "new judicial federalism" when the New Jersey Supreme Court decided *State v. Hunt* in 1982.[1] This set of developments arose because we have a federal system, with a national government and a United States Constitution, as well as fifty state governments, each with its own state constitution. Under such a system, similar matters may sometimes be decided one way by the U.S. Supreme Court (usually first) under the federal Constitution and a different way later by state courts under their state constitutions.

In the 1970s, after the days of the liberal U.S. Supreme Court under the leadership of Chief Justice Earl Warren, the Court began to drift more toward the conservative side. In response, lawyers and state judges who had come of age during the Warren Court years began to look more carefully at their state constitutions, and lawyers started making arguments that state constitutional provisions, even if they were worded similarly or identically to those in the federal Constitution, should be construed more liberally by state courts. As a consequence, even if the claim to particular constitutional rights was lost in the U.S. Supreme Court under the federal Constitution, a similar argument could still be made and won under a state constitution.

Seen from this perspective, it became clear that rulings about federal constitutional rights established a national minimum standard of protection for citizens, but state courts could go beyond that minimum level and provide additional rights for their citizens under their state constitutions. This was true, importantly, even if the state constitution used language identical to that of the federal Constitution. U.S. Supreme Court Justice William J. Brennan Jr., who had served on the New Jersey Supreme Court in the 1950s, described this situation in 1986: "Rediscovery by state supreme courts of the broader protections afforded their own citizens by their state constitutions . . . is probably the most important development in constitutional jurisprudence in our times."[2]

New judicial federalism had its origins in the early 1970s and had gathered a good deal of momentum as the 1980s began. Because many of the cases recognizing more expansive rights under state constitutions dealt with the rights of accused criminals, however, such decisions by state supreme courts drew a lot of criticism, initially from prosecutors and then from the public generally. State supreme court justices were charged with simply "substituting their judgment" for that of the U.S. Supreme Court when they "disagreed" with the latter's interpretations of federal constitutional guarantees.[3]

In a country that had grown used to the Supreme Court issuing definitive pronouncements about rights, this phenomenon seemed strange, at least at first. Of course, when the Supreme Court ruled in favor of expansive federal constitutional rights, that ended the matter and those rights had to be recognized all over the country, including in state courts. However, in the converse situation, where the Supreme Court did not recognize federal rights, or recognized a minimal version of such rights, this quite literally left the matter to the discretion of the fifty states. In this circumstance, it was no surprise that some state courts chose to require greater rights than the national minimum standard. When this occurred in a way that seemed to favor accused criminals or other unpopular people, it raised the kinds of concerns noted in the preceding paragraphs.

By 1982, the year in which *State v. Hunt* was decided, the country, and New Jersey, had a good deal of experience with new judicial federalism. The New Jersey Supreme Court had already issued important interpretations of the state constitution that went well beyond the national minimum standards imposed by the U.S. Supreme Court. For example, the New Jersey court had recognized the rights of poor schoolchildren, of persons who were subjected to searches and seizures by law enforcement personnel, of the terminally ill or injured who wished to die with dignity, and of indigent women who sought medical assistance funding for abortions, as well as expansive state constitutional rights in a number of other controversial areas, including those of persons charged with crimes. All of these decisions went beyond the national minimum standards.

State v. Hunt

By the 1970s, New Jersey had enacted a variety of laws aimed at deterring, or at least punishing, a variety of gambling activities. These were years before casino gambling was legalized in Atlantic City. *State v. Hunt* resulted from Merrell Hunt and Ralph Pirillo Sr. being charged with violating a number of these statutes by their alleged bookmaking activities. Their arrests resulted from a detailed investigation of illegal sports bookmaking activities and from a sequence of New Jersey State Police investigative actions. Illegal sports betting was, and continues to be, a multimillion-dollar enterprise; it often has ties to organized crime, involves bribery of law enforcement officials, and victimizes compulsive gamblers.

First, the state police, conducting an investigation of illegal sports betting, obtained court permission to wiretap the telephone of another gambling suspect, Robert Notaro, and overheard a number of telephone conversations between Notaro and Hunt, then observed both Hunt and Pirillo meeting with Notaro in Atlantic City in 1977.

Second, in 1978, a reliable informant advised the state police that Hunt was conducting an illegal gambling business using two telephones with separate numbers. Based on that information, one of the state police detectives, M. Robert Warner, went to the New Jersey Bell Telephone offices and, without a warrant, obtained the toll billing records for both telephone numbers. Under federal constitutional law, no warrant was required to obtain such information, and there was, at the time, no New Jersey constitutional decision on the matter. These records reflected numerous calls to a service that provided up-to-the-minute information on the results of sporting events.

Third, state police officials listened in on several telephone conversations between another reliable informant and Hunt, without court permission. In these conversations Hunt provided odds on sporting events and accepted bets. The informant told the state police that Hunt was actually working for another person higher up in the operation.

Fourth, the state police applied for and received judicial permission to install pen registers (devices that record telephone numbers that are dialed) on Hunt's two telephones for ten days. The pen registers recorded numerous calls made to Pirillo, as well as to known gamblers in Philadelphia.

Fifth, the state police obtained another court order, this time authorizing the tapping of Hunt's telephones. This provided further information establishing illegal gambling activity, including Hunt giving odds on college football games and accepting bets from callers.

Sixth, the state police obtained search warrants for Hunt and Pirillo and their respective homes and cars. The consequent searches produced a great deal of incriminating evidence, and Hunt and Pirillo were arrested. For example, Hunt had been found at his kitchen table with a bulletin board containing slips of paper with names and dollar figures. More such slips and six thousand dollars in cash were found in Hunt's bedroom.

That led to Hunt and Pirillo being indicted and charged with bookmaking, maintaining a place for gambling, conspiracy to commit bookmaking, and aiding and abetting bookmaking. Represented by well-known criminal defense lawyer Edwin Jacobs, their response was to file a motion to suppress all of the evidence beginning with the toll billing records. A motion to suppress seeks to prohibit the prosecution from utilizing incriminating evidence because it was obtained through an "unreasonable search and seizure." Searches and seizures without a warrant are generally viewed as "unreasonable," subject to important exceptions. Hunt and Pirillo argued that all of the evidence was unreasonably obtained by the state police because the investigation was based on toll billing records that had been obtained without a warrant. This argument was based on Article I, section 7 of the New Jersey constitution: "The right of the people to be secure in their persons, houses, papers, and effects, against unreasonable searches and seizures, shall not be violated; and no warrant shall issue except upon probable cause, supported by oath or affirmation, and particularly describing the place to be searched and the papers and things to be seized."

The trial judge in Atlantic City denied the motion to suppress (probably concluding that Hunt and Pirillo had no expectation of privacy in their telephone billing records), and, in the face of overwhelming evidence against them, they reached a plea bargain. They pled guilty to several of the charges, preserving their right to appeal the search-and-seizure decision, and the other charges were dismissed. A guilty plea may be entered, often resulting in a lesser sentence, while still preserving the right to appeal legal questions such as whether the search and seizure of the telephone call records violated the New Jersey constitution. Hunt and Pirillo were sentenced to terms of a few months in the Atlantic County jail. On appeal to the Appellate Division, New Jersey's intermediate appeals court, the court upheld the trial judge's decision "summarily," meaning that the appeals court was unanimous and was not going to provide an opinion giving its reasons.

Hunt and Pirillo next asked the New Jersey Supreme Court to hear the case, which it agreed to do, according to the court: "primarily to consider the constitutionality of the warrantless search and seizure of defendants' telephone toll billing records."[4] The New Jersey Supreme Court has discretion as to whether to hear cases of this type in which the appellate division decision is unanimous, and it turns down most requests. After Hunt and Pirillo had lost before both the trial and appeals courts, the supreme court's decision to hear the case signaled its interest in the state constitutional search and seizure question.

The New Jersey Supreme Court Opinions

When the *Hunt* case reached the New Jersey Supreme Court it presented starkly the key legal and political question of the new judicial federalism: when is it legitimate for a state supreme court to interpret its state constitution in a fashion that directly contradicts an interpretation by the United States Supreme Court of an identical provision of the United States Constitution?

Three years earlier, in 1979, the U.S. Supreme Court, in a case from Maryland, had considered exactly the issue involved in *State v. Hunt* under the federal Constitution—whether law enforcement officials had to obtain a warrant before placing a "pen register" on a suspect's telephone line, and the Court ruled, albeit in a hotly contested 5–3 opinion, that they did not.[5] The Court reasoned that people do not actually believe the telephone numbers they dial are private because the telephone company necessarily utilizes the number both to connect the call and to bill the caller. Further, the Court concluded that, because this information was voluntarily turned over to the telephone company, there was no "search" and the suspect could have no "legitimate expectation of privacy"[6] in the same way that a person who deposits money in a bank would not have an expectation of privacy in the financial information given to the bank and its employees.[7] Therefore, the search and seizure was not "unreasonable" and no warrant was required. Three of the justices dissented, concluding that numbers dialed from a private telephone, like the actual conversations, were private conduct entitled to constitutional protection. This position, however, did not carry the day. Thus, Hunt and Pirillo's effort in the New Jersey courts started with a substantial legal impediment.

Nonetheless, they were able to persuade the New Jersey Supreme Court to see the matter differently even though the state constitutional language was virtually identical. The *Hunt* case involved long-distance records, rather than a pen register, but this was an insignificant distinction. The court considered the toll billing records first because much of the other evidence stemmed from them. In other words, if the toll billing records were illegally seized, all later evidence attributable to those records would also be illegal. All seven New Jersey Supreme Court justices concluded that the defendants' telephone billing records could not be seized by law enforcement officials without a warrant. Four of the justices joined Justice Sidney Schreiber's opinion for the court. Schreiber, a Republican, had served on the state supreme court since 1975, after three years as a trial judge. He was known as a "lawyers' lawyer," very hardworking and very precise in his opinions, which provided clear direction to the bench and bar. Justice Schreiber retired in 1984, two years after *State v. Hunt* was decided.

The other two justices, while agreeing with the outcome of the majority, wrote separate concurring opinions indicating their differing legal reasoning. Given the New Jersey Supreme Court's record as a leader in new judicial federalism, willing on important occasions to disagree with conclusions of the U.S. Supreme Court, this was not an altogether surprising outcome.

Justice Schreiber first reviewed the key U.S. Supreme Court decisions, indicating that this case would be decided against the defendants, Hunt and

Pirillo, under the federal Constitution. Importantly, however, he continued: "Our inquiry does not end at this point, for we must consider the application of the search and seizure safeguard in the New Jersey Constitution. This Court has seen fit to hold that the search and seizure provisions in the federal and New Jersey Constitutions are not always coterminous, despite the congruity of the language."[8]

Justice Schreiber then referred to several of the New Jersey Supreme Court's earlier decisions in a range of areas, which had "diverged" from U.S. Supreme Court decisions under identical or similar state constitutional provisions. Importantly for this case, he then cautioned that, particularly in the area of criminal law, there was value to "application of uniform rules governing search and seizure." He continued: "Divergent interpretations are unsatisfactory from the public perspective, particularly where the historical roots and purposes of the federal and state provisions are the same. Sound policy reasons, however, may justify a departure. New Jersey has had an established policy of providing the utmost protection for telephonic communications."[9]

Justice Schreiber was referring to the view, held by some, that in the area of criminal procedure rights, which often have to be applied under pressure by law enforcement officials, uniformity rather than diversity in constitutional rights will avoid confusion. Others have countered that where state constitutional standards are higher than federal standards, law enforcement officials only need to know about and enforce the higher state constitutional standards.

Justice Schreiber went on to describe some early laws and court decisions in New Jersey that protected privacy in telephone conversations. He stated that, even before federal constitutional concern for privacy of telephone conversations, New Jersey specifically had "an established policy of providing the utmost protection for telephonic communications." Noting that the telephone in modern times "has become an essential instrument in carrying on our personal affairs," the court found "sound policy reasons" in the New Jersey context to reach a decision in sharp conflict with that of the U.S. Supreme Court.[10] Justice Schreiber noted that a number of other state courts had agreed with the high court's interpretation of the Fourth Amendment to the federal Constitution, but he also noted a variety of academic criticism of that view, as well as a number of other state courts that had declined to follow the U.S. Supreme Court's lead on the matter of warrantless searches and seizures of telephone records. He concluded: "Thus we are satisfied that the police wrongfully obtained the toll billing records of the defendant Hunt in that they were procured without any judicial sanction or proceeding."[11]

Significantly, the New Jersey Supreme Court determined that this decision would not be applied retroactively (other than to Hunt and Pirillo) because its new ruling would cause a "sharp break in the practice of the police authorities" and a number of pending criminal prosecutions were already based on such toll billing records. Further, in a major setback for Hunt and Pirillo, the court concluded that other incriminating evidence (not obtained based on the illegally seized toll billing records) against them was adequate to sustain their convictions and to support the conclusion that the unlawful search and seizure of their telephone billing records constituted "harmless error." So, even though Hunt and Pirillo won their legal argument that the search and seizure was unconstitutional, their convictions were still upheld because of the amount of other evidence against them. An important precedent had been set, however, even though it did not benefit them.

If the decision of the New Jersey Supreme Court had ended there, it would have been only one more example in the new judicial federalism, with state courts interpreting their state constitutions as providing more expansive rights than those recognized by the U.S. Supreme Court under the federal Constitution. As noted earlier, although all seven justices agreed with the outcome, two of them chose to write their own individual "concurring" opinions agreeing with the outcome but presenting additional reasoning. Both concurring opinions were aimed at the methodology and legitimacy questions that arise in this type of case. In other words, they addressed the fundamental question of when it was legitimate for a state court to "disagree" with the U.S. Supreme Court. It is the three opinions in the *Hunt* case taken together that make this such an important, foundational aspect of the new judicial federalism.

First, Justice Morris Pashman, who would retire that same year and who was viewed as consistently the court's most liberal, activist justice and defender of the rights of the underdog, wrote his separate opinion to emphasize the dangers to civil liberties that could arise from warrantless police access to personal telephone records. More important, he wrote separately to respond to both Justice Schreiber's opinion for the court and the other concurring opinion by Justice Alan Handler. Pashman stated: "Because I believe that both opinions define too narrowly the circumstances under which New Jersey courts should independently construe the New Jersey Constitution, I offer my own analysis of the theoretical bases of state constitutional interpretation and its limitations."[12]

Justice Pashman reviewed at some length the development of the new judicial federalism both across the country and in New Jersey, which he had observed during his ten years on the state supreme court. He complimented Justice Handler on his concurring opinion to the extent that it also reviewed this very important development in American constitutional law. However, he criticized the majority opinion for suggesting that "divergent interpretations are unsatisfactory" absent "sound policy reasons." He also read Justice Handler's opinion as arguing "that we follow federal constitutional interpretation unless there are particular reasons to diverge from it."[13]

Justice Pashman saw these approaches as being too narrow because he viewed federal constitutional rights as "the minimum degree of protection a state must give to constitutional rights." He noted that the New Jersey Supreme Court had never attempted to set forth "rules, principles, or theories" to guide it in determining when and under what circumstances it would diverge from these national minimum standards established by the U.S. Supreme Court.

He went on to assert that uniformity in federal and state constitutional rights was not necessarily beneficial. In a federal system like that in the United States, he argued, the possibility of differing views about constitutional rights could be preferable. Justice Pashman asserted that the "path chosen by the United States Supreme Court is not necessarily the best, the most protective of our constitutional rights, or the most reflective of the intent of the Framers."[14]

He also pointed out that because, in the federal system, many areas of governmental authority are reserved for the states, in interpreting the federal Constitution's limitations on state authority the U.S. Supreme Court is often somewhat constrained (or the rights it enforces are somewhat "diluted") by concerns over "federalism" or over interfering with sovereign prerogatives or authority of states. In Pashman's view, this made U.S. Supreme Court decisions not the most appropriate precedents for state courts to follow when interpreting similar or even identical provisions of their own state constitutions: "The United States Supreme Court has also been hesitant to impose on a national level far-reaching constitutional rules binding on each and every state. This reluctance derives, first, from the nationwide jurisdiction of the Court. Once it settles a rule, experimentation with different approaches is precluded."[15]

Based on all of these reasons, Justice Pashman contended that the New Jersey Supreme Court should not be "reluctant" to act to protect rights under circumstances where it perceives that the U.S. Supreme Court has protected New Jersey citizens "inadequately." He concluded: "It is our role alone to say what those rights are, and it is our solemn obligation to enforce them."[16]

Justice Alan Handler, who had served as a trial judge and on the supreme court since 1977 and was known for his intellectual and scholarly approach to the law, wrote his concurring opinion to propose a different approach to state constitutional rights adjudication under circumstances where the U.S. Supreme Court had, under similar factual circumstances, already interpreted an identical or similar provision of the federal Constitution. Handler, who published numerous law review articles about judging, was described by his colleague Justice Robert Clifford, as "one of the four maybe honest-to-goodness, gold-plated, legitimate intellectuals to serve on the court since the 1947 Constitution—the other three being Joseph Weintraub, Nathan Jacobs, and Robert Wilentz."[17] As Justice Pashman noted, Justice Handler reviewed the background of the new judicial federalism extensively. Yet, as Justice Schreiber had done, Handler warned: "There is a danger, however, in state courts turning uncritically to their state constitutions for convenient solutions to problems not readily or obviously found elsewhere. The erosion or delusion of constitutional doctrine may be the eventual result of such an expedient approach."[18]

At this point in his opinion, Justice Handler inserted a footnote referring to events in California, where, after the California Supreme Court had diverged from U.S. Supreme Court interpretations, the voters had amended several provisions of the California state constitution to require that they be interpreted by state courts to conform to interpretations of counterpart federal constitutional provisions. Justice Handler thought this development "may affect the ability of the California courts to give their own charter independent force," and wrote that it would be "unfortunate if our decision today were cast in that light."[19] Handler went on to urge that careful attention be given to interpretations of the federal Constitution, noting that state constitutions may expand, but never contract, federal constitutional rights and that federal decisions are "nevertheless important guides on the subjects which they squarely address." The possibility that a state's voters can vote to overturn their state supreme court's interpretations of the state constitution beyond national minimum standards, and even further mandate that in the future the state courts must interpret the state and federal decisions in "lockstep," is an important feature of state constitutional law. Justice Handler apparently saw this as a more likely possibility in New Jersey if the court was viewed as "turning uncritically to [our] state constitution[s] for convenient solutions to problems not readily or obviously found elsewhere."[20]

Based on this view of the relationship between state and federal constitutional rights, Justice Handler made the following proposal: "It is therefore appropriate, in my estimation, to identify and explain standards or criteria for determining when to invoke our State Constitution as an independent source for protecting individual rights."[21] He then listed seven "standards or criteria" that might justify state constitutional divergence from federal minimum constitutional standards:

- Differing textual language where the state constitution protects a right not included in the federal Constitution, or where the phrasing of the provision is significantly different from the federal Constitution.
- Legislative or constitutional history indicating that when the state constitutional provision was adopted it was intended to provide a more expansive right.
- Previously established bodies of state law that support a more protective interpretation of the state constitution (this would be the early New Jersey laws protecting telephone conversations that were relied upon in Justice Schreiber's majority opinion).

- Differences in the structure of federal and state constitutions, such as the federal Constitution's central function of enumerating powers, in contrast to state constitutions' central function of limiting governmental power, as well as the inclusion of affirmative rights within state constitutions.
- Matters of "peculiar state interest or local concern" where there is no need for uniformity throughout the country.
- A state's particular history and traditions that might support a more protective interpretation of the state constitution.
- "Distinctive attitudes of a state's citizenry" that might support a more expansive interpretation of a state constitution's guarantees of rights.[22]

For each of these standards or criteria, Justice Handler provided extensive citations to decisions from New Jersey and other states relying on these factors to justify state constitutional interpretations of rights beyond the national minimum standards. In this sense, Justice Handler's opinion provided a concise, textbook-like primer for students, lawyers and judges, as well as members of the public, on the new judicial federalism.[23] It was on this basis that Justice Pashman complimented the opinion. Justice Pashman, however, was concerned that Justice Handler's list of standards or criteria could be viewed as a limiting approach. Justice Pashman had stated: "Although the factors listed are potentially broad, they impose clear limits. At bottom, Justice Handler's approach effectively entails a presumption against divergent interpretations of our constitution unless special reasons are shown for New Jersey to take a path different from that chosen at the federal level."[24]

Justice Handler, after his articulation of standards or criteria for divergence, was satisfied that the circumstances presented in the *Hunt* case justified the court in going beyond the federal minimum standards of search-and-seizure protections. He concluded: "New Jersey's long history of statutory and legal protection for telephonic communications makes independent resort to the State charter appropriate in the face of conflicting federal law. . . . Consistent with this longstanding statutory and legal tradition of extending the utmost solicitude to telephonic communications, I am satisfied that the New Jersey Constitution protects the privacy of all aspects of telephone use, including toll billing records. Therefore, I concur in the opinion of the Court."[25] Even though Justice Handler's concurring opinion in 1982 was not joined by any of the other six justices, it became the majority view of the New Jersey Supreme Court the very next year.[26]

Hunt's National Influence

The New Jersey Supreme Court's trilogy of opinions in *Hunt* framed the fundamental practical, political, and jurisprudential issues of the emerging new judicial federalism. Should state courts follow in "lockstep" the decisions of the United

States Supreme Court interpreting the federal constitution?[27] Should there, at the very least, be a presumption in favor of following these decisions? Alternatively, should there not only be no such presumption, but should state courts hesitate to follow U.S. Supreme Court interpretations of identical or similar provisions of the federal Constitution because of their possible dilution based on federalism or other prudential concerns?[28] Because of the New Jersey Supreme Court's stature both generally and as a leader in new judicial federalism even before 1982, its *Hunt* decision, which responded directly to all of these questions in clear and well-researched form, became widely influential in state courts across the nation.

Known as the "criteria approach," the *Hunt* decision was adopted by the Washington Supreme Court in 1986.[29] Thereafter, states like Illinois, Michigan, Massachusetts, Connecticut, Pennsylvania, Delaware, Wyoming, and a number of others have adopted this approach as well, and continue to follow it with varying degrees of rigor.[30]

Hunt's New Jersey Influence

Interestingly, after such a detailed debate over these methodology and legitimacy questions in the early 1980s, the New Jersey Supreme Court has not been particularly rigorous in following its own criteria approach.[31] Many of its most important later new judicial federalism decisions do not explicitly follow the methodology set forth in *Hunt*. For example, in 1990, the court held that household garbage that had been set out at the curb could not be searched without a warrant.[32] The garbage-search cases are classic examples of new judicial federalism. Two years earlier, the U.S. Supreme Court had upheld an identical warrantless search of curbside garbage, based on its reasoning that telephone records and bank records were not protected by a "reasonable expectation of privacy." This prompted New Jersey Justice Robert Clifford to make the following memorable statement, in his inimitable style, about the relationship between state constitutional interpretation and U.S. Supreme Court interpretations of similar or identical federal constitutional rights guarantees: "In interpreting the New Jersey Constitution, we look for direction to the United States Supreme Court, whose opinions can provide 'valuable sources of wisdom for us.' . . . But although that Court may be a polestar that guides us as we navigate the New Jersey Constitution, we bear ultimate responsibility for the safe passage of our ship. Our eyes must not be so fixed on that star that we risk the welfare of our passengers on the shoals of constitutional doctrine. In interpreting the New Jersey Constitution, we must look in front of us as well as above us."[33]

Justice Clifford noted that the U.S. Supreme Court might be "especially cautious" in search-and-seizure cases because "the Court must take note of the disparity in warrant-application procedures among the several states, and must consider whether a warrant requirement in that situation might overload the procedure in any one state." He continued, however, that "we are fortunate to have in New Jersey a procedure that allows for the speedy and reliable issuance of search warrants based on probable cause. A warrant requirement is not so great a burden in New Jersey as it might be in other states."[34] Justice Clifford's opinion for the court in the garbage search case took a different view of the reasonableness of a property owner's expectation of privacy in garbage that has been put out at the curb. The opinion disagreed with and authoritatively rejected the majority opinion of the U.S. Supreme Court on the same issue, which had to view the matter from a national, fifty-state perspective rather than New Jersey's state-specific perspective. The opinion, however, did not apply the *State v. Hunt* criteria approach. Justice Daniel O'Hern dissented, stating: "This case is not about garbage. This case is about the values of federalism. . . . The issue is the basis on which we shall depart from Supreme Court precedent in interpreting counterpart guarantees of our Constitution. . . . For me, it is not enough to say that because we disagree with a majority opinion of the Supreme Court, we should invoke our State Constitution to achieve a contrary result."[35]

Justice Marie Garibaldi also dissented, relying on the earlier U.S. Supreme Court decision. She stated: "An examination of the 'divergence criteria' developed in *State v. Hunt* . . . and reaffirmed in *State v. Williams* . . . indicates that there are no independent state-constitutional grounds to justify our divergence from federal law in this area."[36] Thus, as early as 1990, the New Jersey Supreme Court reached a result quite similar to *State v. Hunt*, but it did not follow the earlier prescribed methodology in arriving at that similar result.

New Judicial Federalism

Cases like these involving search and seizure of telephone records and garbage and similar cases in other contexts serve to illustrate quite clearly the dilemmas of constitutional interpretation in our dual federal system. In difficult cases there is no "right" or "correct" answer to the constitutional question posed by the litigation. State courts must decide, when the question is properly presented to them, whether a rights guarantee in the state constitution, even if similar or identical to the rights guarantee in the federal Constitution, should necessarily be interpreted in a way to follow what the U.S. Supreme Court has already decided. Many state courts do, in fact, tend to follow the U.S. Supreme Court in "lockstep" when they interpret similar state constitutional provisions.[37] Others diverge from the U.S. Supreme Court based on a variety of considerations, such as those illustrated by the New Jersey cases.

Wisconsin Chief Justice Shirley Abrahamson, in discussing the garbage search cases, addressed the lingering controversial question of disagreement between state judges and the U.S. Supreme Court: "But should not different opinions about individual rights in search and seizure cases be expected and accepted? . . . Differences in interpretation of the state and federal constitutions should be viewed, I believe, as examples of the difficulties of interpreting language, especially the broad phrases of a bill of rights. . . . We accept division of opinion within the United States Supreme Court on interpretations of constitutional language. . . . Why should state courts not closely examine a federal decision to determine whether it is sufficiently persuasive to warrant adoption into state law?"[38]

These views recognize the legitimacy of a reasoned difference of opinion, not as a "mere" result-oriented disagreement, but rather as the product of honestly held alternative ways of looking at a problem of constitutional interpretation and the consequences of resolving it in a certain way.

The telephone records and garbage search cases involve a disagreement about people's reasonable expectation of privacy. Justice Abrahamson reported that she conducted "her own unscientific survey of Wisconsinites' views on garbage." The "general consensus" was that one's garbage is private. "These views raise questions about how a court determines society's reasonable expectation of privacy."[39] Simply to say that protection under a state constitution may be more extensive than under the federal Constitution fails to confront the question of what those protections should and will be. Justice Abrahamson's forthright recognition of the real locus of discretion in the state high courts is refreshing, but the questions still linger on.

Possibly the concern expressed by Justice Pashman in *Hunt* that Justice Handler's criteria might serve to limit development of independent state constitutional rights protections has not materialized. The "criteria approach" has not been rigidly followed by the New Jersey Supreme Court. In 2006, Justice Virginia Long, in a decision rejecting the U.S. Supreme Court's view in *New York v. Belton* that a warrantless search of an automobile could be conducted even after the occupants had been removed, wrote for a unanimous court:

> We decline to adopt *Belton* and its progeny because to do so would require us to accept a theoretically rootless doctrine that would erode the rights guaranteed to our own citizens by Article I, Paragraph 7 of our constitution—the right to be free from unreasonable searches and seizures. To us, a warrantless search of an automobile based not on probable cause but solely on the arrest of a person unable to endanger the police or destroy evidence cannot be justified under any exception to the warrant requirement and is unreasonable.
>
> We do not view Article I, Paragraph 7 as a procedural matter but as a reaffirmation of the privacy rights guaranteed to our citizens and our duty as judges to secure them. So viewed, the *Belton* rationale simply does not pass muster.[40]

Conclusion

New Jersey's *State v. Hunt* decision was clearly a central element of the important and enduring new (not so new anymore) judicial federalism. It continues to provide guidance about the terms of the debate concerning expansive or more protective state constitutional rights. In 2007, former Chief Justice Deborah Poritz described *State v. Hunt* as an example of the New Jersey Supreme Court's leadership in the area of individual rights.[41] As Dr. John Kincaid explained:

> The new judicial federalism, however, suggests a model that would enable rights advocates to continue pressing for vigorous national and even international rights protections, while also embedding in regional constitutions and local charters rights that cannot be embedded in the national constitution, effectively enforced by the national government, or enforced only at minimal levels. Such an arrangement would produce peaks and valleys of rights protection within a nation, but this rugged rights terrain is surely preferable to a flat land of minimal or ineffectual national rights protection. The peak jurisdictions can function, under democratic conditions, as rights leaders for a leveling up process.[42]

The discussions of whether, and how, to climb to the state constitutional "peaks" or to remain in the federal constitutional "valley" continue to turn on the arguments presented over a generation ago in the three *State v. Hunt* opinions.

NOTES

1. 91 N.J. 338 (1982).
2. G. Alan Tarr, *Understanding State Constitutions* (Princeton, NJ: Princeton University Press, 1998): 165 (quoting William J. Brennan Jr. in "State Constitutional Law," *National Law Journal*, September 29, 1986, S-1); Accord William J. Brennan Jr., "Foreword: Remarks of William J. Brennan, Jr.," *Vermont Law Review* 13 (1988): 11.
3. Robert Williams, *The Law of American State Constitutions* (New York: Oxford University Press, 2009), 127, 137.
4. *Hunt*, 91 N.J. at 340–341.
5. *Smith v. Maryland*, 442 U.S. 735 (1979).
6. Ibid. at 740.
7. *United States v. Miller*, 425 U.S. 435 (1976).
8. *Hunt*, 91 N.J. at 344.
9. Ibid. at 345.
10. Ibid. at 346.
11. Ibid. at 348.
12. Ibid. at 350 (Pashman, J., concurring).
13. Ibid. at 355.
14. Ibid. at 356.
15. Ibid. at 358.
16. Ibid.

17. Daniel J. O'Hern, *What Makes a Court Supreme: The Wilentz Court From Within* (Newark, NJ: New Jersey Law Journal Books, 2009), 43.

18. *Hunt*, 91 N.J. at 361 (Handler, J., concurring).

19. Ibid. at 362n. 1; ibid. at 362.

20. Ibid. at 361.

21. Ibid. at 363.

22. Ibid. at 364–367.

23. I have referred to such opinions as "teaching opinions." Williams, *American State Constitutions*, 144.

24. *Hunt*, 91 N.J. at 354 (Pashman, J., concurring). In a law review article, Justice Handler stated: "I wrote separately in *Hunt* to express my view that resort to the state constitution as an independent source for protecting individual rights is most appropriate when supported by sound reasons of state law, policy, or tradition." Alan B. Handler, "Expounding the State Constitution," *Rutgers Law Review* 35 (1983): 202, 204; see also ibid. 206n. 29; *Hunt*, 91 N.J. at 367n. 3 (Handler, J. concurring).

25. *Hunt*, 91 N.J. at 368, 372.

26. *State v. Williams*, 93 N.J. 39, 57–58 (1983).

27. See Williams, *American State Constitutions*, chapter 7.

28. Ibid., 169–177, 185.

29. *State v. Gunwall*, 720 P.2d 808 (Wash. 1986); Williams, *American State Constitutions*, 148–150.

30. Williams, *American State Constitutions*, 150–162, 178–185.

31. Ibid., 154–155.

32. *State v. Hempele*, 120 N.J. 182 (1990).

33. Ibid. at 196.

34. Ibid. at 197.

35. Ibid. at 225–226 (O'Hern, J., dissenting).

36. Ibid. at 230 (Garibaldi, J., dissenting).

37. Williams, *American State Constitutions*, 193–232.

38. Shirley Abrahamson, "Divided We Stand: State Constitutions in a More Perfect Union," *Hastings Constitutional Law Quarterly* 18 (1991): 723, 725–733; quote 731.

39. Ibid., 729n. 26, 731.

40. *State v. Eckel*, 185 N.J. 523, 540 (2006).

41. Deborah T. Poritz, "The 2007 Chief Justice Joseph Weintraub Lecture: The New Jersey Supreme Court: A Leadership Court in Individual Rights," *Rutgers Law Review* 60 (2008): 705, 711–713.

42. John Kincaid, "Foreword: The New Federalism Context of the New Judicial Federalism," *Rutgers Law Journal* 26 (1995): 913, 946–947.

7

In the Matter of Baby M (1988)

Reining in Surrogate Parenting and
Defining Children's Best Interests

SUZANNE A. KIM

The case of *In the Matter of Baby M* has been called the "custody trial of the twentieth century."[1] The baby girl at its center was born on March 27, 1986, in the coastal town of Long Branch, New Jersey.[2] Her birth certificate listed her name as Sara. The certificate also listed her mother as Mary Beth Whitehead, who carried and gave birth to her, and her father as Richard Whitehead, Mary Beth's husband. Unlike the other babies born at Monmouth Medical Center that day, however, Sara had two additional visitors; they also considered themselves her father and mother.

Sara's genetic father was William Stern, known as Bill. Bill Stern and his wife, Elizabeth, known as Betsy, came to visit the newborn baby daughter they would call Melissa. *In the Matter of Baby M* was the case in which the New Jersey Supreme Court decided who were the parents of the baby known as both Sara and Melissa.

While the story of the struggle over the baby, who came to be known as Baby M, drew a media frenzy, Baby M's origins were not all that extraordinary, at least not technologically. She was born of what the law has called traditional surrogacy, by which a woman is inseminated with semen. The surrogate provides both her egg and womb. The technology is essentially the same as the artificial insemination used by millions of couples throughout the world. The difference between traditional surrogacy and more standard uses of artificial insemination is that, through a surrogacy agreement, the genetic and gestational mother contracts to relinquish her parental rights to the child's genetic father.

At issue in the *Baby M* case was whether the agreement reached between Bill Stern and Mary Beth Whitehead to give him full parental rights over the child they conceived through artificial insemination and whom Whitehead carried and delivered, was valid. And, if the agreement was not valid, who should have custody of the baby?

The Story

The tale of Baby M often starts with a focus on the Sterns or the Whiteheads. But these couples did not come together by chance. The nation would probably have never heard of Baby M had Noel Keane not brought Mary Beth Whitehead and the Sterns together.

Commonly known as the "father of surrogate motherhood," Michigan attorney Noel Keane founded the Infertility Center of New York (ICNY) in 1981.[3] Keane sought out surrogate-mother candidates through ads in college newspapers after mainstream newspapers rejected his requests to purchase ad space.[4] He arranged his first surrogacy in 1976 in Michigan, where the law did not expressly forbid it. Thereafter, Keane quickly gained national status as a pioneer in surrogacy, frequently appearing in popular media outlets.

Keane was committed to surrogacy because, as he said, "I believe there are thousands of people who want it and need it, including surrogate mothers. I intend to help them. . . . If you have not been there, if you have not wanted children or had no problem in having your own, then you cannot presume to know what drives these childless people."[5] He often situated his commitment to surrogacy in the context of his Catholic beliefs, although the Catholic Church does not approve of surrogacy.[6]

Keane was a middleman. He found mothers to act as surrogates and matched them up with couples who wanted to have children but could not. For this service, he charged a nonrefundable $7,500 fee paid upfront by the prospective parents. At the time of the *Baby M* case, Keane was one of a small number of lawyers and doctors arranging surrogate births in the United States. New York was a good place to do this in 1984, the year the Sterns signed a contract with ICNY and began the process of identifying a surrogate mother; New York law, like Michigan's, did not prohibit surrogacy. Indeed, while surrogacy was certainly not unheard of, its legal status was unclear at the time Keane began to arrange surrogate births. Few courts had considered explicitly whether and how to enforce such arrangements if they went sour, as would happen with Whitehead and the Sterns.

At the time Mary Beth Whitehead learned of ICNY and its need for surrogate mothers, she was a twenty-six-year-old stay-at-home mother living in Brick Township, New Jersey, with Richard Whitehead, her husband of eleven years, and their two children. Mary Beth had married young, when she was sixteen, and Richard was twenty-four. They met at the deli where she worked as a waitress. The daughter of Joseph and Catherine Messer, she was the sixth of eight children and had dropped out of high school at fifteen.

Once the Whiteheads had their two children, Richard underwent a vasectomy. The early years of their marriage have often been characterized as tumultuous.[7] The couple struggled over money, moved frequently, and separated at one point.[8] By the early 1980s, the couple's situation had stabilized, with Richard holding a job as a garbage truck driver, and the couple owning a home (albeit heavily mortgaged).

On the other side of the struggle over Baby M were the Sterns. Bill and Betsy had met while they were graduate students at the University of Michigan. At the time, Bill was pursuing a doctorate in biochemistry, and Betsy was simultaneously pursuing a doctorate in human genetics and a medical degree. They were both twenty-eight when they married in 1974.

By 1985, the year the Sterns met the Whiteheads, Bill and Betsy lived in the affluent town of Tenafly, New Jersey.[9] The Sterns had no biological children. After marrying, they had planned to wait to start a family until Betsy finished her medical training. After Betsy completed her medical residency, she showed signs of having multiple sclerosis. Concerned about the potential medical complications surrounding pregnancy, the couple decided not to have a biological child.[10]

They considered adoption but were concerned about their ability to adopt because of their age and the interfaith nature of their marriage. Bill had been born in Berlin, Germany, in 1946, and his parents were the only members of his extended Jewish family to survive the Holocaust. By the time Bill and Betsy learned of ICNY, both of Bill's parents had died. As an only child with no other surviving relatives, Bill wished to have biological offspring.

By August of 1984, the Sterns had begun considering surrogacy as an alternative to adoption. They had initially wanted a surrogate mother who would carry Betsy's egg fertilized with Bill's sperm. But since the in vitro fertilization this would require was still considered experimental, they did not view this as a viable option. After seeing an advertisement placed by ICNY, the Sterns signed up with the surrogacy center.

Several months earlier, Whitehead had responded to an ad placed by ICNY in her local newspaper. It stated: "surrogate mother wanted, Couple unable to have children willing to pay $10,000 fee and expenses to woman to carry husband's child. Conception by artificial insemination. All replies strictly confidential."[11]

In her memoir about the eventual legal battle with the Sterns over the parentage of the baby to whom she would give birth, Whitehead described her motivations as both altruistic and financial. She hoped to do something to "improve the lives of an infertile couple," and to help her family economically.[12]

The Whiteheads met the Sterns at a restaurant in New Brunswick, New Jersey. During the meeting the couples discussed the potential surrogacy arrangement. The Sterns were pleased that Mary Beth Whitehead said that all she would want was an "annual picture and letter report of progress" about the baby.[13] Richard Whitehead reportedly even jokingly said he would leave his wife if she kept the baby.[14]

In February 1985, Mary Beth Whitehead entered into a surrogacy agreement with Bill Stern, in which she agreed to be artificially inseminated with Bill's sperm, deliver a child, and give the child to him. She was to renounce any parental rights to the child. She was to "assume all risks, including the risk of death, which are incidental to conception, pregnancy, childbirth, including but not limited to, postpartum complications."[15]

Bill had the right to terminate the contract without compensation to Mary Beth if she experienced a miscarriage in the first four months of her pregnancy. Also, if a test of the fetus demonstrated that it was "physiologically abnormal," the contract allowed for abortion "upon demand of William Stern."[16]

Bill was to be listed on the birth certificate as the child's father, and he was to name the child. If he died prior to the child's birth, Betsy was to gain custody of the baby. Upon delivery of the child, Bill was to pay Mary Beth $10,000, in addition to any medical expenses not covered by the Whiteheads' medical insurance. Mary Beth was entitled to $1,000 if her pregnancy ended after the fourth month in stillbirth, miscarriage, or mandated abortion.

After a series of inseminations with Bill Stern's semen, Mary Beth Whitehead became pregnant. The relationship between the Sterns and Whitehead was cordial initially, although clashes arose over whether she should submit to an amniocentesis and take particular medications.

Whitehead wrote in her memoir of the baby's birth, "It wasn't until the day I delivered my daughter that I fully comprehended the fact that it wasn't Betsy Stern's baby. It was the joy, and the pain, of giving birth that finally made me realize I wasn't giving Betsy Stern her baby, I was giving her my baby."[17] The day after the baby was born, Whitehead told the Sterns of her inability to give Sara to them, and that she did not think she could go on living if she had to give up the baby. She declined the $10,000 to which she was contractually entitled.

Whitehead did, however, give the baby to the Sterns two days later. The day after that Whitehead went to the Stern residence in great distress and asked to have the baby for a week. Fearing that she would take her own life, they gave her the baby. What followed was a two-year struggle that drew national attention over the parentage of Baby M. During this time, the Sterns repeatedly sought the baby's return. The Whiteheads repeatedly refused.

The Sterns sought and obtained a paternity order declaring Bill Stern to be the baby's father from the Florida courts, where Whitehead had previously taken the baby for a brief visit. In addition, they filed a civil complaint in a New Jersey court seeking to enforce the surrogacy agreement between Mary Beth Whitehead and Bill Stern. Based on the Florida paternity order, the Sterns obtained a New Jersey court order transferring custody of the baby to Bill.

When the New Jersey police presented the Whiteheads with an order to surrender the baby, the Whiteheads showed the police the baby's birth certificate with Mary Beth and Richard Whitehead listed as her parents. During the ensuing confusion, Mary Beth Whitehead secretly handed the baby out a window in their home to Richard Whitehead. Baby M traveled with the Whiteheads from New Jersey to Florida and over the course of nearly three months stayed in fifteen hotels, motels, and relatives' homes.[18] During this time, the Sterns hired a private detective to locate the Whiteheads and the baby.

After Mary Beth Whitehead became ill in Florida and had to enter the hospital, the Florida police took custody of the baby while she was staying at her maternal grandparents' home. Nearly three months after being handed out of the Whiteheads' window, Baby M returned to New Jersey. The Sterns obtained temporary custody and Mary Beth Whitehead was granted two supervised visitation periods per week. On January 5, 1987, when the baby was nearly nine months old, the trial in the case began in a New Jersey state court before Judge Harvey Sorkow.

The Court Case

Whether Baby M belonged with Bill Stern or Mary Beth Whitehead depended on whether the agreement they reached before Mary Beth became pregnant with the baby was enforceable and what the courts thought was in the "best interests of the child." Regarding the contract, Bill Stern argued that the contract was enforceable and binding. Whitehead argued that it was not. Moreover, each side argued that it was in the baby's "best interests" to be with them.

Interestingly, the trial court and the New Jersey Supreme Court treated these two inquiries differently. The trial court treated the best interests of the child as the umbrella under which to consider whether the contract between Stern and Whitehead was a good one. The New Jersey Supreme Court treated the two as distinct issues, so that the court might choose not to enforce the contract but still give custody to Stern.

After a thirty-two-day trial spanning two months (with thirty-eight witnesses, including fifteen expert witnesses), the trial court agreed with the Sterns and ordered that sole custody of the baby be awarded to Bill Stern and that Mary Beth Whitehead's parental rights be terminated.

In a lengthy written opinion, the trial judge framed his discussion entirely in terms of "the best interests of the child." The court characterized its discussion of the validity of the contract as "commentary" within the best interests legal analysis.[19] If the contract was not enforceable, the judge said, he must determine the custodial, visitation, and support rights of the parties.

Mary Beth Whitehead attacked the contract's validity on a number of grounds. She argued that it was invalid because she had not given informed consent to its terms. The court rejected this argument outright, stating that the concept of informed consent was limited to medical malpractice cases and had no relevance to this case. The trial court also found no evidence of problems with the contract's formation. Whitehead was not coerced into signing it. She had the ability to alter it or bargain for different terms, and she was not defrauded into signing it.

Whitehead argued that she was fraudulently induced to sign the contract because she had not been informed that ICNY's psychologist's evaluation of her included reservations about her suitability to be a surrogate mother based on her perceived tendency to deny her feelings. The court concluded, however, that the Sterns could not be held responsible for ICNY's failure to share this finding and that, even if the Sterns were somehow responsible, Whitehead did not rely on this alleged misrepresentation to her detriment. Instead, the court found that she raised her fraud arguments "after the fact," because, in the court's view, "Mrs. Whitehead wanted to enter a surrogate contract."[20]

Beyond the contract and its formation, the trial court examined whether the child's best interests were better served by being in the custody of Mary Beth Whitehead or Bill Stern. In opting for Bill Stern's custody, the judge stressed differences in the parties' "emotional stability," "ability . . . to recognize and respond to the child's physical and emotional needs," attitudes toward education, "ability . . . to make rational judgments," and ability to "help the child cope with her own life."[21]

The court focused significantly on what it viewed as Mary Beth Whitehead's troubling relationships with her husband and her children. Referring to the parties' relative "emotional stability," the court wrote, "Mrs. Whitehead dominates the family," and "Mr. Whitehead is clearly in a subordinate role." The court suggested that he was not well situated to engage in "rational judgments" because "Mr. Whitehead permits his wife to make most of the important decisions in their family."[22] Despite Mary Beth Whitehead's calls to the police alleging domestic violence by her husband, the court described Mr. Whitehead as "a benign force in the Whitehead household."[23]

Mary Beth Whitehead's attitude toward the baby and her older children came under scrutiny. The court found her too "overbearing" and "thoroughly enmeshed with Baby M, unable to separate her own needs from the baby's." Similarly, the court found "from clear and convincing proofs presented to it that Mrs. Whitehead has been shown to impose herself on her children" and that she "exhibit[ed] an emotional over-investment." The court was concerned by the assertion of Whitehead's lawyer that "she loved her children too much." In the court's words, "Too much love can smother a child's independence. Even an infant needs her own space."[24]

In its exposition of the best interests of the child, the court also variously described Mary Beth Whitehead as "impulsive" for dropping out of high school, removing her son from a second-grade classroom, and fleeing to Florida with the baby; "manipulative" for threatening to kill herself and the baby if she didn't get to keep the baby; "exploitative" for bringing her older daughter to court with her; "untruthful" to advance her position; and "a woman without empathy."[25]

The trial court's opinion noted that, while Mary Beth Whitehead did not complete high school, the Sterns both held doctoral degrees, and that Betsy Stern was a medical doctor.[26] Their relationship appeared more equal to the court than the Whiteheads' relationship, insofar as they seemed to share a "mutually supportive relationship wherein each respects the other and there is a balancing of obligations." Moreover, "The Sterns [had] a private, quiet, and unremarkable life which augers [sic] well for a stable household environment." Whereas Mary Beth Whitehead flouted a court order for custody to be transferred to Bill Stern, said the trial court, the Sterns "obeyed the law." In contrast with its finding of Whitehead's mendacity, the court found that the Sterns were "credible, sincere, and truthful people."[27]

For these reasons, among others, the court concluded that it was in the child's best interests to be in the custody of Bill Stern and his wife. The trial court also issued an immediate order allowing Betsy Stern to adopt Baby M.

Mary Beth Whitehead appealed the trial court's decision to the New Jersey Supreme Court, which, in February 1988, one month before Baby M's second birthday, reversed the trial court decision and declared that a surrogacy contract for pay, like that between Bill Stern and Mary Beth Whitehead, was "illegal, perhaps criminal."[28]

The court provided two main reasons. First, the contract directly conflicted with existing family law–related statutes. For instance, the law prohibits payment or acceptance of money when placing a child for adoption. The surrogacy agreement was, in effect, payment for adoption, a form of "baby-bartering."[29] Moreover, New Jersey law requires proof of parental unfitness or abandonment before parental rights can be involuntarily terminated. According to the court, the surrogacy agreement attempted an end run around this statutory requirement.

Second, the contract conflicted with a number of weighty state policies. For example, enforcing the agreement would run counter to the state's policy that "to the extent possible, children should remain with and be brought up by both of their natural parents. . . . The impact of failure to follow that policy is nowhere better shown than in the results of this surrogacy contract. A child, instead of starting off its life with as much peace and security as possible, finds itself immediately in a tug-of-war between contending mother and father."[30]

Moreover, the surrogacy agreement violated New Jersey's policy that the "rights of natural parents are equal concerning their child, the father's right no greater than the mother's."[31] The agreement effectively gave priority to the father's parental rights over the mother's.

In the court's judgment, the contract also violated the state policy favoring voluntary surrender of children through informed consent. Mary Beth Whitehead did not receive counseling, nor was the psychological evaluation that ICNY conducted of Whitehead put to any use. The contract committed the natural mother to relinquish her baby "before she knows the strength of her bond with her child." Of equal concern to the court was that the natural father and adoptive mother apparently did not benefit from any meaningful investigation of the surrogate mother: "They know little about the natural mother, her genetic makeup, and her psychological and medical history."[32]

Perhaps most importantly, in the court's view, the contract entirely failed to accord deference to the "best interests of the child." There had been no investigation into the fitness of the Sterns as custodial parents, of Betsy Stern as adoptive parent, of the Sterns' superiority to Mary Beth Whitehead as custodians, or of the effects on Baby M of the contractually agreed upon custodial arrangement.

In addition to all of these concerns, the New Jersey Supreme Court was troubled by what it observed as the "profit motive" that "predominates, permeates, and ultimately governs the transaction."[33] Moreover, enforcement of contracts such as this one posed the dangerous potential for exploitation of the poor and for the degradation of women.

Even though Mary Beth Whitehead may have "agreed" to the contract, for the New Jersey Supreme Court this was not the end of the matter. The morality of the deal was up for consideration, and the court weighed in with a series of broad social statements. "There are, in a civilized society, some things that money cannot buy," wrote the court. "Employers can no longer buy labor at the lowest price they can bargain for, even though that labor is 'voluntary,' or buy women's labor for less money than paid to men for the same job, or purchase the agreement of children to perform oppressive labor, or purchase the agreement of workers to subject themselves to unsafe or unhealthful working conditions." There is a limit to allowing bargains or exchanges just because they are "voluntary." "There are, in short, values that society deems more important than granting to wealth whatever it can buy, be it labor, love, or life."[34]

Bill Stern sought enforcement of the contract on constitutional grounds as well, contending that failing to enforce the agreement would violate his constitutional right to procreation. The court rejected this argument, drawing a distinction between the right to procreate and the right to the "custody, care, companionship, and nurturing that follow birth."[35] Stern also argued that he and his wife were being unequally compared to couples in which the wife conceives a child with a sperm donor. In the latter case, parental rights are honored, unlike in the Sterns' case, in which the husband conceives a child with a surrogate mother.

According to the New Jersey Supreme Court, these situations were different enough from one another to justify different treatment under the law. The sperm donor is not in the same position as the surrogate mother, at the very least because of the "difference [in] time it takes to provide sperm for artificial insemination and the time invested in a nine-month pregnancy."[36]

Deciding that the contract was invalid and that William Stern had no constitutional claims to support its enforcement, the New Jersey Supreme Court decided the case as a custody dispute between a biological mother and biological father. Short of adoption by Betsy Stern, the court concluded, Whitehead was the baby's mother. And it was clear that Bill Stern was the baby's father. Custody cases are decided based on what is in the "best interests of the child."[37] After reviewing the trial record upon which the trial court based its custody award to Stern, the New Jersey Supreme Court concluded that this earlier custody award was reasonably based on sufficient credible evidence. This evidence was strongly persuasive in contrasting both the "family life of the Whiteheads and the Sterns and the personalities and the characters of the individuals."[38] And so the New Jersey Supreme Court sustained the award of Baby M's custody to Bill Stern, but it terminated Betsy Stern's adoption of Baby M and granted Mary Beth Whitehead parental visitation rights.

The Impact

The world watched eagerly as the drama surrounding Baby M unfolded. News articles about surrogate parenting appeared periodically in the early 1980s in U.S. newspapers, with the annual combined total of articles on the subject in the *New York Times, Los Angeles Times*, and *Washington Post* ranging from eight to twenty-five from 1980 to 1983. In 1987, the year of the custody trial in the *Baby M* case, 270 articles on surrogacy appeared in these three major newspapers.[39] Given this level of coverage, it would have been difficult to remain ignorant of the case. And, indeed, public opinion polls conducted at the time showed just how aware the public was of Baby M. Nearly everyone had heard of the *Baby M* case.[40]

While Bill Stern may have come across as the more sympathetic party compared to Mary Beth Whitehead in the court of public opinion, views sharply divided over whether surrogacy should be allowed in general. According to reports, "a CBS/New York Times poll and a U.S. News & World Report poll found that most respondents favored Stern receiving custody of the baby (74 percent and 75 percent, respectively); at the same time, when asked about whether such contracts should be legal or whether it was right or wrong for a woman to be a surrogate mother, respondents were evenly divided."[41]

This split was unsurprising, given the range of issues the case encompassed. According to law professor Carol Sanger, "The case provoked philosophical

debate, political organizing, and legislative action as ethicists, feminists, theologians, lawmakers, and local men and women weighed in on surrogacy's moral,
legal, and practical significance."[42]

The *Baby M* case brought to the forefront, in a very public and immediate
way, questions about rights and interests in the context of women and their bodies, children, and family. According to Sanger, the case "set the stage for debates
about the commoditization of children, women's reproductive autonomy, and
the meaning of family in an era of technological possibilities, concerns now
directed at the ever more sophisticated forms of assisted reproduction that have
come into being since 1985."[43]

The dispute between Mary Beth Whitehead and Bill Stern can claim, as part
of its legacy, the creation of a body of law relating to surrogacy, which sought
to begin to answer some of the questions the case had raised. In 1985, the year
Mary Beth Whitehead entered into the surrogacy agreement with Bill Stern,
there were no surrogacy laws in place in any state.[44] The case prompted widespread efforts among lawmakers and lawyers to develop legal rules regarding
surrogacy. By 1987, the year of the trial in the case, about half of the states had
introduced legislation regulating surrogacy.[45]

Today, as with early legislative approaches, the law of surrogacy varies
considerably by state. About half of the states have statutes in place that deal
directly or indirectly with surrogacy. In some of the remaining states, case law
alone indicates the status of surrogacy agreements. In other states, the enforce-
ability of surrogacy agreements is unclear.

Of those states that do have something to say about surrogacy, a variety
of approaches have emerged since *Baby M*. Some states, like New Jersey, refuse
to recognize surrogacy contracts. Of these, some impose criminal penalties for
participating in or facilitating surrogacy arrangements.[46] Other states permit
surrogacy but regulate it. For example, some states limit the intended parents in
surrogacy agreements to married couples.[47] Others explicitly bar compensation
for surrogacy.[48] Another approach has been to enforce surrogacy agreements
and recognize the intended parents.[49]

The law of surrogacy that the *Baby M* case precipitated continues to evolve.
Since *Baby M*'s time, gestational surrogacy has become a popular form of surrogacy. In contrast with the traditional surrogacy engaged in by the Sterns and
Whitehead, in gestational surrogacy the surrogate does not contribute any of
her own genetic material (namely, her egg) but does provide her womb by carrying the baby. As with traditional surrogacy, gestational surrogacy's status varies from state to state. Some states permit one form of surrogacy but not the
other,[50] other states permit or bar both,[51] and other states' laws are unclear on
either or both forms of surrogacy.[52]

Epilogue

What happened to those involved in the custody struggle over Baby M? Mary Beth and Richard Whitehead divorced in 1987, when the appeal to the New Jersey Supreme Court was still pending, and Mary Beth married accountant Dean Gould, with whom she went on to have two children.[53]

Richard Whitehead moved to Florida in 1988 to be closer to family and worked as a cement truck driver until his retirement in 1994. He died in a hospice in 2001.[54]

Harold J. Cassidy, the chief counsel for Mary Beth Whitehead, continues to practice law in Shrewsbury, New Jersey, at the three-lawyer Cassidy Law Firm. Its Web site lists fifteen "practice areas," including "Surrogate mother and gestation carrier cases."[55]

Noel Keane died in 1997 at the age of fifty-eight after a lengthy battle with cancer. According to his son and law partner, Christopher, his father helped arrange more than six hundred surrogate births during his career, starting in 1976.[56]

Gary N. Skoloff, the Sterns' chief counsel, is still one of New Jersey's most prominent family law practitioners at the twenty-lawyer firm, which he and Saul Wolfe cofounded more than fifty years ago. Skoloff almost had a twofer in this book since he was counsel to the plaintiff in *Lepis v. Lepis*, a case that just missed being included.

Bill and Betsy Stern still live quietly in Tenafly, New Jersey, in the house where they raised Baby M. Bill still works at the same job, and Betsy continues to fight medical problems that have afflicted her for many years.

Baby M, or Melissa Elizabeth Stern, grew up in Tenafly with the Sterns. In March 2004, immediately after she became eighteen, Melissa legally terminated Mary Beth Whitehead's parental rights and formalized Betsy Stern's maternity through adoption proceedings. Referring to the Sterns, she told a reporter for *New Jersey Monthly* magazine, "I'm very happy I ended up with them. I love them, they're my best friends in the whole world, and that's all I have to say about it."[57]

After graduating from George Washington University in 2008 with a major in religious studies, Melissa completed a dissertation at King's College, London, entitled "Reviving Solomon: Modern Day Questions Regarding the Long-Term Implications for the Children of Surrogacy Arrangements."[58] In October 2011, Judge Harvey Sorkow, the trial court judge in the Baby M case who had coined the name Baby M, presided at Melissa's wedding to a neuroscientist from New Jersey. The couple lives in London.

In 2007, Melissa was listed in *USA Today* as one of twenty-five "Lives of Indelible Impact" for the preceding twenty-five years, alongside Nelson Mandela, Pope John Paul II, the passengers of United Flight 93 and New York City firefighters on September 11, 2001, Mother Teresa, and Diana, Princess of Wales.[59]

NOTES

1. Carol Sanger, "Developing Markets in Baby-Making: In the Matter of Baby M," *Harvard Journal of Law and Gender* 30 (2007): 69.
2. The baby was born at Monmouth Medical Center. *In the Matter of Baby M*, 217 N.J. Super. 313, 346 (Ch. Div. 1987), affirmed in part and reversed in part, 109 N.J. 396 (1988).
3. Sanger, "Developing Markets," 83.
4. Ibid., 83–84.
5. Ibid., 83 (quoting Noel P. Keane with Dennis L. Breo, *The Surrogate Mother* [Everest House, 1981], 23–24).
6. Ibid.; see also Vatican, Congregation for the Doctrine of the Faith: Instruction Dignitas Personae on Certain Bioethical Questions, December 12, 2008, http://www.vatican.va/roman_curia/congregations/cfaith/documents/rc_con_cfaith_doc_20081208_dignitas-personae_en.html (accessed October 26, 2012).
7. See, for example, Sanger, "Developing Markets," 67; *Baby M*, 217 N.J. Super. at 339–40.
8. According to the trial court, "from the date of their marriage through 1981 the Whiteheads moved at least 12 times," and "[i]n or about 1978, the Whiteheads separated during which time Mrs. Whitehead received public assistance." *Baby M*, 217 N.J. Super at 339; see also Sanger, "Developing Markets," 67.
9. Sanger, "Developing Markets," 67.
10. *Baby M*, 217 N.J. Super. at 336.
11. Henry M. Butzel, "The Essential Facts of the *Baby M* Case," in *On the Problem of Surrogate Parenthood*, ed. Herbert Richardson, 12 (Lewiston, NY: Edwin Mellen Press, 1987); *Baby M*, 217 N.J. Super. at 381.
12. Mary Beth Whitehead and Loretta Schwartz-Nobel, *A Mother's Story* (New York: St. Martin's Press, 1989), 7.
13. *Baby M*, 217 N.J. Super. at 344.
14. Bill Stern testified that "[Richard Whitehead], in fact, had said if Mary Beth wanted to keep the kid, he'd walk right out on her." Sara Robbins, *Baby M Case: The Complete Trial Transcripts* (Buffalo, NY: William S. Hein, 1988), 119.
15. *Baby M*, 109 N.J. at 472 App. A.
16. Ibid. at 473.
17. Butzel, "Problem," 12. According to the trial court, "[Whitehead] testified that throughout her pregnancy, she recognized the child being carried was not to be hers but was Mr. Stern's. . . . She testified that at the moment of birth she realized that she could not and would not give up the child." *Baby M*, 217 N.J. Super. at 347.
18. "During their almost three months in Florida, Mr. and Mrs. Whitehead lived with [Whitehead's parents] for approximately two to three weeks. They left their son and daughter in the care of [Whitehead's parents] and began a fugitive existence, staying in no less than 15 hotels and motels, as well as with an assortment of relatives and friends." *Baby M*, 217 N.J. Super. at 350.
19. Ibid. at 323.
20. Ibid. at 383.
21. Ibid. at 393–95.
22. Ibid. at 393, 394.
23. Ibid. at 396.
24. Ibid. at 392, 393
25. Ibid. at 393, 397

26. Ibid. at 394.

27. Ibid. at 397, 398.

28. *In the Matter of Baby M*, 109 N.J. 396, 411 (N.J. 1988).

29. Ibid. at 425.

30. Ibid. at 434.

31. Ibid. at 435.

32. Ibid. at 437.

33. Ibid. at 439.

34. Ibid. at 440.

35. Ibid. at 448.

36. Ibid. at 450.

37. Ibid. at 445.

38. Ibid. at 457.

39. Susan Markens, *Surrogate Motherhood and the Politics of Reproduction* (Berkeley: University of California Press, 2007), 20.

40. According to Markens, "a Gallup poll conducted during the 1987 trial found that 93 percent of those surveyed had heard of the Baby M case." Ibid.

41. Ibid., 22.

42. Sanger, "Developing Markets," 69.

43. Ibid., 69–70.

44. Joanna L. Grossman, "Time to Revisit Baby M?: A Trial Court Refuses to Enforce a Surrogacy Agreement, Part One," *Find Law* (January 2010), http://writ.news.findlaw.com/grossman/20100119.html; Laura M. Katers, "Arguing the 'Obvious' in Wisconsin: Why State Regulation of Assisted Reproductive Technology Has Not Come to Pass and How it Should," *Wisconsin Law Review* 2000 (2000): 445.

45. Katers, "Arguing the Obvious," 455; Marilyn Adams, "Surrogate Parenting Contract Legislation Enacted: 1987, 1988 and 1989 Legislative Sessions," *State Legislative Report* 15 (1990): App. A, 9; Richard L. Roe, *Childbearing by Contract: Issues in Surrogate Parenting* (Madison: Wisconsin Legislative Reference Bureau, 1988), 1.

46. See, for example, D.C. Code, sec. 16–402 (LexisNexis 2005) (prohibiting surrogacy contracts and subjecting to one year in prison and $10,000 fine); Michigan Compiled Laws Service., sec. 772.855–722.859 (LexisNexis 2005) (barring surrogacy contracts for compensation and imposing imprisonment and fines for participating in or helping to arrange such contracts).

47. For example, New Hampshire and Virginia limit "intended parents" to married couples. New Hampshire Revised Statutes Annotated, sec. 168-B1 (LexisNexis 2001); Virginia Code Annotated, sec. 20–156 (2004).

48. For example, Washington State permits surrogacy arrangements so long as they are not for compensation, for the surrogate or anyone who facilitates the arrangement. *See* Washington Revised Code Annotated, sec. 26.26.210 (West 2005) (defining a "surrogate parentage contract" as a contract for either traditional or gestational surrogacy); ibid., sec. 26.26.240 (voiding any surrogate parentage contract for compensation); ibid., sec. 26.26.230 (prohibiting compensation to any person, organization, or agency assisting in the formation of a surrogate parentage contract).

49. See, for example, *Johnson v. Calvert*, 851 P.2d 776, 782 (Cal. 1993) (enforcing gestational surrogacy agreement and determining parental status based on intent).

50. See Texas Family Code Annotated, sec. 160.754(c) (West 2008) (permitting only gestational surrogacy by prohibiting a surrogate from donating her own egg); North Dakota Century Code, sec. 14–18–04 (2005) (voiding traditional surrogacy arrangements);

ibid., sec. 14–18–08 (vesting parental rights in the intended parents of a gestational surrogacy arrangement).

51. See Florida Statutes, sec. 742.15 (2010) (permitting gestational surrogacy arrangements); ibid., sec. 63.212 (permitting traditional surrogacy arrangements); New York Domestic Relations Law, sec. 122–123 (McKinney 2010) (voiding surrogacy contracts and subjecting intended parents and surrogate to $500 fine, $10,000 fine for arranging a surrogacy contract, and felony charges for multiple violations of arranging surrogacy contracts).

52. See Tennessee Code Annotated, sec. 36–1–102(48) (2005) (defining "surrogate birth" as both traditional and gestation surrogacy, but cautioning that "[n]othing in this subdivision (48) shall be construed to expressly authorize the surrogate birth process in Tennessee unless otherwise approved by the courts or the general assembly"); Louisiana Revised Statutes Annotated, sec. 9:2713 (2005) (seemingly excluding gestational surrogacy arrangements from surrogacy contract prohibition by limiting ban's scope to surrogacy by insemination.).

53. See Robert Hanley, "Whiteheads Divorce and Cite Battle for Baby M, Not Pregnancy, as Cause," *New York Times*, November 13, 1987, http://query.nytimes.com/gst/fullpage.html ?res=9B0DEEDD1438F930A25752C1A961948260 (last accessed October 26, 2012); Donald P. Myers, "After Baby M: Mary Beth Whitehead Has a New Storybook Life, and Some Tough Talk About Surrogate Motherhood," *Los Angeles Times*, March 6, 1989, http:// articles.latimes.com/1989–03–06/news/vw-65_1_mary-beth-whitehead (last accessed October 26, 2012).

54. Sanger, "Developing Markets," 97.

55. Attorneys, The Cassidy Law Firm, http://www.thecassidylawfirm.com/Attorneys/ (accessed June 2012).

56. Lawrence Van Gelder, "Noel Keane, 58, Lawyer in Surrogate Mother Cases, Is Dead," *New York Times*, January 28, 1997, http://www.nytimes.com/1997/01/28/nyregion/noel-keane -58-lawyer-in-surrogate-mother-cases-is-dead.html (last accessed October 26, 2012).

57. Jennifer Weiss, "Now It's Melissa's Time," *New Jersey Monthly*, March 2007.

58. Newsletter, George Washington University Department of Religion, 2008, http://www .gwu.edu/~religion/news/Newsletter2008.pdf (last accessed October 26, 2012).

59. "Lives of Indelible Impact," *USA Today*, May 29, 2007, http://www.usatoday.com/news/ top25-people.htm (last accessed October 26, 2012).

8

Lehmann v. Toys 'R' Us (1993)

Protecting Employees from Sexual Harassment and a Hostile Work Environment

FREDRIC J. GROSS

When Terri Lehmann began working at Toys 'R' Us headquarters in Paramus, New Jersey, in 1981, the law of sexual harassment was still in its infancy. In 1986, the United States Supreme Court first addressed the issue, condemning a supervisor's extortionate demands for sex. In 1991, a federal court of appeals denounced the U.S. Postal Service for allowing a male to return to the workplace of a female coworker whom he had been sexually harassing. In the meantime, trial court decisions went off in every imaginable direction precisely because the appellate courts had barely begun to clarify the law.

The New Jersey Supreme Court's 1993 landmark decision in *Lehmann v. Toys 'R' Us*[1] addressed hostile workplace sexual harassment as a violation of New Jersey's Law Against Discrimination ("LAD"),[2] which forbids discrimination in employment based on a person's sex. In a decision penned by New Jersey's first female supreme court justice, Marie Garibaldi, a unanimous court set down strict standards for assessing workplace sexual harassment and put employers on notice that failing to control such harassment would make employers liable for damages caused by the harassers' misconduct. *Lehmann* would be the first decision from a court of last resort specifying that a woman's claim of hostile work environment must be assessed from the victim's perspective and deeming severe or pervasive harassment to be sufficient to state a claim.

Dramatis Personae and the Story Behind *Lehmann v. Toys 'R' Us*

There are two principal actors in the events underlying the decision: Theresa Lehmann, known as Terri, and her immediate supervisor, Donald Baylous. The story of their employment relationship is the story of this case.

Toys 'R' Us hired Lehmann in 1981 to work as a clerk at corporate headquarters. During the next five years, she progressed through a series of positions with increasing responsibilities, some of them supervisory. In September 1986, she was promoted to a technical position, that of systems analyst in the purchasing department.

Lehmann loved her work and did not want to leave it. The company's management acknowledged that she performed her work very well and did not want to lose her.

Donald Baylous came to work at Toys 'R' Us in November 1985, after Lehmann had been there for more than four years. Baylous was hired as director of purchasing administration, a middle management position. He got his job, as it turned out, by falsely claiming to have a college degree, when in fact he was about six credits short.[3]

By Christmas 1986, Baylous had earned a reputation as a "touchy" person—not in the traditional sense of an emotionally sensitive soul, but rather in the sense of one who did not hesitate to grab, rub, poke, and rake his fingers over his subordinates. This touchiness manifested itself almost exclusively toward women.[4] Baylous also was prone to make blatantly sexist comments to his female subordinates. But, in all fairness, Baylous neither propositioned any employees nor asserted that corporate success grows out of sexual intimacy.

The facts developed in the litigation confirmed that Baylous's numerous incidents of touching and offensive comments discomfited more than half a dozen women, not only Terri Lehmann. The multiple targets of his touching and comments likely influenced the *Lehmann* court's decision to look to the totality of the evidence, including proofs of harassment of nonparties, when assessing whether a sexually hostile workplace existed.

Sexist Comments

Until Mary L., a bottom-level supervisor, was able to obtain a transfer, she reported directly to Baylous. On one occasion, she had come to work wearing business clothes for a meeting. The business meeting ended before lunch, and Mary L. returned from lunch wearing her usual workplace garb, jeans. That afternoon, at a routine meeting of supervisors who reported to him, Baylous asked Mary L. if she had gone home "for a quickie."[5] On another occasion, Baylous told both Mary L. and Terri Lehmann to "dress more seductively to get ahead."[6] Mary L. never protested; she "felt intimidated" because Baylous was her boss.[7]

During a business meeting when others, including Lehmann, were present, Baylous told another of his supervisees, Gail Z., that she had "a cute rump."[8] Baylous told Marlene P., another subordinate, that her hair "looked seductive"—something nobody else had ever told her.[9] When Baylous and another female supervisee, Linda N., were both at work while suffering from colds, Baylous gratuitously assured Lehmann and all others in attendance at a business meeting that the colds were just a coincidence and not the result of any intimacy. That non-intimacy comment did not amuse Linda N., particularly since earlier in the day Baylous had made the same comment to her when they were alone, "and she told him that she didn't like it."[10]

Baylous targeted Terri Lehmann with sexist remarks a number of times. He once instructed her to tell a male buyer that his three-hundred-page order would have to be redone. When Lehmann protested to Baylous that the buyer would be livid, Baylous told Lehmann that to calm him down, "just lean over his desk and show him your tits."[11] Lehmann found that instruction both "weird" and "disgusting."[12] She said nothing to Baylous because, she explained, "I was afraid that I could lose my job."[13]

On still another occasion, a computer problem arose, which the programmer stated was not the fault of Baylous's purchasing department. Baylous immediately told Lehmann "to write a memo to cover your ass," and then gratuitously added, "because you have such a cute little ass."[14]

Uninvited Touchings

At his very first meeting with the women who reported directly to him, Baylous forced Mary L., the woman seated closest to him, to play "kneesies." Mary L. found, to her consternation, that "[Baylous'] knee was up against my knee," and this was *not* accidental.[15] Mary confided her dismay to Terri Lehmann, who had observed the incident, as soon as they were away from Baylous.

Once, as Mary was leaving the building with Baylous a couple of steps behind her, "[h]e just raked his fingers down my back." On another occasion, Baylous grabbed Mary around the hips or the waist.[16] According to Lehmann's and another witness's accounts, while Baylous held Mary, he asked her if she had gone home during lunch time "for a quickie."[17]

Once, while Patty K. was talking to her immediate supervisor, Baylous "came up behind me and put his hands on my neck." Patty testified that another time, without invitation, Baylous "put his hands on my shoulders while he wanted me to explain my job to Sanford Bollinger," his new boss.[18] This was no fleeting touching. Baylous's hands remained on Patty K.'s shoulders throughout the time she spoke to Bollinger, a period of "a few minutes."[19] She did not complain, she explained, because Baylous "was my boss; . . . I felt intimidated."[20] Baylous also rubbed Ms. Lehmann's back without invitation.

Barbara C., who reported directly to a superior of Baylous's, was not intimidated by Baylous's rank. At the Christmas party, when Baylous came up from behind and put his hands on her, Barbara C. told him loudly enough for others to hear, "Get your F'in' hands off of me."[21] The whole group that Ms. Lehmann was sitting with then "talked about what a pain in the neck Don was being and how we wished he would just leave us alone."[22]

Baylous's repeated touching cannot be dismissed as innocuous, and his sexist comments cannot be dismissed, as the defense would have it, as mere banter; on occasion Baylous's actions clearly belied that characterization. In particular, Lehmann testified about a private meeting with Baylous as follows: "I noticed something out of the corner of my eye out of the window, and I said, 'what's going on out there?' At this, [Baylous] lifted the back of my shirt up over my shoulders. I know my bra strap was exposed, and he said, 'give them a show.' And I pulled my shirt down, ran out of the office crying."[23]

The Antiharassment Policy of Toys 'R' Us

Toys 'R' Us had a strong written corporate policy forbidding sexual harassment. Its policy manual defined sexual harassment as follows: "While it is difficult to specifically define sexual harassment, it certainly includes unwelcome sexual advances, requests for sexual favors, verbal or physical conduct of a sexual nature, such as uninvited touching or sexually related comments."[24] Theoretically, any Toys 'R' Us employee could be fired for "[m]aking unwelcome sexual advances, requests for sexual favors, or any other verbal or physical contact of a sexually harassing nature."[25] Moreover, the policy asserted that managers who observe harassment should "[t]ake immediate action to stop it and Notify Area Management." In theory, at Toys 'R' Us, "All reports of sexual harassment must be fully investigated. Violations of Toys 'R' Us harassment policy will not be permitted and may result in discipline or discharge."[26]

This corporate policy proved to be "more honour'd in the breach than in the observance," however.

The Employer's Investigation

Terri Lehmann first complained of sexual harassment after her boss, Baylous, "started telling me to lean over desks and show my tits and cover my ass."[27] On January 22, 1987, she went to Baylous's immediate supervisor, William Frankfort, to complain for the first time about the hostile environment Baylous had created. Lehmann told Frankfort that Baylous had been acting in a sexually harassing manner toward her and a number of other women in the organization.

Instead of taking "immediate action to stop" the sexual harassment as the corporate policy required, Frankfort told Ms. Lehmann to handle the problem herself.[28] She remonstrated, "I was afraid to tell Don," but Frankfort insisted that she should tell Baylous, handling the problem herself.[29]

Four days later, Terri Lehmann and Mary L. took their complaints to the company's human resources department, which agreed to investigate their accusations of sexual harassment against Baylous. Eric Jonas, the corporation's manager of employee relations, was responsible for undertaking this investigation.

At an initial meeting on January 26, 1987, Mary L. and Terri Lehmann both told Jonas about the trouble they were having with Baylous. They also gave Jonas a list of corroborating witnesses, including Jermel M., Linda N., Barbara C., Patty K., and Debbie A.

Before the women had left his office that day, Jonas was already making excuses for Baylous. "Eric [Jonas] said that Don behaved this way because that was the difference between North and South and that being Don was from the South, that's why he acted this way." At that meeting, Jonas asked the two women what they wanted. Lehmann said, "[T]ransfer him, promote him, just make it stop." Mary L. suggested that the company "fire him."[30]

Although the company's own guideline required that the investigator "maintain the confidentiality of the individual who is complaining of harassment,"[31] according to Lehmann Jonas's initial response to the complaints was that "he couldn't do anything about it if Mary and I wanted to remain confidential."[32] Nevertheless, Jonas promised not to tell Baylous who had complained.

Jonas next reviewed this promise of confidentiality with his immediate supervisor, attorney Richard Cudrin, the Toys 'R' Us vice president for employment and labor relations and author of the company's sexual harassment policy. Cudrin agreed that Lehmann's identity should not be disclosed to Baylous since "she was very insistent."[33]

After Jonas consulted with Cudrin, Jonas told Baylous's immediate supervisor, William Frankfort (to whom Lehmann already had complained), to speak to Baylous. Baylous later testified that Frankfort told him, "I should try to control my hands, even to the point that if I felt that I was going to touch, put my hands in my pockets."[34] Jonas also spoke to Baylous, merely telling Baylous to "be very careful about how you approach individuals from this point on."[35] Jonas failed to document the fact, let alone the content, of that vague and weak caution.

By contrast, Jonas kept notes of Lehmann's remarks, but not of any other interviews. In violation of the company's own written guidelines to "document each phase of the investigation," Jonas did not keep a list of his other interviews or the dates of those interviews.[36] At best, Jonas tried to carry around the whole investigation in his head.

Not surprisingly, Jonas's memory was not up to the task. At deposition and trial, he couldn't remember what Lehmann and Mary L. said at the January 26 meeting. He couldn't remember how many persons he interviewed. He couldn't remember in which of three meetings Lehmann provided the names of witnesses. Jonas was so befuddled that he could not even remember whether prior to the trial he had ever heard about Baylous's two "show your tits" comments to Lehmann.

Although Jonas's promise of confidentiality had been very narrow—not to disclose to Baylous who had complained, Jonas treated it as though he was not allowed to tell any of the witnesses he questioned that a complaint had been made against Baylous. For example, when Jonas interviewed Jermel M., he never mentioned Baylous. Nor did he mention Mary L., the woman Jermel had seen Baylous grab around the hips and ask if she had gone home for a quickie. When Jonas interviewed Marlene P., to whom Lehmann had spoken tearfully immediately after the shirt-lifting incident, Jonas did not ask for corroboration of Lehmann's account. Likewise, Jonas did not interview Patty K. about the shirt-lifting incident, even though she was on Lehmann's original list of witnesses. Patty K. would have told Jonas that Terri Lehmann was "very upset, shaking, flushed" the day when "she told me that he had lifted her shirt." In fact, Jonas never went to the purchasing department to ask if anyone had seen or known of the shirt-lifting incident or recalled seeing Lehmann in tears afterward.

Jonas showed little concern for what Baylous said and did. Jonas knew that, after Frankfort had cautioned Baylous to keep his hands in his pockets, Baylous had walked up to Terri Lehmann's sister, Laura, also a Toys 'R' Us employee, and without invitation started rubbing Laura's back. Terri Lehmann told Jonas of this, yet Jonas did not interview Laura. If Jonas is to be believed, he blinded himself so thoroughly to all that was happening that he knew nothing of Baylous's reputation.

The deficiencies in Jonas's investigation were paralleled by Jonas's incredibly constrictive standard for what is important in a claim of sexual harassment. Jonas presumed that patently offensive conduct did not even constitute a sexually harassing act. Worse, Jonas swore under oath that he saw no significance at all in the fact that Baylous supervised most of the offended women:

Q: Did you ever talk to Barbara C. about this matter?

A: Yes.

Q: And did she tell you that at the Christmas party of 1986, Mr. Baylous had put [his] hands on [her] shoulders and she told him, get your F'in hands off of me?

A: She didn't define it that graphically, but she said she told him to take his hands off of her.

Q: Didn't you think that was a sexually harassing act?

A: No, not isolated by itself, no.

Q: Certainly it wasn't welcome, was it?

A: Well, she objected to it.

Q: And it was done by a manager to an employee, wasn't it?

A: That's not important.[37]

Baylous's immediate supervisor, William Frankfort, was no more interested than Jonas in getting to the bottom of the matter. It appears that Frankfort did nothing more responsive to Lehmann's complaint than tell Baylous to keep his hands in his pockets and tell Barbara C. that she was in error when she "told him the same things were [still] happening" two months later. Frankfort's inaction is perhaps explained by his comment to Barbara C., who reported directly to Frankfort, that Frankfort would "hate to see Don's career affected by Ms. Lehmann's complaint."[38] Frankfort's effort to protect Baylous is exemplified by his cautioning Lehmann, when she first complained, not to tell Frankfort's superior, Executive Vice President Howard Moore, a member of the Toys 'R' Us board of directors, what Baylous had been doing. Frankfort explained that Moore "was very straitlaced, and he was a family man."[39] Frankfort, Baylous's supervisor, apparently well understood that Baylous's conduct would offend a straitlaced family man, precisely because Baylous's conduct was sexually harassing.

The old boys' network did a good job of protecting Baylous. He was not disciplined in the slightest. His career was not impaired, even though his harassing actions continued after he was told to "be very careful." Top management found Baylous "guilty of poor judgment on several occasions," but nothing about that misconduct ever found its way into Baylous's personnel file.[40]

The Forced Confrontation

On April 7, 1987, Terri Lehmann felt compelled to give two weeks' notice to Toys 'R' Us. She did so for several reasons: she could not tolerate the pattern of unwanted touching and sexist comments that her immediate supervisor, Donald Baylous, inflicted upon her and other women in the workplace; ten weeks after her in-house complaint against Baylous, the Toys 'R' Us investigation of her complaint obviously had been bogus; and the physical consequences of the stress she was experiencing were so severe that her physician had urged her to quit.

Once Lehmann gave notice, upper management panicked and forced her into an unwanted confrontation with Baylous. As chief lawyer Richard Cudrin testified: "If we're sitting in a situation where somebody is threatening to quit the company and sue the company, because she's contacted NOW and contacted other organizations— . . . it [the forced confrontation] was our way of attempting to resolve [the situation]." Cudrin continued: "There was talk of getting an attorney. There was talk of sexual harassment and getting an attorney. In my mind that conjures up litigation."[41] The prospect of litigation prompted Cudrin and his immediate superior, Jeffrey Wells, not merely to breach the promised confidentiality but to do so in the most offensive way imaginable.

Specifically, seeking to induce Lehmann to drop her sexual harassment complaint, Cudrin and Wells forced her into a surprise confrontation with Baylous on the day she gave notice. They did this while knowing that she did not want to confront her boss. Thus, instead of acting to correct the problem—Baylous—the company chose to humiliate the victim.[42]

By the time Terri Lehmann left Toys 'R' Us headquarters that afternoon, she had been so thoroughly traumatized by the forced confrontation that she could not even come to work for the final two weeks after she gave notice. As a result of the psychological trauma caused by that forced confrontation, she would never again be able to work where men were also employed unless she first received extensive therapy.

Five weeks after the forced confrontation, Cudrin wrote to Lehmann's attorney asserting that she "met with her supervisor who in turn investigated the matter and concluded there was no harassment."[43] Surely Lehmann's supervisor, Baylous, did not investigate his own actions and was in no position to exonerate himself of sexual harassment. Likewise, Baylous's supervisor, Frankfort, cannot be said to have "investigated the matter and concluded there was no harassment." Designated investigator Jonas definitely was not Lehmann's "supervisor," and his so-called investigation was a sham. Nevertheless, Toys 'R' Us, speaking through Cudrin, falsely insisted that an unnamed supervisor had determined that the company and Baylous had done nothing wrong.

The Legal Proceedings

The Trial Court

Terri Lehmann's lawsuit against Toys 'R' Us was tried by a New Jersey Superior Court judge, Benedict E. Lucchi, sitting without a jury. During the trial, Judge Lucchi had asked Richard Cudrin, "Do you think Mr. Jonas did a thorough job investigating this?" After receiving an evasive answer, the judge commented, "I was a police officer at one time. I was in the Prosecutor's Office criminal section. I'm saying, what's going on here? How do you investigate this? Right now, after listening, I'm concluding that Jonas didn't break his back on this one."[44] Later in the day, Judge Lucchi expanded on this criticism: "Do you have anything that says that Mary L. today came and says that she was touched? I was touched? Nothing. Everything is—that's no kind of investigation."[45]

The next day, when Cudrin's boss, Jeffrey Wells, vice president of human relations, was on the stand, Judge Lucchi expressed in no uncertain terms his tentative conclusions about the investigation: "There's no notes in this great investigation, no writing about the investigation except when he spoke to the plaintiff? . . . And yet you have an investigation such as this, and Jonas says, well, this is it? It was very poor. Do you think it was great shakes, that investigation?"[46] When Wells responded that Jonas was hamstrung by the promise of confidentiality (even though the promise only extended to nondisclosure to Baylous of the complainant's identity), Judge Lucchi countered, "But how about these other things? The rump or putting the hands on thighs or around the waist? The incident at the Christmas party where some little girl gave some rough language? Nobody seems to know about it. These people weren't interviewed."

In his *Lehmann* decision, Judge Lucchi made it a point to denounce the investigation as a sham: "[T]his Court wishes to note that it was unimpressed with Toys 'R' Us' investigation of plaintiff's complaints. It appears from the testimony that the Toys 'R' Us employees in charge of investigating this matter did not properly and thoroughly attend to plaintiff's allegations, thus exacerbating plaintiff's problems."[47]

Nevertheless, while accepting the truth of Lehmann's evidence, Judge Lucchi did not see Baylous's behavior as violating New Jersey's Law Against Discrimination, evidently because Baylous never sought sexual activity with Lehmann. Nor did the judge find in the forced confrontation a violation of the LAD's prohibition against retaliation. He did find that the shirt-lifting incident constituted a battery, and he awarded Terri Lehmann five thousand dollars in compensatory damages for this. But the judge found no evidence that Baylous acted with malice toward Lehmann, and he therefore concluded there was no basis for awarding punitive damages.

The Appellate Division

Terri Lehmann appealed Judge Lucchi's decision to the superior court's appellate division, New Jersey's intermediate appeals court. A three-judge panel of that court unanimously ruled that, even if Baylous had acted in jest, "raising the female subordinate's sweater and telling her to give others a show would be an obvious violation of her right to remain free from such a touching, and was in wanton disregard of her privacy and feelings." The lead opinion of three written by the panel continued, "[T]he wanton disregard of plaintiff's personal rights and sensitivities would, if believed, be sufficient to permit the award of [punitive] damages."[48]

Although all three judges concluded that the facts, as related by Judge Lucchi, amounted to a violation of the LAD, they disagreed about the legal standard to be applied in cases of sexual harassment. The lead opinion by Judge Thomas Shebell found that Judge Lucchi's trial-level decision was so murky that remanding the case for additional fact finding was necessary; that Judge Lucchi had erred by refusing to consider an award of punitive damages in conjunction with Baylous's battery, the unwarranted touching of Lehmann; that Toys 'R' Us, while liable for workplace sexual harassment by a supervisory employee, could not be subjected to punitive damages absent evidence that it had engaged in independent misconduct; and that Judge Lucchi correctly dismissed claims relating to the confrontation with Baylous that was forced on Lehmann, whether the claims were based on invasion of privacy, intentional invasion of privacy, intentional infliction of emotional distress, or reprisal in violation of the LAD.

Although Judge Shebell used a five-part test drawn from a federal court decision, as did Judge Lucchi, Shebell ruled that Lucchi had misapplied the test.[49] Appellate Division Judge Steven Skillman, by contrast, would use the federal EEOC guidelines as the test for liability.[50] Judge William D'Annunzio, the third appellate division judge sitting on the *Lehmann* case, concurred in the result but found that "strict liability for damages is inappropriate in this type of case. I would posit employer liability on traditional principles of respondeat superior and, alternatively, on an employer's inadequate response when it knows or has reason to know that one or more of its employees has created a sexually offensive environment."[51]

The New Jersey Supreme Court

Both sides sought and obtained review in the New Jersey Supreme Court. The seven justices accepted Lehmann's appeal as the vehicle for adopting a legal standard explicitly designed to eradicate sexual harassment from the workplace. They did so within the framework announced in the first paragraph of the decision:

> This appeal presents this Court with two questions concerning hostile work environment sexual harassment claims under the New Jersey Law Against Discrimination. . . . First, what are the standards for stating a cause of action for hostile work environment sex discrimination claims? Second, what is the scope of an employer's liability for a supervisor's sexual harassment that results in creating a hostile work environment? We hold that a plaintiff states a cause of action for hostile work environment sexual harassment when he or she alleges discriminatory conduct that a reasonable person of the same sex in the plaintiff's position would consider sufficiently severe or pervasive to alter the conditions of employment and to create an intimidating, hostile, or offensive working environment.[52]

QUESTION 1: LEGAL STANDARDS FOR A HOSTILE WORK ENVIRONMENT CLAIM. In the state supreme court's view, the facts developed by Terri Lehmann clearly established a violation of the LAD. However, no single precedent supported the court's novel, but careful, analysis of what standards should govern a hostile workplace claim.

To establish standards for actionable hostile work environment claims, the court had to determine a number of subsidiary issues. One was from whose viewpoint conduct should be assessed to determine whether it was harassing. The victim's? A hypothetical reasonable person's? Or perhaps the harasser's? The *Lehmann* court's resolution of this issue departed radically from traditional tort law concepts.

The law traditionally assesses conduct by asking whether a hypothetical "reasonable person" would act in a particular way or, in the present context, would a reasonable person conclude Baylous's acts and comments were harassing. Answering this question presents a practical problem. Conduct that would offend many women could be dismissed by many men as mere joking. When sexual harassment is at issue, should the hypothetical "reasonable person" be a woman or a man? Or should judges and juries be allowed to answer this question on a case-by-case basis?

The *Lehmann* court concluded that sexual harassment must be examined from the viewpoint of a person of the same sex as the one claiming to have been harassed: "In evaluating whether the harassment alleged was sufficiently severe or pervasive to alter the conditions of employment and to create a hostile or intimidating work environment for a female plaintiff, the finder of fact shall consider the question from the perspective of a reasonable woman. If the plaintiff is male, the perspective used shall be that of a reasonable man."[53] Accordingly, "[t]o state a claim for hostile work environment sexual harassment, a female plaintiff must allege conduct that occurred because of her sex and that a reasonable woman would consider sufficiently severe or pervasive to alter the conditions of employment and create an intimidating, hostile, or offensive working environment."[54]

Thus, instead of adhering to tort law's traditional hypothetical "reasonable person" doctrine, the *Lehmann* court worked a radical but appropriate shift by adopting a reasonable victim analysis. This better protects those entitled to protection and concomitantly strengthens enforcement of the LAD.

A second issue the court had to deal with was whether the sexual harassment complaint was reasonable. On that issue as well, the New Jersey Supreme Court departed from the common law tradition. In this instance, the tradition was that a jury should assess a complainant's reasonableness by the jury's own understanding of community standards. That tradition could excuse offensive conduct because it was not sufficiently outrageous to upset the jury's concept of a reasonable woman. Such an approach would withhold protection from harassment for those most needing it. For example, persons not from the mainstream culture may be hugely offended by touching or language, which members of the mainstream might view as borderline. Likewise, those who take employment in a field historically reserved to the opposite sex often suffer from workplace banter that merely perpetuates the standards of conduct of the single-sex workplace.

The court explained: "We believe that in order to fairly evaluate claims of sexual harassment, courts and finders of fact must recognize and respect the difference between male and female perspectives on sexual harassment. The reasonable person standard glosses over that difference, which is important here, and it also has a tendency to be male-biased, due to the tendency of courts and our society in general to view the male perspective as the objective or normative one."[55]

The court elaborated: "We emphasize that the LAD is remedial legislation. Its very purpose is to change existing standards of conduct. Thus, the reasonableness requirement must not be used to hold that the prevailing level of discrimination is per se reasonable, or that a reasonable woman would expect sexual harassment on entering a historically male-dominated workplace. The LAD is designed to remediate conditions of hostility and discrimination, not to preserve and immunize pre-existing hostile work environments."[56]

Furthermore, a reasonable complaint must be rational or fact based, rather than a statement reflecting community standards. The court explained:

> The category of reasonable women is diverse and includes both sensitive and tough people. A woman is not unreasonable merely because she falls toward the more sensitive side of the broad spectrum of reasonableness. Nor should "reasonable" be read as the opposite of "emotional." Perhaps because "reasonable" contains the word "reason," some have interpreted reasonableness as requiring a Vulcan-like rationality and absence of feeling. The reasonable woman standard should not be used to reject as unreasonable an emotional response to sexual harassment. On the contrary, such a response is normal and common. Only an idiosyncratic response of a hypersensitive plaintiff to conduct that a reasonable woman would not find harassing is excluded by the reasonable woman standard.[57]

The *Lehmann* court thus held that the harassing conduct must have actually occurred and been based on the victim's sex. But once liability is determined, the court noted that individualized responses to harassment will affect the measure of damages: "Of course, the subjective reaction of the plaintiff and her individual injuries remain relevant to compensatory damages."[58]

A third issue that the court had to tackle was when the allegedly harassing conduct is so offensive as to violate the law. Some courts had held that under Title VII of the Civil Rights Act of 1964, the parallel federal equal employment opportunity enactment, sexual harassment must be "regular and pervasive." Building upon that standard, Toys 'R' Us, as well as the New Jersey attorney general, urged that "severe and pervasive" be adopted as the governing LAD legal standard. Under that approach, a single incident, no matter how severe—even a forcible rape—could never be pervasive and so would not violate Title VII.

The *Lehmann* court rejected that approach, holding that the LAD is violated when offending conduct is either severe or pervasive: "Although it will be a rare and extreme case in which a single incident will be so severe that it would, from the perspective of a reasonable woman, make the working environment hostile, such a case is certainly possible. The LAD was designed to prevent the harm of hostile working environments. No purpose is served by allowing that harm to go unremedied merely because it was brought about by a single, severe incident of harassment rather than by multiple incidents of harassment."[59]

When pervasive harassment is at issue, the fact finder has to examine the totality of the circumstances. About that, the court said: "Rather than considering each incident in isolation, courts must consider the cumulative effect of the various incidents, bearing in mind 'that each successive episode has its predecessors, that the impact of the separate incidents may accumulate, and that the work environment created may exceed the sum of the individual episodes.' 'A play cannot be understood on the basis of some of its scenes but only on its entire performance, and similarly, a discrimination analysis must concentrate not on individual incidents but on the overall scenario.'"[60] Moreover, in all cases, it is only the harasser's conduct, not the plaintiff's injury, that must be severe or pervasive.[61]

Yet another issue, the fourth that the court had to address, was whether it mattered if the plaintiff was not the intended target of the offending conduct. Terri Lehmann contended that Baylous established a hostile working environment for women by verbally and physically harassing a number of women, including her. If all that mattered were conduct where she was the target, proof of pervasive harassment would be elusive.

The New Jersey Supreme Court recognized in *Lehmann* that the societal goal of eliminating workplace sex discrimination, including sex-based harassment, could not be reached if a plaintiff's standing to complain were limited to incidents where she was the direct target of the harasser. "The LAD was enacted to protect not only the civil rights of individual aggrieved employees but also to protect the public's strong interest in a discrimination-free workplace."[62] Put differently, the overarching goal of the LAD, which is "eradication of the cancer of discrimination," would not be attained if courts blinded themselves to the totality of the circumstances.

> [A] plaintiff in a hostile work environment sexual harassment case establishes the requisite harm if she shows that her working conditions were affected by the harassment to the point at which a reasonable woman would consider the working environment hostile.
>
> In making that showing, the plaintiff may use evidence that other women in the workplace were sexually harassed. . . . A woman's perception that her work environment is hostile to women will obviously be reinforced if she witnesses the harassment of other female workers. Therefore, we hold that the plaintiff need not personally have been the target of each or any instance of offensive or harassing conduct.[63]

A fifth issue for the New Jersey Supreme Court regarding the legal standard for a hostile work environment was whether sexual harassment had to involve sexual content. At the trial level, Judge Lucchi failed to find sexual harassment because little of Baylous's conduct had been explicitly sexual. Correcting that not uncommon view, the supreme court made clear that what is critically important is not the sexual content of the harassing conduct, but that the victim's gender spurred on the harasser. "[T]he harassing conduct need not be sexual in nature; rather, its defining characteristic is that the harassment occurs because of the victim's sex."[64]

The court went on to make clear that the LAD does not prescribe a code of civility: "Common sense dictates that there is no LAD violation if the same conduct would have occurred regardless of the plaintiff's sex. For example, if a supervisor is equally crude and vulgar to all employees, regardless of their sex, no basis exists for a sex harassment claim. Although the supervisor may not be a nice person, he is not abusing a plaintiff because of her sex."[65]

Baylous's conduct undeniably had been influenced by the sex of his subordinates. He would not have told any male employee to display his breasts or his penis when he encountered an irate customer. Neither would Baylous have lifted any male's sweater or pulled down any male's pants to "give them a show." His comments about dressing seductively and using bodies to get ahead were reserved for females. So were his neck rubbing, knee grabbing, back scratching, and palm holding. Had his subordinates not been female, there is no evidence that any of those things would have happened.

The New Jersey Supreme Court also took care to note in *Lehmann* that "not all sex-based harassment is sex-based on its face."[66] For example, male police officers hostile to the hiring of female police officers might "st[ea]l their case files and vandalize their personal property," and such non-sex-based harassment might or might not be accompanied by "obviously sex-based" harassment. Both types of harassment could be used to prove a hostile workplace claim under the LAD. "All that is required is a showing that it is more likely than not that the harassment occurred because of the plaintiff's sex."[67]

The court also had to address whether the harasser's intent mattered. Under federal law, intent to discriminate is an essential element that must be proved to win any Title VII claim. Departing far from the federal standard, in *Lehmann* the court ruled that intent is not an element of an LAD claim:

> The LAD is not a fault- or intent-based statute. A plaintiff need not show that the employer intentionally discriminated or harassed her, or intended to create a hostile work environment. The purpose of the LAD is to eradicate discrimination, whether intentional or unintentional. Although unintentional discrimination is perhaps less morally blameworthy than intentional discrimination, it is not necessarily less harmful

in its effects, and it is at the effects of discrimination that the LAD is aimed. Therefore, the perpetrator's intent is simply not an element of the cause of action. Plaintiff need show only that the harassment would not have occurred but for her sex.[68]

The New Jersey Supreme Court also dealt with the requisite level of harm in *Lehmann*. It made clear that "[h]arassment need not be so severe as to affect the psychological well-being of the plaintiff." The court continued: "Given the breadth of individual and societal harms that flow from discrimination and harassment, to limit the LAD's application to only those cases in which the victim suffered, or could have suffered, serious psychological harm would be contrary to its remedial purpose."[69] Accordingly, what has come to be called "garden variety" psychological harm, which does not disable or require professional treatment, is compensable under the LAD.

QUESTION 2: THE SCOPE OF AN EMPLOYER'S LIABILITY. The second broad question the New Jersey Supreme Court had to address in *Lehmann* was "What is the scope of an employer's liability for a supervisor's sexual harassment that results in creating a hostile work environment?"[70]

Shortly before the court considered the *Lehmann* case, it had ruled that the LAD provided only equitable, and not monetary, remedies for which there was no right to jury trial.[71] The Legislature responded quickly by amending the LAD so that it afforded a jury trial and all remedies traditionally available in tort actions including monetary damages.[72]

Lehmann provided the first opportunity for the New Jersey Supreme Court to expound upon the new range of remedies available against an employer, typically a business organization, for a supervisor's sexual harassment. In addition to equitable relief, these remedies included both compensatory and punitive money damages. Most important, in discussing these remedies the *Lehmann* court repeatedly made clear that employers must act firmly to prevent and remedy sexual harassment.

In dealing with the available remedies for sexual harassment in the workplace, the New Jersey Supreme Court explicitly addressed in the *Lehmann* decision what equitable relief the LAD allowed. After noting that the employer is the party who controls the workplace, the court reaffirmed that in cases of supervisory sexual harassment, whether the harassment is of the quid pro quo or the hostile work environment type, the employer is directly and strictly liable for all equitable damages and relief. Equitable damages may include hiring or reinstating the harassment victim, disciplining, transferring, or firing the harasser, providing back pay and/or front pay, and taking preventative and remedial measures at the workplace.[73]

This broad panoply of equitable remedies is in part illusory. The frequency with which courts have ordered employers to discipline or fire a harasser roughly equals the frequency with which hens have teeth. By all appearances, Baylous's career suffered no adverse impact from his sexual harassment. Nevertheless, in the years following *Lehmann,* large employers with increasing frequency disciplined or fired harassers before any complaints went to litigation. To this day, however, small businesses usually fall behind the curve.

In turning to the further remedial question of when the employer will be held liable for compensatory damages in supervisory sexual harassment cases, the court looked first to a well-known legal treatise, the *Restatement of Agency (2d),* section 219, for guidance in imposing vicarious liability for damages: "[A]n employer whose supervisory employee is acting within the scope of his or her employment will be liable for the supervisor's conduct in creating a hostile work environment. Moreover, even in the more common situation in which the supervisor is acting outside the scope of his or her employment, the employer will be liable in most cases for the supervisor's behavior. . . . For example, if an employer delegates the authority to control the work environment to a supervisor and that supervisor abuses that delegated authority, then vicarious liability . . . will follow."[74]

The court next looked to negligence as a legal basis for requiring an employer to pay compensatory damages caused by supervisory harassment:

Another basis for employer liability under agency law is negligence. . . .

In light of the known prevalence of sexual harassment, a plaintiff may show that an employer was negligent by its failure to have in place well-publicized and enforced anti-harassment policies, effective formal and informal complaint structures, training, and/or monitoring mechanisms. We do not hold that the absence of such mechanisms automatically constitutes negligence, nor that the presence of such mechanisms demonstrates the absence of negligence. However, the existence of effective preventative mechanisms provides some evidence of due care on the part of the employer.[75]

The court continued, "[G]iven the foreseeability that sexual harassment may occur, the absence of effective preventative mechanisms will present strong evidence of an employer's negligence."[76] Thus, the *Lehmann* decision all but required employers to adopt programs to prevent sexual harassment.

Next, the court permitted liability to be imposed on the employer based on studied indifference: "If a plaintiff can show that an employer had actual knowledge of the harassment and did not promptly and effectively act to stop it, liability . . . may be appropriate."[77]

Then the court addressed the possibility of an employer being held directly, not vicariously, liable for sexual harassment in the workplace: "Although an employer's liability for sexual harassment of which the employer knew or should have known can be seen to flow from agency law, it also can be understood as direct liability. When an employer knows or should know of the harassment and fails to take effective measures to stop it, the employer has joined with the harasser in making the working environment hostile. The employer, by failing to take action, sends the harassed employee the message that the harassment is acceptable and that the management supports the harasser."[78]

Hammering home management's need to become proactive if workplace sexual harassment is to be eliminated, the New Jersey Supreme Court declared in *Lehmann* that "[t]he most important tool in the prevention of sexual harassment is the education of both employees and employers. Consensus among employees and employers should be the goal. We think that providing employers with the incentive not only to provide voluntary compliance programs but also to insist on the effective enforcement of their programs will do much to ensure that hostile work environment discrimination claims disappear from the workplace and the courts."[79]

To complete the discussion of remedies, the court dealt with when an employer might be held liable for punitive damages. It set forth the standards as follows: "[T]he employer should be liable for punitive damages only in the event of actual participation by upper management or willful indifference."[80]

Conclusion

After the legal details are said and done, what motivated the New Jersey Supreme Court to take on, as it did, the issue of hostile workplace sexual harassment? In *Lehmann,* the court demonstrated a clear understanding that its decision radically departed from traditional tort doctrine. The court justified its zeal to stamp out workplace sexual harassment by declaring that its decision would make it easier for all concerned to stay within the law: "[W]e cannot deny legal redress to the victims of discrimination and harassment merely because the perpetrators may be unaware of the illegality of their conduct. In order to ensure fairness for all, both employees and employers must be able to understand what constitutes a claim for gender-hostile work environment. A clear and intelligible legal standard will protect employees from the damage wrought by a hostile working environment and will enable employers to conform their conduct to the law."[81]

At the time of its *Lehmann* decision, the New Jersey Supreme Court was already being criticized in some quarters for supposedly having a pro-employee bias, which purportedly made it difficult to do business in New Jersey. The court sought to defuse any such criticism of its *Lehmann* holdings by pointing out that sexual harassment is hugely costly to employers even in the absence of litigation.[82] It observed:

Sex discrimination and sexual harassment also cause serious economic harms. Dr. Freada Klein, a researcher and consultant to large companies on sexual harassment, has estimated that the cost of sexual harassment for a typical Fortune 500 service or manufacturing company of 23,784 employees is over $6.7 million per year, exclusive of costs of litigation, processing state or federal charges, and destructive behavior or sabotage. The $6.7 million figure derives from the costs of employee turnover, absenteeism, reduced productivity, and the use of internal complaint mechanisms. That harm to the productivity and profitability of corporations necessarily harms the economy of the State and the welfare of its citizens.

Moreover, the Legislature has declared that discrimination is "a matter of concern to the government of the State, and that such discrimination threatens not only the rights and proper privileges of the inhabitants of the State but menaces the institutions and foundation of a free democratic State."[83]

Thus, the *Lehmann* decision was guided both by concern for the business costs of tolerating and perpetuating a sexually hostile workplace and by concern for the personal costs, financial and psychological, of being victimized by workplace harassment. By trumpeting the full panoply of harms its decision was correcting, the New Jersey Supreme Court successfully adopted in *Lehmann* a revolutionary approach to an intractable problem without drawing any substantial adverse criticism from within or beyond the legal profession.

From an even broader perspective, in *Lehmann v. Toys 'R' Us*, the New Jersey Supreme Court addressed a contentious area of law in its infancy and nursed it into early adulthood. The decision made history not only in vindicating Terri Lehmann's demand for justice but also in protecting countless other workers from a sexually charged hostile work environment. The decision is replete with novel and sometimes radical legal holdings, adopted to promote compliance with New Jersey's Law Against Discrimination. The decision provided a road map to employers for avoiding liability, while at the same time it ensured employees' freedom from sexual harassment, or substantial compensation for suffering such harassment. And the decision is so carefully wrought that it generated no outcry for legislative correction.

By virtually any standard, therefore, the *Lehmann* decision has been a resounding success in New Jersey. Its impact goes far beyond this state's borders, however. Although it directly expresses New Jersey law and controls only lower courts in this state, the case has been widely read and cited with approval by a multitude of state and federal courts throughout the country, including the United States Supreme Court. A more completely successful landmark decision construing a single state's unique statute would be hard to imagine.

NOTES

The author, who, with E. Carter Corristan and the late Audrey Scharff, represented Terri Lehmann, acknowledges the assistance of his former associate attorney, Susan E. Babb, and of retired journalist Carl A. Winter in writing this chapter.

1. 132 N.J. 587 (1993).
2. *New Jersey Statutes Annotated*, sec. 10:5–1–5–42 (West 2012).
3. Baylous's explanation for this irregularity defied credulity. He testified that, at the time he applied for employment, he incorrectly believed he had graduated and did not learn otherwise until after he had falsely answered interrogatories in the *Lehmann* litigation.
4. The defense portrayed Baylous's conduct as asexual because he also touched men. The record of the case reveals exactly two occasions when Baylous was seen touching men: He once walked with his arm around his immediate supervisor, and Toys 'R' Us vice president Wells testified without elaboration that Baylous had touched him on occasion. Baylous did not outrank either of those men. He did outrank each woman he touched in the workplace.
5. Trial Transcript at 94–95, *Lehmann v. Toys 'R' Us*, No. L-37521–87 (N.J. Super. Ct. Law Div., June 6, 1990).
6. Trial transcript at 169, *Lehmann v. Toys 'R' Us*, June 11, 1990.
7. Trial transcript at 23, *Lehmann v. Toys 'R' Us*, June 7, 1990.
8. Trial transcript at 61, *Lehmann v. Toys 'R' Us*, No. June 11, 1990.
9. Trial transcript at 35, *Lehmann v. Toys 'R' Us*, June 7, 1990.
10. Trial transcript at 70, *Lehmann v. Toys 'R' Us*, June 11, 1990.
11. Ibid. at 28.
12. Ibid. at 29. The term "tits" was not commonly used in the Toys 'R' Us workplace. The only other time Lehmann encountered this term in the workplace came shortly after Christmas 1986. At that time, Baylous informed her that his new boss, Sanford Bollinger, had a short temper. Lehmann responded by saying, "[T]hat's all we need, is somebody with a quick temper," because that makes me nervous, and Baylous said, "Well, just stick your tits out at him as if you're brave and act as if you're brave." Ibid. at 36.
13. Ibid. at 29.
14. Ibid. at 40.
15. Trial transcript at 115, *Lehmann v. Toys 'R' Us*, June 6, 1990.
16. Ibid. at 94.
17. Trial transcript at 128, *Lehmann v. Toys 'R' Us*, June 11, 1990.
18. Trial transcript at 56, *Lehmann v. Toys 'R' Us*, June 7, 1990.
19. Ibid. at 77.
20. Ibid. at 58.
21. Ibid. at 109.
22. Trial transcript at 22, *Lehmann v. Toys 'R' Us*, June 11, 1990.
23. Ibid. at 32.
24. Trial transcript at 51, *Lehmann v. Toys 'R' Us*, June 14, 1990.
25. Trial transcript at 71, *Lehmann v. Toys 'R' Us*, June 13, 1990.
26. Trial transcript at 51, *Lehmann v. Toys 'R' Us*, June 14, 1990.
27. Trial transcript at 133, *Lehmann v. Toys 'R' Us*, June 11, 1990.
28. Ibid. at 143.
29. Trial transcript at 147, *Lehmann v. Toys 'R' Us*, June 12, 1990.
30. Trial transcript at 53, *Lehmann v. Toys 'R' Us*, June 11, 1990.

31. Ibid. Trial transcript at 137, *Lehmann v. Toys 'R' Us*, June 13, 1990.
32. Trial transcript at 54, *Lehmann v. Toys 'R' Us*, June 11, 1990.
33. Trial transcript at 141, *Lehmann v. Toys 'R' Us*, June 13, 1990.
34. Trial transcript at 10, *Lehmann v. Toys 'R' Us*, June 14, 1990.
35. Trial transcript at 80–81, *Lehmann v. Toys 'R' Us*, No. June 13, 1990.
36. Ibid. at 112–113.
37. Ibid. at 113.
38. Ibid. at 119.
39. Trial transcript at 44, *Lehmann v. Toys 'R' Us*, June 11, 1990.
40. Trial transcript at 40, *Lehmann v. Toys 'R' Us*, June 14, 1990.
41. Trial transcript at 171–177, *Lehmann v. Toys 'R' Us*, June 13, 1990.
42. In recent years, many hospitals and physicians have recognized that a sincere apology, together with an early offer of reasonable compensation, will dramatically reduce the cost of medical malpractice claims. If the behavior of Toys 'R' Us toward Terri Lehmann is any indication, employers may not yet have learned that an apology can go a long way toward preventing or resolving lawsuits.
43. Trial transcript at 61, *Lehmann v. Toys 'R' Us*, June 14, 1990.
44. Trial transcript at 149, *Lehmann v. Toys 'R' Us*, June 13, 1990.
45. Ibid. at 179.
46. Trial transcript at 47, *Lehmann v. Toys 'R' Us*, June 14, 1990.
47. *Lehmann v. Toys 'R' Us*, 132 N.J. 587, 600 (1993) (quoting the trial transcript, *Lehmann v. Toys 'R' Us*).
48. *T.L. v. Toys 'R' Us*, 255 N.J. Super 616, 642 (App. Div. 1992).
49. *Andrews v. City of Philadelphia*, 895 F.2d 1469, 1482 (3d Cir.1990). Lucchi, the trial judge, had applied *Andrews*'s five-part test in *Lehmann:* (1) the employees suffered intentional discrimination because of their sex; (2) the discrimination was pervasive and regular; (3) the discrimination detrimentally affected the plaintiff; (4) the discrimination would detrimentally affect a reasonable person of the same sex in that position; and (5) the existence of respondeat superior [agency] liability.
50. The EEOC guidelines state, in pertinent part: "Harassment on the basis of sex is a violation of section 703 of title VII. Unwelcome sexual advances, requests for sexual favors, and other verbal or physical conduct of a sexual nature constitute sexual harassment when . . . (3) such conduct has the purpose or effect of unreasonably interfering with an individual's work performance or creating an intimidating, hostile, or offensive working environment." 29 C.F.R. § 1604.11(a)(3) (2012).
51. *Toys 'R' Us*, 255 N.J. Super at 644 (D'Annunzio, J., concurring).
52. *Lehmann v. Toys 'R' Us*, 132 N.J. 587, 592 (1993).
53. Ibid. at 611–612.
54. Ibid. at 603.
55. Ibid. at 614.
56. Ibid. at 612.
57. Ibid. at 613–614.
58. Ibid. at 613.
59. Ibid. at 606–607.
60. Ibid. at 607 (citations omitted).
61. Ibid. at 609.
62. Ibid. at 600.
63. Ibid. at 610–11.
64. Ibid. at 602.

65. Ibid. at 604.

66. Ibid. at 605.

67. Ibid. at 606.

68. Ibid. at 604–605.

69. Ibid. at 608–609.

70. Ibid. at 592.

71. *Shaner v. Horizon Bancorp*, 116 N.J. 433, 455 (1989).

72. L. 1990, c.12, s 2, codified at N.J.S.A. 10:5–13.

73. *Lehmann*, 132 N.J. at 617.

74. Ibid. at 619–620.

75. Ibid. at 621.

76. Ibid. at 622.

77. Ibid.

78. Ibid. at 623.

79. Ibid. at 626.

80. Ibid. at 625.

81. Ibid. at 602.

82. Here the court drew freely from a friend of the court, or amicus, brief, filed by the New Jersey chapter of the National Organization for Women and the Rutgers Law School Women's Rights Clinic.

83. *Lehmann*, 132 N.J. at 609 (citations omitted).

9

Doe v. Poritz and Megan's Law (1995)

The Subtle Art of Judicial Deference to the Legislature

RONALD K. CHEN

The New Jersey Supreme Court has often been accused of usurping legislative functions to further social policy objectives. Particularly during the tenure of the late Chief Justice Robert Wilentz, judicially imposed mandates drew the ire of critics who made the familiar accusations of "judicial activism" and "super legislature." Two of the most notable examples are dealt with in other chapters of this book—the *Mount Laurel* doctrine requirement that municipalities in every region of the state provide a realistic opportunity for the production of housing affordable to low- and moderate-income households, and the requirement in *Abbott v. Burke* that the state fund poor urban school districts at least on par with successful suburban districts.

Doe v. Poritz, in which the court upheld the sex offender community notification provisions of Megan's Law, is in marked contrast.[1] In *Doe*, the court, also speaking through Chief Justice Wilentz, addressed the registration and community notification provisions of Megan's Law, a legislative response to the brutal abduction and murder of Megan Kanka. The court found that those Megan's Law provisions did not violate the ex post facto, double jeopardy, cruel and unusual punishment, or bill of attainder clauses of the federal Constitution or analogous state constitution provisions. In addition, the court found that the legislation does not deprive sex offenders of their constitutional rights to equal protection under the laws or to privacy.

By ruling in that way, the court ostensibly deferred to the legislature's superior policy-making competence in crafting a solution to a situation that had attracted widespread public apprehension—the release of convicted sex offenders into the community without the knowledge of or notice to those who might encounter those offenders. The court accepted, largely at face value and with a studied credulity that it otherwise did not often demonstrate with regard to the legislature, assurances that the intent underlying the law was not to impose additional punishment on convicted sex offenders but was solely to protect against future offenses, despite the punitive effects that community notification would have.

In upholding Megan's Law, however, the court also imposed both substantive limitations and a set of procedures for initial determination and review of community notification decisions that made implementation considerably different than what was contemplated in the original 1994 attorney general's guidelines promulgated under the statute. In many ways, the New Jersey Supreme Court could be considered effectively a coauthor of Megan's Law along with the legislative branch. Given the court's approach, the judiciary also could be considered effectively a coadministrator of Megan's Law, along with the executive branch.

The Enactment of Megan's Law

The horrific circumstances surrounding the death of Megan Kanka forced the public to confront explicitly a pathology traditionally left unspoken in open discourse. Jesse Timmendequas, a previously convicted sex offender and child molester, lived with two other convicted sex offenders across the street from the Kanka family in a suburban neighborhood of split-level homes in Hamilton Township, New Jersey. On July 29, 1994, Timmendequas lured Megan into his house by offering to show her a puppy. After sexually assaulting her, he slammed her head onto a dresser, strangled her to death with a belt, then placed the body in a wooden toy chest and dumped it in nearby Mercer County park. The next day, he confessed to investigators and led police to the site. Timmendequas was eventually found guilty of kidnapping, four counts of aggravated sexual assault, and two counts of felony murder.

Apart from the appalling nature of the crime itself, public outrage was triggered in particular by the fact that Timmendequas and his other offender housemates had been released into the community without any public notification. The New Jersey legislature responded quickly by enacting a series of provisions that collectively became known as Megan's Law. The provisions requiring registration of sex offenders and subsequent community notification of the offenders' release into the community attracted the most attention.

The expedited legislative process was criticized by some as hasty.[2] The speaker of the general assembly took the unusual step of treating passage of the bills as "an emergency" need, which allowed a floor vote in the assembly without the regular committee process. On August 29, within a month after Megan Kanka's death, a bill had passed the general assembly. After the state senate proposed amendments that were agreed to by the assembly, the bill passed both houses on October 20. Governor Christine Todd Whitman signed it into law on October 31, 1994, just over three months after Megan's death.

Megan's Law imposed a number of substantial requirements. The first is that those who had been convicted of enumerated sex offenses were required to register with local law enforcement agencies.[3] The second requirement was that the attorney general had to promulgate guidelines and procedures for community notification and identify particular factors relevant to risk of re-offense (although the statute itself already mandated a long list of such factors). The guidelines, in turn, were to provide for three levels of notification depending upon the degree of the risk of re-offense. A third Megan's Law requirement was that county prosecutors of the counties where the registrant both was convicted and intended to reside had to assess the risk of re-offense by the registered person and assign a tier classification (Tier One for the lowest risk of re-offense and Tier Three for the highest).

The county prosecutor where the registrant intended to reside also selected the means of notification, which was linked to the level of risk.[4] Under Tier One (low risk), the prosecutor had to notify law enforcement agencies likely to encounter the registrant.[5] Under Tier Two (moderate risk), the prosecutor, working with local law enforcement agencies, had to notify schools, licensed day care centers, summer camps, and designated community organizations involved in the care of children or the support of battered women or rape victims.[6] Under Tier Three (high risk), law enforcement agencies were required to notify members of the public likely to encounter the registrant.[7]

In early December 1994, the attorney general released an initial version of those guidelines, prompted by the imminent release of sex offenders who fell within the community-notification provisions applied retroactively. The guidelines, for the most part, closely tracked the statutory language, with a few illustrative examples added, such as a history of arson, animal cruelty, or bed wetting, to assist the county prosecutors in assessing the risk of re-offense, and determining the manner of notification.[8] But the guidelines repeatedly stressed that the ultimate determination of whether the offender constituted a low, moderate, or high risk of re-offense, and the extent and methodology of any notification, was left to the complete and ostensibly unreviewable discretion of the county prosecutors.

The Legal Challenges

Legal challenges to Megan's Law began almost immediately after the law became effective.[9] The most immediate issue raised in those challenges was whether community notification was permissible with regard to those whose offenses occurred before October 31, 1994, the statute's effective date. Retroactive application of Megan's Law was considered essential to assuage public outcry against sex offenders living in effective anonymity in the community and, if community notification were limited to prospective application against those who offended after October 31, 1994, it might very well be years before the law would be implemented.

Megan's Law also was challenged on procedural due process grounds. The attorney general's guidelines vested essentially complete discretion in the relevant county prosecutor to assess the risk of re-offense and to determine the manner and extent of any community notification. No explicit provision was made for judicial review of those determinations, and the absence of such review raised concerns from judges hearing the initial challenges.

Doe v. Poritz

"John Doe" was a first time sex offender. In February 1986, more than eight years before Megan's Law was enacted, he was sentenced to a ten-year term of imprisonment at the Adult Diagnostic and Treatment Center (ADTC) in Avenel, based on a plea agreement he entered into after being indicted and charged with sexual assault for molesting two teenage boys.[10]

Doe successfully completed treatment at ADTC within six years and was paroled. This was unusual for offenders sentenced to Avenel, most of whom are forced to serve their maximum sentence. After successfully completing his parole, Doe had been living and working in the community without incident. He had not re-offended to anyone's knowledge and, when Megan's Law was enacted, he apparently was totally reintegrated in the community.[11]

Doe brought an action in New Jersey Superior Court seeking to enjoin the implementation of Megan's Law against those, like himself, who believed that exposure through community notification would lead them to lose their jobs and destroy their efforts to reintegrate into the community. Doe's constitutional challenges were based upon the ex post facto clause, the equal protection clause, and the due process clause.[12]

Near the time the case came before Judge Harold Wells in the superior court's law division in early 1995, several challenges brought by former offenders in federal court had led to some initial success.[13] In the midst of this foment, on February 22, 1995, Judge Wells ruled that retroactive application of community notification did not constitute new punishment that would violate the ex post facto clause, and he therefore upheld the statute. Judge Wells did rule, however, that "fundamental concepts of fairness and due process . . . require that Doe be given a prenotification hearing in the event the prosecutor determines that Tier Two or Tier Three notification may be appropriate."[14] In referring to the procedures that due process would require, Judge Wells wrote: "In the instant case, these procedures are non-existent, let alone not clearly defined. Local prosecutors are given only the Attorney General's rather soft guidelines to help evaluate the risk of re-offense. . . . The prosecutor has broad and untrammeled discretion to decide what information he or she deems relevant or necessary. The prosecutor, with the aid of the guidelines and police input, then makes the final decision on what the risk of re-offense is and thereby the level and manner of notification."[15]

Judge Wells also found that, as a statutory matter, the attorney general's guidelines constituted administrative rules, which should have been adopted in compliance with the APA. He therefore invalidated the guidelines and ordered that the attorney general promulgate new guidelines in conformity with the APA's notice and comment procedures, and only thereafter would Judge Wells conduct an in camera hearing on what degree of risk of re-offense, if any, Doe presented, and what level and what manner of public notification would occur.[16]

The New Jersey Supreme Court's Opinion

At the time it was rendered, Judge Wells's decision was perceived by many as a substantial and welcome vindication of Megan's Law, in contrast to the contemporaneous federal court decisions in *Diaz v. Whitman* and *Artway v. Attorney General of New Jersey* that at least predicted, if not outright declared, constitutional infirmity. Given the pressure created by strong public desire for immediate implementation of Megan's Law, the supreme court agreed to bypass the appellate division, the intermediate appeals court, and hear the appeal directly.

Particularly with the benefit of fifteen years of hindsight, it is possible to understand and sympathize with the court's dilemma when it agreed to decide the *Doe* case. It was presented with a statute that was hastily crafted by the legislature, which delegated to the administrative expertise of the attorney general's office the task of crafting guidelines that supplied the necessary detail to permit immediate implementation. The original attorney general's guidelines, however, which even Judge Wells described somewhat sarcastically as "rather soft," were drafted under the same pressures and with the same haste as the legislation, and thus were, as the court itself ultimately described them, "to a great extent merely a formalization of the classification requirements explicitly set forth in the statute."[17]

The court also was faced with a difficult legal issue as to whether retroactive application of Megan's Law met constitutional muster. There were forceful arguments, at least indirectly supported by then prevailing United States Supreme Court precedent, that community notification constituted additional "punishment," a characterization that would have rendered retroactive application violative of the ex post facto, double jeopardy, and bill of attainder clauses of the federal Constitution. Simply put, the legislative and executive branches of government had not given the judicial branch much ammunition to protect Megan's Law from constitutional attack.

Chief Justice Wilentz's response in *Doe v. Poritz*, paradoxically, could be described as both judicial activism and judicial restraint. Understanding his and the court's complex methodology is difficult but offers fascinating insights into the subtle interplay among the three branches of government on a highly charged issue.

Step One: Reinventing the Statute and Rewriting the Attorney General's Guidelines

The court began with an extensive reinvention of Megan's Law, essentially performing the role (originally intended by the legislature for the attorney general) of defining the factors to be considered in determining the three levels of risk of re-offense and then identifying the permissible mechanisms to be used in community notification. The statute itself explicitly identified a number of factors that were relevant to assessing the risk of re-offense but left to the attorney general the task of further refining and supplementing those criteria.[18]

The original draft of the guidelines promulgated in December 1994 added several criteria but omitted some contained in the statute. Of those omitted, said the court, "Most important is the statutory factor requiring consideration of the offender's 'behavior in the community following service of sentence.'"[19] The court, therefore, required that all the statutory criteria be considered before any "tier" decision was made.

In recrafting the guidelines, however, the court focused primarily on the statutory language describing the consequences of each level of risk assessment:

(1) If risk of re-offense is low, law enforcement agencies likely to encounter the person registered shall be notified;

(2) If risk of re-offense is moderate, organizations in the community including schools, religious and youth organizations shall be notified in accordance with the Attorney General's guidelines, in addition to the notice required by paragraph (1) of this subsection;

(3) If risk of re-offense is high, the public shall be notified through means in accordance with the Attorney General's guidelines designed to reach members of the public likely to encounter the person registered, in addition to the notice required by paragraphs (1) and (2) of this subsection.[20]

The court found that the phrase "likely to encounter" should be read into the requisite showing for offenders at all risk assessment levels, even though the statute includes the phrase only for low and high risks of re-offense, and not for notification to institutions such as schools and victims' shelters for those posing moderate risks.

Chief Justice Wilentz then used a clever interpretive device that leveraged the affirmative requirement that notification must be made to those "likely to encounter" the offender into a limitation that such notification could be made only to those likely to encounter the offender. The court thus significantly restricted the scope of the notification contemplated by the attorney general's guidelines, which would have permitted Tier Three notification through "community meetings, speeches in schools and religious congregations" as well as "such other methods as determined by the prosecutor with the input of local law enforcement," without assessing whether those audiences would be likely to encounter the offender.

Chief Justice Wilentz, therefore, shifted the focus of the tier classification process away from the speculative and subjective process of estimating the possibility that an individual offender would have the mindset to re-offend—the comparative assessment that was the major underpinning of Megan's Law— and directed it toward the more objectively measurable criterion of whether the offender is "likely to encounter" that portion of the public to whom notice would be directed. The latter "likelihood" is arguably more amenable to empirical assessment and judicial review, since it depends upon measuring the probability of commonplace social interactions, rather than predicting individual idiosyncratic (and often pathological) behavior.

The court was thus able to avoid defining on an absolute evaluative scale the murky distinctions among "low," "moderate," and "high" risks of re-offense. On this issue—ostensibly the analytic core of the tiered notification system—the court merely required that, in order to find that an offender was a moderate risk for re-offense, the prosecutor adduce "some proof, in the form of expert opinion or otherwise, that the moderate-risk offender class poses a risk of re-offense substantially higher than the low-risk class."[21] Similarly, to find that an offender was a high risk, the prosecutor must adduce evidence that he poses a risk that is "substantially higher" than the moderate-risk class. The court essentially acknowledged that the analysis of whether a risk was "substantially" higher than the preceding class could be described as somewhat indeterminate:

> We realize the generality of the standard against which the court will decide the correctness of the Tier level decision, but given the unavoidable uncertainties in this entire area, we do not believe it is realistic to impose requirements of proof of some statistical differentiation of the risk of re-offense between the classes or between the offender before the court and the typical offender of the other classes. We can say no more about the meaning of "substantially higher" other than that it is intended to portray a difference in risk so significant as to warrant the

conclusion that the Legislature intended this most substantial difference in the level and therefore the manner of notification.[22]

The court found that the original attorney general's guidelines impermissibly varied from the intent of the statute by omitting reference to the likelihood that the offender would encounter those members of the public who would receive notification and to the offender's behavior in the community following service of sentence. It then found that the guidelines, as rewritten by the court itself, were now sufficiently unremarkable in comparison to the statute that they did not require the notice and comment period required for formal rule making under the APA.[23]

The court thus subtly assigned to itself the power that the legislature had delegated to the executive branch to use its administrative expertise to refine the process of risk assessment and method of notification. Then, after restricting the guidelines to a close rewording of the statute, the court found unnecessary the procedural protections, with the concomitant delays, that the legislature had also enacted under the APA when an administrative agency engages in a significant exercise of rule-making discretion. In another context this could aptly be described as judicial usurpation of the legislative and executive functions, but in this case, understandably, there was little outcry when the result was to preserve the overall constitutionality of Megan's Law and permit immediate implementation.

Step Two: Defining the Concept of "Punishment"

Only after the scope of community notification was limited by Chief Justice Wilentz's restrictive interpretation of the statute did the court address the most immediately pressing doctrinal issue: whether community notification constituted "punishment." Using somewhat florid language that on the surface paid homage to the legislature's "pure" motives, the court found that it did not.

The initial challengers of Megan's Law and its community notification provisions were convicted sex offenders whose sexual offenses had occurred before October 31, 1994, the date the provisions were enacted into law. Their challenges were based on retroactive application of community notification.

Under the ex post facto clause, the government may not, among other things, apply a law retroactively if it "changes the punishment, and inflicts a greater punishment than the law annexed to the crime, when committed."[24] The bill of attainder clause forbids legislatures from engaging in "legislative acts, no matter what their form, which apply either to named individuals or to easily ascertainable members of a group in such a way as to inflict punishment on them without a judicial trial."[25] Finally, the double jeopardy clause prohibits "a second prosecution for the same offense after conviction[,] and multiple punishments for the same offense."[26]

The key issue under each of these clauses was whether retroactive application of Megan's Law's community notification provisions amounts to new "punishment." At the time Doe v. Poritz was being decided, courts and commentators disagreed strongly on the methodology for defining and identifying punishment. And the United States Supreme Court had recently expressed unwillingness "to articulate a single 'formula' for identifying those legislative changes that have a sufficient effect on substantive crimes or punishments to fall within the constitutional prohibition."[27]

The state, and those who argued for a restrictive interpretation of the three constitutional clauses, maintained that the judicial inquiry should focus solely on whether the legislature had a pure, nonpunitive motive. The challengers, on the other hand, argued that whether a state-imposed sanction is "punishment" does not depend only on the alleged purity of the legislative motive, but also depends upon an "assess[ment of] the character of the actual sanctions imposed on the individual by the machinery of the state,"[28] in other words, an "effects" test.

Chief Justice Wilentz and the majority of the court came down firmly on the side of looking at legislative motive. They adopted a predominantly subjective definition of "punishment," explicitly rejecting the use of any objective factors, such as those articulated in Kennedy v. Mendoza-Martinez.[29] Rather, as Justice Stein observed in dissent, "the Court's inquiry both begins—and ends—with legislative intent."[30]

The Doe opinion concluded, "A law does not become punitive simply because its impact, in part, may be punitive unless the only explanation for that impact is a punitive purpose: an intent to punish." Doe further explained that demonstrating subjective legislative intent increases the challenger's burden of proof: "Where the stated legislative intent is remedial, the burden on those claiming there is a hidden punitive intent is 'the clearest proof' of that intent."[31]

At the time that Doe v. Poritz was decided, it was by no means clear that the essentially self-proving "legislative intent" test would overcome concerns that the effects of community notification would be punitive. Language from some United States Supreme Court decisions strongly adverted to an inquiry into the punitive and deterrent effects of a challenged measure as determining whether a government-imposed restriction constituted punishment.

In United States v. Halper, for example, the Court articulated a test for punishment that appears to lower the threshold for finding a legislative sanction to be punitive, although it did so in language that generated confusion and lent support to both sides of the issue:

> We have recognized in other contexts that punishment serves the twin aims of retribution and deterrence. Furthermore, retribution and deterrence are not legitimate nonpunitive governmental objectives. From

these premises, it follows that a civil sanction that cannot be fairly said solely to serve a remedial purpose, but rather can only be explained as also serving either retributive or deterrent purposes, is punishment, as we have come to understand that term.[32]

In *Austin v. United States*, the Court extended the reliance on extrinsic evidence by introducing a historical analysis of a statute's punitive nature. Recalling the *Halper* qualitative factors, *Austin* reiterated the inquiry into whether "a civil sanction that cannot fairly be said solely to serve a remedial purpose, but rather can only be explained as also serving either retributive or deterrent purposes."[33] The Court then ruled that civil forfeiture is "punishment" subject to the excessive fines clause of the Eighth Amendment.

Based on these and other U.S. Supreme Court cases that were at least equivocal on whether a deterrent or retributive effect was sufficient to cast a government restriction as "punishment," the federal courts that had been considering community notification under Megan's Law had already been establishing a foundation for striking down retroactive application of the statute as violative of the ex post facto clause.

The most noteworthy of these cases was *Artway v. Attorney General*, decided nine months after *Doe v. Poritz* by the United States Court of Appeals for the Third Circuit, which covers New Jersey.[34] Judge (later Chief Judge) Edward R. Becker engaged in an exhaustive analysis of the case law and crafted a three-pronged approach—actual purpose, objective purpose, and effect—to determine whether the measure constituted punishment. Judge Becker was clearly attempting to stake a jurisprudential claim, but he acknowledged that the doctrine in this area was still murky. "We have thus attempted to harmonize a body of doctrine that has caused much disagreement in the federal and state courts. We realize, however, that our synthesis is by no means perfect. Only the Supreme Court knows where all the pieces belong."[35]

One opinion that was not particularly persuasive to the Third Circuit Court of Appeals, however, was *Doe v. Poritz*. In a footnote, Judge Becker cataloged what he perceived to be *Doe*'s analytical errors:

Although the New Jersey Supreme Court recognized in *Doe* that *Mendoza-Martinez* does not apply to this analysis, we disagree with that court's approach insofar as it failed to take this recognition to its logical conclusion (in addition to its neglect of history under *Austin* and its total disregard of effects). The *Doe* Court notes that *Mendoza-Martinez* does not apply to the relevant "punishment" analysis, but continues to rely on other authorities that, like *Mendoza-Martinez*, pertain to the question of whether a proceeding is sufficiently criminal in nature to warrant protection under the Fifth and Sixth Amendments.

For example, although the *Doe* Court nominally applies the *Halper* and *Austin* tests, it loads its analysis with the assertion that "where the stated legislative intent is remedial, the burden on those claiming there is a hidden punitive intent is the 'clearest proof' of that intent." *Doe*, 142 N.J. at 162. . . . *Austin, Kurth Ranch*, and *Morales* have further changed the analysis, sensibly we think, to include an increasing focus on objective, effect-oriented aspects of the measure in question.[36]

Thus, *Doe v. Poritz* did not appear to have an immediate impact on the analysis of courts not subject to its supervisory power.

As it turns out, however, the New Jersey Supreme Court was proven to be largely correct to the extent that it predicted how the United States Supreme Court would ultimately define punishment for purposes of the ex post facto and double jeopardy clauses. In *United States v. Ursery*, decided approximately one year after *Doe v. Poritz*, the Court discussed how to determine whether a civil forfeiture proceeding conducted after a criminal proceeding was a successive punishment prohibited by the double jeopardy clause.[37] Its conclusion was that "First, we ask whether Congress intended [the] proceedings . . . to be criminal or civil. Second, we turn to consider whether the proceedings are so punitive in fact as to 'persuade us that the forfeiture proceeding[s] may not legitimately be viewed as civil in nature,' "despite Congress' intent."[38]

Many courts, including courts that were originally inclined to find community notification to be a form of punishment, took *Ursery* as a signal that the test for defining punishment was predominantly, albeit not exclusively, one of legislative intent and not effects.[39] A year later, in *Kansas v. Hendricks*, the U.S. Supreme Court put a finer point on it.[40] It clearly ruled that determining whether civil commitment of convicted sexually violent predators constituted ex post facto punishment was "first of all a question of statutory construction," calling for judicial deference to the legislature's stated intent.[41]

Although *Hendricks* held open the theoretical possibility that the legislature's manifest intent might be rebutted, a party challenging the statute must provide "the clearest proof" that "the statutory scheme [is] so punitive either in purpose or effect as to negate [the State's] intention" to deem it "civil."[42] As a practical matter, barring monumental collective indiscretion by the legislature, such a showing would be essentially impossible for a challenger to make, and it is now fairly settled that community notification under Megan's Law does not constitute punishment.

Nevertheless, the issue of how "punishment" should be defined is, at least theoretically, one in which the New Jersey Supreme Court's jurisprudence is still at variance with the federal appellate court embracing New Jersey. The Third Circuit has continued to maintain that its *Artway* standard for defining "punishment" has survived the U.S. Supreme Court's decisions in *Ursery* and *Hendricks*.

In *E.B. v. Verniero*, for example, the court found that "the holding of *Ursery* is a narrow one limited to civil forfeitures. Neither of the principal rationales supporting its conclusion is pertinent here and we find nothing in the Court's reasoning that is inconsistent with the *Artway* standard. It necessarily follows that *Ursery* provides no justification for abandoning that standard."[43]

The court similarly distinguished *Hendricks:*

> Like *Ursery, Hendricks* does not establish "a single 'formula'" for identifying which legislative measures constitute punishment and which do not. However, the context involved in *Hendricks*—civil commitment of sex offenders—is, obviously, more closely related to the context involved here than was the context of *Ursery*. In determining the continuing viability of *Artway*, therefore, we must give careful consideration to how *Hendricks* addressed the question of whether civil commitment is punishment. We find substantial overlap between the factors relied on in *Hendricks* and those that comprise the *Artway* test and we discern no need to abandon (or overhaul) *Artway*.[44]

At the same time that it preserved the doctrinal validity of the *Artway* standard, the Third Circuit in *E.B. v. Verniero* upheld New Jersey's community notification against claims that the law's notification requirements violated the ex post facto and double jeopardy clauses of the Constitution. The Third Circuit did so by using the *Artway* standard (over Judge Becker's partial dissent), rather than abandoning it.[45]

Whether Judge Becker or Chief Justice Wilentz had the better of the intellectual argument may be a debatable point, but the question of whether *Doe v. Poritz* or *Artway v. Attorney General* had a greater impact on real-life outcomes is not. Retroactive application of community notification was sustained and expeditiously implemented, allowing the institution of Megan's Law to engraft itself onto law enforcement processes, where it remains today.

Step Three: Separating Substance from Process

Having disposed of the constitutional objections to retroactive application of community notification, the New Jersey Supreme Court then addressed the argument that community notification violated a substantive federal or state constitutional right to privacy. While the court eventually concluded that it did not, it distinguished between an invasion of a right to privacy that was so severe that it must be prohibited outright and a deprivation of an interest in privacy that, while justified by the state's interest in protecting the community, was sufficiently tangible that it required a further procedural due process analysis.

Although the court rejected the existence of any absolute, independent, and self-executing constitutional right to be free from community notification, it did establish a framework within which the judiciary could rein in excessive application of Megan's Law under the rubric of procedural due process and New Jersey's doctrine of fundamental fairness. To do so, the court was required to construct a defensible distinction between denying a substantive right to be free from public notification and at the same time identifying a sufficiently palpable liberty interest to trigger procedural protections against indiscriminate publication of the offender's personal information.

It is arguably in this area that Chief Justice Wilentz utilized the flexible nature of New Jersey's state constitution to greatest advantage. While it was clearly his goal to allow community notification to proceed in some form, it was not his goal to permit widespread notification to the public at large, many of whose members were not likely to encounter the offender. It was a daunting task to thread the doctrinal needle in a way that would both recognize a liberty interest sufficient to impose procedural notice and judicial review requirements and avoid constructing a complete barrier to all forms of notification.

Previous federal cases, such as *Paul v. Davis*, had found that "reputation alone, apart from some more tangible interests such as employment, is [not] either 'liberty' or 'property' by itself sufficient to invoke the procedural protection of the Due Process Clause."[46] Standing alone, such a rule would suggest that community notification regarding sex offenders would not deprive them of a cognizable interest that would even trigger a procedural due process inquiry.

Chief Justice Wilentz responded by noting that even these federal cases recognized a liberty or property interest in "stigma plus," in other words, "damage to reputation and impairment of some additional interest."[47] He then set out to identify the "plus" applicable to Megan's Law offenders. He discovered it in the distinct privacy interest, separate and apart from the reputational interest, in being free from disclosure of personal information that, while insufficient to prevent community notification outright, was enough to warrant inquiry into the adequacy of the procedural protections in place before notification took place. "Thus, we conclude that because the stigma resulting from notification is tied to the protectible interest in privacy, which has been grounded in the Fourteenth Amendment, plaintiff has a protectible interest in his reputation."[48]

For good measure, noting that liberty interests sufficient to trigger procedural due process may be created by state law or by the federal constitution itself, the court then found a parallel protection for reputation and privacy in the New Jersey state constitution.

> Under the State Constitution, we find protectible interests in both privacy and reputation. Our analysis differs from that under the Federal Constitution only to the extent that we find a protectible interest in reputation without requiring any other tangible loss. In interpreting the State Constitution, we "look to both the federal courts and other state courts

for assistance . . . [but] [t]he ultimate responsibility for interpreting the New Jersey Constitution . . . is ours." In fulfilling that responsibility, we have generally been more willing to find State-created interests that invoke the protection of procedural due process than have our federal counterparts.[49]

The court found that "the right of a person to be secure in his reputation is a part of the right of enjoying life and pursuing and obtaining safety and happiness which is guaranteed by our fundamental law."[50] The reputational interest, therefore, fell within the terms of Article I, paragraph 1 of the New Jersey Constitution: "All persons are by nature free and independent, and have certain natural and unalienable rights, among which are those of enjoying and defending life and liberty, of acquiring, possessing, and protecting property, and of pursuing and obtaining safety and happiness."

As one further bulwark against indiscriminate application of Megan's Law, Chief Justice Wilentz relied upon the New Jersey "doctrine of fundamental fairness" to support the limitation that community notification could not occur without the availability of individualized judicial review:

> Even if principles of due process did not require that defendants classified as Tier Two or Three be granted a pre-notification hearing, such process would be required by considerations of fundamental fairness. New Jersey's doctrine of fundamental fairness "serves to protect citizens generally against unjust and arbitrary governmental action, and specifically against governmental *procedures* that tend to operate arbitrarily. [It] serves, depending on the context, as an augmentation of existing constitutional protections or as an independent source of protection against state action.[51]

Having thus concluded through multiple analytical paths that the registration and notification provisions of Megan's Law implicate protectable liberty interests in privacy and reputation and therefore trigger the right to due process, the court set out to determine what type of process was due. Using the well-known factors laid out in *Mathews v. Eldridge*,[52] it required that a hearing be conducted prior to community notification under Tier Two and Tier Three. The court allocated to the state the initial burden of introducing evidence to justify notification, but, if the state did so, the burden then shifted to the offender to rebut that evidence:

> In these proceedings, the State shall have the burden of going forward, that burden satisfied by the presentation of evidence that *prima facie* justifies the proposed level and manner of notification. Upon such proof, the offender shall have the burden of persuasion on both issues, that burden

to remain with the offender. In other words, the court, assuming the State has satisfied its burden of going forward, shall affirm the prosecutor's determination unless it is persuaded by a preponderance of the evidence that it does not conform to the laws and Guidelines.[53]

The Third Circuit, in *E.B. v. Verniero*, agreed that the due process clause was triggered by a sufficient liberty interest. It ratcheted up the procedural protections even further and allocated the ultimate burden of proof to the state and not the offender, finding that the due process clause required that the State make its case by the heightened constitutional standard of "clear and convincing evidence."[54]

This requirement of judicial review established by *Doe* and refined by subsequent federal decisions has now evolved into a comprehensive system in which each of New Jersey's court regions or vicinages has at least one Megan's Law judge assigned to review risk assessments and notifications, and a special panel of the appellate division to hear appeals. The existence of the extensive Megan's Law system of tier classification, judicial review, and community notification is now the template that has been duplicated to some degree by every state in the country and demonstrates the lasting practical significance of *Doe v. Poritz*.[55]

Despite recent empirical research strongly suggesting that Megan's Law is not particularly effective, the political realities are such that the system of sex offender registration and community notification begun in New Jersey is embedded in the nation's law enforcement and crime prevention structure.[56]

The Lingering Legacy of *Doe v. Poritz*

Ironically, although the New Jersey Supreme Court sustained the major components of Megan's Law against constitutional attack, one of the most immediate public reactions to *Doe v. Poritz* was to overrule it partially through amendment to the state constitution. By happenstance, the technological and sociological phenomenon of the Internet was becoming universally appreciated at nearly the same time that the court ruled. Thus the public's ability—leading quickly to the public's demand—to access large amounts of information instantaneously led to a desire for an online sex offender registry by which members of the public could acquire the same information about an offender as would be received through community notification simply by accessing the database through a home computer. Such immediate access to information on demand, however, was inconsistent with the laboriously crafted safeguards that *Doe v. Poritz* had imposed, requiring individual notice and a hearing before notification could occur. Since the court had ruled as a matter of state constitutional law that those safeguards were mandated, the legislature proposed a constitutional amendment that was approved by public referendum in November 2000:

Notwithstanding any other provision of this Constitution and irrespective of any right or interest in maintaining confidentiality, it shall be lawful for the Legislature to authorize by law the disclosure to the general public of information pertaining to the identity, specific and general whereabouts, physical characteristics and criminal history of persons found to have committed a sex offense. The scope, manner and format of the disclosure of such information shall be determined by or pursuant to the terms of the law authorizing the disclosure.[57]

Directly thereafter, the legislature enacted a law authorizing creation of the Internet Sex Offender Registry, which today allows the public to access personal information, including a recent photograph, home address, and the nature of the underlying offense, for all moderate (Tier Two) and high (Tier Three) offenders. This was ultimately upheld against federal constitutional challenge by the Third Circuit.[58]

Nevertheless, the New Jersey Supreme Court's methodology of deference to the overall scheme of the legislature, but with significant procedural safeguards attached, has had a salutary effect, both with regard to community notification in particular and the treatment of sex offenders generally. A system of judicial review of risk assessments, absent in the statute and the original attorney general's guidelines, is now in place to curtail the exercise of unbridled executive discretion.

This system of review is obviously not without cost to the court system and prosecutors' offices: resources are required to implement risk assessment, tier classification, and judicial review. Given the now well known capacity of the Internet to grant public access at low cost to massive amounts of information, the temptation may soon be great to dispense with the tier classification system completely and simply allow the public free access to all criminal conviction data for all offenders living in a proscribed geographical area, regardless of the offender's real or perceived risk of re-offense. If that development takes place and is upheld, Megan's Law as originally conceived may become obsolete. It may have been made moot by technological advances that create efficiencies in information delivery which outweigh the state's desire to provide more carefully tailored notifications.

The general requirement of procedural fairness has been extended to other areas as well. For instance, in *State v. Bellamy*, the court concluded, citing *Doe*, that fundamental fairness requires that the trial court inform a defendant of the possible consequences under the Sexually Violent Predator Act of a guilty plea to a sexual offense covered by the act that might result in the defendant being faced with commitment under the act for a period in excess of his or her sentence.[59]

In *Jamgochian v. New Jersey State Parole Bd.*, the court also relied on *Doe* in finding that both due process and the doctrine of fundamental fairness required a hearing before a sex offender on community parole for life is subjected to a curfew [60] Lower courts have extended *Doe*'s rationale of due process and fundamental fairness to require hearings before a parent accused of abuse,[61] or a teacher accused of sexual misconduct,[62] can be included by an administrative agency in a central registry. Indeed, *Doe v. Poritz* has become the standard citation for describing New Jersey's doctrine of fundamental fairness, which "serves to protect citizens generally against unjust and arbitrary governmental action," including situations unrelated to the procedural rights of sex offenders.[63]

The lasting significance of *Doe v. Poritz* is not measured by the doctrinal law it announced or the breadth of its actual holding. Indeed, with the passage of years, the precise issue of whether community notification can be applied retroactively to those whose offenses occurred before October 31, 1994, has become increasingly moot. Given the relatively small number of persons subject to its provisions, the decision did not have the same effect on public policy and institutions as did *Mount Laurel* or *Abbott v. Burke*. However, the methodology the court used of stating its deference to the legislature, but at the same time circumscribing the implementation of the law to keep it safely within constitutional boundaries, has become a model courts have used in subsequent cases to salvage an uncertain statutory scheme from invalidity.

NOTES

1. 142 N.J. 1 (1995).
2. See, for example, Jenny Montana, "An Ineffective Weapon in the Fight against Child Sexual Abuse," *Journal of Law and Policy* 3 (1995): 569, 571n. 15.
3. New Jersey Statutes Annotated, sec. 2C:7–2 (West 2012).
4. Ibid. sec. 2C:7–8(d).
5. Ibid. sec. 2C:7–8(c)(1).
6. Ibid. sec. 2C:7–8(c)(2).
7. Ibid. sec. 2C:7–8(c)(3).
8. See *Doe v. Poritz*, 142 N.J. 1, 99 (1995) (attorney general guidelines' "contents are largely dictated either explicitly or implicitly by the language of the statute").
9. I was appointed as pro bono counsel to the first such legal challenge. See *Diaz v. Whitman*, No. 94–6376 (D.N.J. Jan. 6, 1995) (order granting preliminary injunction). See also *Artway v. Attorney General*, 876 F. Supp. 666 (D.N.J. 1995), aff'd in part and vacated in part, 81 F.3d 1235 (3d Cir. 1996).
10. See *Doe v. Poritz*, 283 N.J. Super. 372, 377 (Law Div. 1995), aff'd as modified, 142 N.J. 1, 26 (1995).
11. *Doe v. Poritz*, 142 N.J. at 26.
12. *Doe* also raised a challenge under the New Jersey Administrative Procedures Act (APA) that the attorney general's guidelines were invalid since they were not adopted under the normal rule-making procedures of the APA, which requires notice and an opportunity for public comment before promulgation of administrative regulations. See generally *Metromedia v. Division of Taxation*, 97 N.J. 313, 331–32 (1984) (describing six

factors to be considered when determining whether an agency action constitutes rule making that must conform to the requirements of the APA).

13. In *Diaz v. Whitman*, Chief Judge John Bissell had issued a preliminary injunction against community notification, finding that the plaintiff had satisfied the standard for preliminary relief that he would be likely to succeed after a trial in establishing that retroactive application of Megan's Law would be found to violate the ex post facto clause, and that implementation without the availability of judicial review would violate the due process clause. *Diaz v. Whitman*, No. 94–6376 (D.N.J. January 6, 1995) (order granting preliminary injunction).

    A few days after Judge Wells decided *Doe*, Federal District Court Judge Nicholas Politan ruled in *Artway v. Attorney General* that retroactive application of community notification violated the ex post facto clause. *Artway v. Attorney General*, 876 F. Supp. 666 (D.N.J. 1995), aff'd in part and vacated in part, 81 F.3d 1235 (3d Cir. 1996). These decisions, to say the least, heightened public concern about whether Megan's Law could be implemented immediately.

14. *Doe v. Poritz*, 283 N.J. Super. at 401.

15. Ibid. at 403.

16. Ibid. at 409.

17. *Doe v. Poritz*, 142 N.J. at 97.

18. New Jersey Statutes Annotated, sec. 2C:7–8(b) (West 2012):

    Factors relevant to risk of re-offense shall include, but not be limited to, the following:

    (1) Conditions of release that minimize risk of re-offense, including but not limited to whether the offender is under supervision of probation or parole; receiving counseling, therapy or treatment; or residing in a home situation that provides guidance and supervision;

    (2) Physical conditions that minimize risk of re-offense, including but not limited to advanced age or debilitating illness;

    (3) Criminal history factors indicative of high risk of re-offense, including:

        (a) Whether the offender's conduct was found to be characterized by repetitive and compulsive behavior;

        (b) Whether the offender served the maximum term;

        (c) Whether the offender committed the sex offense against a child;

    (4) Other criminal history factors to be considered in determining risk, including:

        (a) The relationship between the offender and the victim;

        (b) Whether the offense involved the use of a weapon, violence, or infliction of serious bodily injury;

        (c) The number, date and nature of prior offenses;

    (5) Whether psychological or psychiatric profiles indicate a risk of recidivism;

    (6) The offender's response to treatment;

    (7) Recent behavior, including behavior while confined or while under supervision in the community as well as behavior in the community following service of sentence; and

    (8) Recent threats against persons or expressions of intent to commit additional crimes.

19. *Doe v. Poritz*, 143 N.J. at 24n. 5.

20. New Jersey Statutes Annotated, sec. 2C:7–8(c) (West 2012).

21. *Doe v. Poritz*, 142 N.J. at 33.

22. Ibid. at 33–34.

23. Ibid. at 97–98.

24. *Calder v. Bull*, 3 U.S. 386, 390 (1798); accord *Collins v. Youngblood*, 497 U.S. 37, 42–43 (1990).

25. *United States v. Brown*, 381 U.S. 437, 448–49 (1965).

26. *United States v. Halper*, 490 U.S. 435, 440 (1989).

27. *California Dep't of Corr. v. Morales*, 514 U.S. 499, 509 (1995).

28. *Halper*, 490 U.S. at 447.

29. 372 U.S. 144 (1963). The *Mendoza-Martinez* factors were identified by the United States Supreme Court in order to determine whether proceedings had become so punitive that they triggered the procedural protections of the Fifth and Sixth Amendments that attach to criminal trials. *Mendoza-Martinez* set forth a multifactor analysis to determine whether a measure constitutes "punishment" triggering criminal process guarantees: "[w]hether the sanction involves an affirmative disability or restraint, whether it has historically been regarded as a punishment, whether it comes into play only on a finding of scienter [intent or knowledge of wrongdoing], whether its operation will promote the traditional aims of punishment-retribution and deterrence, whether the behavior to which it applies is already a crime, whether an alternative purpose to which it may rationally be connected is assignable for it, and whether it appears excessive in relation to the alternative purpose assigned." Ibid. at 168–169.

30. *Doe v. Poritz*, 142 N.J. at 128 (1995) (Stein, J., dissenting).

31. Ibid. at 62.

32. 490 U.S. 435, 448–449 (1989).

33. 509 U.S. 602, 602 (1993).

34. 81 F.3d 1235 (3d Cir. 1996).

35. Ibid. at 1263.

36. Ibid. at 1262n. 26.

37. 518 U.S. 267 (1996). See also *Hudson v. United States*, 522 U.S. 93 (1997) (disavowing double jeopardy analysis of *Halper*).

38. *Ursery*, 518 U.S. at 288.

39. Chief Judge Bissell, who granted a preliminary injunction to Carloz Diaz based in part on a prediction of likelihood of success on the ex post facto claim, reversed his position once he had read the *Ursery* decision.

40. 521 U.S. 346 (1997). *See also Smith v. Doe*, 538 U.S. 84 (2003) (Alaska sex offender registration statute did not violate ex post facto clause).

41. *Hendricks*, 521 U.S. at 361.

42. Ibid.

43. 119 F.3d 1077, 1094 (3d Cir. 1997).

44. Ibid. at 1095. Another panel of the Third Circuit subsequent to *E.B.* alluded to the possibility that "the continued viability of *Artway* is arguably in doubt in the wake of recent Supreme Court precedent" but was not required to reach the question. *United States v. Edwards*, 162 F.3d 87, 90 (3d Cir. 1998).

45. Later, in *Paul P. v. Verniero*, 170 F.3d 396 (3d Cir. 1999), and *Paul P. v. Farmer*, 227 F.3d 98 (3d Cir. 2000), the Third Circuit also rejected claims that the notification requirement violated registrants' privacy rights.

46. 424 U.S. 693 (1976) (inaccurate publication of plaintiff's name on list of customers of prostitute did not deprive plaintiff of liberty or property under Fourteenth Amendment). Ibid. at 701.

47. *Doe v. Poritz*, 142 at 103.

48. Ibid. at 104.

49. Ibid. (internal quotations and citations omitted).

50. Ibid. at 105.

51. Ibid. at 107–08.

52. 424 U.S. 319 (1976).

53. *Doe v. Poritz*, 142 N.J. at 32.

54. *E.B. v. Verniero*, 119 F.3d 1077, 1107–11 (3d Cir. 1997).

55. At the federal level, the Jacob Wetterling Crimes Against Children and Sexually Violent Offender Registration Act of 1994, 42 U.S.C. § 14701 (2012) et seq. requires each state receiving federal law enforcement funding to impose registration requirements on sex offenders, and the Adam Walsh Child Protection and Safety Act, 42 U.S.C. § 16911 (2012) et seq. requires each state to establish a system of tiered risk assessment and notification similar to Megan's Law.

56. See Kristen Zgoba, Philip Witt, Melissa Dalessandro, and Bonita Veysey, "Megan's Law, Assessing the Practical and Monetary Efficacy," *National Criminal Justice Reference Series* (December 2008), http://www.ncjrs.gov/pdffiles1/nij/grants/225370.pdf. This report by the New Jersey Department of Corrections Office of Policy and Planning (under a grant from the National Institute of Justice) reached several critical conclusions:

    ■ Megan's Law has no effect on community tenure (i.e., time to first re-arrest).
    ■ Megan's Law showed no demonstrable effect in reducing sexual re-offenses.
    ■ Megan's Law has no effect on the type of sexual re-offense or first time sexual offense (still largely child molestation/incest).
    ■ Megan's Law has no effect on reducing the number of victims involved in sexual offenses.
    ■ Costs associated with the initial implementation as well as ongoing expenditures continue to grow over time. Start up costs totaled $555,565 and current costs (in 2007) totaled approximately $3,900,000 for the responding counties.
    ■ Given the lack of demonstrated effect of Megan's Law on sexual offenses, the growing costs may not be justifiable.

57. New Jersey Constitution, article IV, sec. 7, par. 12.

58. *A.A. v. State of New Jersey*, 341 F.3d 206 (3d Cir. 2003).

59. 178 N.J. 127, 138 (2003).

60. 196 N.J. 222 (2008).

61. *New Jersey Div. of Youth and Family Services v. M.R.*, 314 N.J. Super. 390 (App. Div. 1998).

62. *Matter of Allegations of Sexual Abuse at East Park High School*, 314 N.J. Super. 149 (App. Div. 1998).

63. See *Oberhand v. Director, Division of Taxation*, 193 N.J. 558, 578 (2008) (citing *Doe* as support for doctrine of fundamental fairness that forbids retroactive application of tax on decedent estates).

10

New Jersey's School Funding
Litigation, *Robinson v. Cahill* and
Abbott v. Burke (2011)

The Epitome of the State Supreme Court as an Independent,
Progressive Voice in Guaranteeing Constitutional Rights

PAUL L. TRACTENBERG

In many ways, New Jersey's school funding and education reform litigation is the centerpiece of this book. No cases better represent that than *Robinson v. Cahill* and *Abbott v. Burke*, the tandem that has revolutionized New Jersey's school funding and educational system and has shaken the nation in the process. *Robinson* dominated much of the 1970s, and *Abbott* has been at the center of the state's legal, fiscal, educational, and political universes since the 1980s.

To understand their collective dominance, you need to know how they are connected. Although they bear different names and are technically separate cases, they are really aspects of one litigation stream. The plaintiffs in *Robinson* successfully challenged two school funding statutes in the early 1970s, but in 1976 the New Jersey Supreme Court found that a third statute—the Public School Education Act of 1975—was "facially constitutional."[1] That meant the court had concluded the statute, adopted by the legislature but not yet being implemented, was sufficiently likely to produce a constitutional result that it could go forward despite challenges to its ability to do so.

However, this ruling was not quite the end of *Robinson:* the legislature failed to appropriate the money for its own newly adopted and judicially validated funding law. After weighing a variety of more intrusive affirmative remedies, the New Jersey Supreme Court wound up with a traditional negative remedy— enjoining the expenditure of any funds, state or local, on the public schools.[2] Although the educational impact of that order was minimized by its timing—it went into effect in July—it was sufficient to galvanize prompt legislative action. The state's first income tax was adopted in short order to provide funding for the schools, the injunction was lifted, and the Public School Education Act of 1975 went into effect.

When that substantial dust settled, the court made clear that the *Robinson* plaintiffs could return to the court whenever they believed they could prove that the statute "as applied" was not meeting the constitutional standards articulated by the court. The court's invitation was accepted by the filing of *Abbott v. Burke* more than four years later in 1981. The rest, as they say, is history—a history that will be addressed briefly later in this chapter.

Another introductory point, though, is the extent of the Rutgers Law connection to this litigation. *Robinson* was filed in 1970 by a young Jersey City lawyer, Harold Ruvoldt Jr. Ruvoldt reportedly was compensated for his work by Jersey City, whose interest was in reducing local property taxes by attracting more state education aid to districts like it. When the case started to heat up in late 1971, I became involved on behalf of two "friends of the court," the ACLU of New Jersey and the NAACP Newark Chapter Education Committee. Having recently joined the Rutgers Law faculty, I enlisted the assistance of two colleagues in the law school's recently founded Constitutional Litigation Clinic and a team of clinic students, as well as students from my own Public Education Law seminar. Together we participated fully in the case before the trial judge, Theodore Botter, and the New Jersey Supreme Court, submitting a seminal hundred-page brief to the court in late 1972 detailing our legal arguments. I presented oral arguments to the court repeatedly during the nearly four years that *Robinson* was before the New Jersey Supreme Court.

In 1973, thanks to generous funding from the Ford Foundation, I was able to establish the Education Law Center (ELC), which has been representing the plaintiffs throughout *Abbott's* long, and still uncompleted, history. Since I directed ELC for its first three years, it became the primary locus of my engagement in *Robinson*, although law students continued to be engaged in the effort.

Between 1976, when I returned to full-time law teaching, and 1979 when Marilyn Morheuser, a Rutgers Law alumna and former research assistant of mine, became ELC's executive director, there was a sort of interregnum director, Michael Lottman. Morheuser immediately turned her formidable energies and skills toward New Jersey's school funding laws, and in February 1981 filed *Abbott v. Burke* on behalf of students in the state's poor urban school districts. These districts, with their more than 300,000 students, became known as the "Abbott districts." ELC was and remained their lawyer for the intervening thirty-one years, and I have been involved, officially and unofficially, for most of that period.

The Rutgers Law imprint goes beyond that. Alumni judges also played an enormously important role in this litigation. Steven Lefelt, as an administrative law judge, conducted a 100-day trial in 1986 and 1987 and issued a 607-page opinion in 1988 that became the basis of the New Jersey Supreme Court's 1990 decision that struck down the Public School Education Act of 1975. More recently, Judge Peter Doyne has twice been called on by the New Jersey Supreme Court, once in 2009 and once in 2011, to serve as a special master conducting remand hearings and submitting reports to the court. Supreme court justices Virginia Long and especially Jaynee LaVecchia have played important roles in recent years.

The Significance of *Robinson/Abbott*

One of the triggers for case selection in this book was a poll conducted in late 1999 by the *New Jersey Lawyer*, a publication of the state bar association. It asked New Jersey judges and lawyers to identify the most important state court and federal court decisions of the almost completed twentieth century. Based on the survey, the *New Jersey Lawyer* listed the five leading decisions in each category. *Robinson/Abbott* was far and away the leading state court decision; interestingly, another education case, *Brown v. Board of Education*, was the runaway leader among federal court decisions.

In a Master's Report to the New Jersey Supreme Court on March 22, 2011, Judge Peter Doyne made clear why the state's school funding and educational reform cases were top-rated, "Educational reform in the State of New Jersey has been a crusade waged in the courts for nearly four decades producing twenty Supreme Court opinions in an effort to provide the schoolchildren of New Jersey with their constitutional right to a thorough and efficient education. No other issue has, even remotely, been the focus of such scrutiny and controversy."[3]

Judge Doyne's reference to a "thorough and efficient education" (popularly known over the years as T&E) is central to this litigation of unprecedented proportions, not just for New Jersey but also for the nation. That phrase relates to the state constitution's education clause, added in 1875 and only construed once regarding unequal school funding prior to *Robinson* in the 1895 decision of *Landis v. Ashworth*.[4] Ironically, in that case the beneficiaries of unequal funding were students in urban schools who received free secondary school education while students in outlying districts received only elementary education.

In *Robinson* and *Abbott*, the disparity was reversed. It was low-income, mostly minority urban students who were receiving far less funding for their educations than students, typically more educationally advantaged and mostly white, in the suburbs. A legal challenge on behalf of urban students was filed in February 1970 and eventually led to the first New Jersey Supreme Court decision in 1973. The court reached the same bottom line as trial judge Botter—that the state's school funding law was unconstitutional—but it did so in a manner that was doctrinally the opposite of Botter. He had found that the funding law violated the federal and state equal protection and state tax uniformity clauses, but, if fully funded, probably not the education clause. By contrast, the state supreme court turned its decision solely on the education clause.[5]

The phrase "thorough and efficient" was central to the decision, but neither the phrase "thorough and efficient education" recited by Judge Doyne nor the word "education" actually appears in the constitutional provision. In its entirety, the provision reads: "The Legislature shall provide for the maintenance and support of a thorough and efficient system of free public schools for the instruction of all the children in the State between the ages of five and eighteen years."[6]

In an article I wrote in 2008, I pondered the meaning of that enormously important constitutional language and suggested that it might be read more productively backward. That is to say, "free public schools" were the essential building blocks of the state's educational program. Only if those schools were combined into an "efficient system," was there the possibility of affording students a "thorough" education. My conclusion was that we had, quite possibly, spent too little time and attention on ensuring that we had in place an "efficient system of free public schools" and that that impeded our effort to provide the "thorough education," which I believe is the ultimate intention of the constitution's education clause.[7]

In the *Robinson* and *Abbott* litigation, we had taken a more direct approach by penetrating to the core of the education clause and asserting that its purpose was to guarantee all New Jersey's students a "thorough" education, one designed to provide them with an equal opportunity to become effective citizens and competitors in the contemporary labor market with their more advantaged peers. But perhaps in doing so we made the realization of that objective more difficult.

What May Be Next

If there needs to be a next generation of education litigation in New Jersey, its focus might be on assuring the existence of an "efficient system of free public schools." In all likelihood, that would thrust into the foreground such long-recognized inefficiencies as:

- The state's crazy quilt of more than six hundred school districts, many of them too small to operate a full kindergarten to twelfth grade (K–12) educational program;
- The woeful and increasing incapacity of the state education department to effectively oversee New Jersey's educational system, given its notable paucity of research and data capability and lack of staff qualified to monitor districts let alone provide meaningful technical assistance;

- The legislative and executive branches' penchant for regularly underfunding the state's education formula and typically leaving the state aid details to the eleventh hour of the appropriations process in June so school districts do not learn how much money they will have for the next school year until it is too late to do any real planning;
- The seemingly intractable problems surrounding establishment of an effective database of student-level data that would permit the tracking of changes in educational performance of individual students;
- The ever changing statewide tests of student achievement in relation to the Core Curriculum Content Standards, the determinant of a constitutionally sufficient education, that make it virtually impossible to determine even in the aggregate how New Jersey students are performing; and
- The growing influence of private funders, both organizations and individuals, in devising and implementing educational reforms that have blurred the line between public and private and obscured the genesis and even the details of those reforms from effective public scrutiny.

Historic Impact

For better or worse the extensive New Jersey litigation to date has focused on the dollars and cents of funding public education, initially on the intricacies of the statutory school finance formulae and, increasingly as the litigation has proceeded from *Robinson* to *Abbott*, on the programmatic uses of that money. Throughout the process there has been an effort to connect the dollar input with the educational outcomes. Little sustained attention has been paid, however, to the structure and delivery system that converts the dollars into the programs, and we may come to rue that.

By any standard, the *Robinson/Abbott* litigation is extraordinary. In duration—six years for *Robinson* and thirty-one years and counting for *Abbott*—it has to be among the longest running cases of all time.[8] It has accounted for at least twenty-seven opinions and orders of the New Jersey Supreme Court, as well as a 607-page opinion by an administrative law judge and lengthy opinions by lower court judges. This is almost certainly another world record. The main trial in *Abbott* occupied about one hundred trial days. There have been thousands of pages of legal briefs, affidavits, and expert reports.

These records are rivaled by the dollar impact of the litigation. To a vastly greater extent than any other state's school funding litigation, the *Robinson/Abbott* litigation has resulted in tens of billions of dollars in state education aid being directed to New Jersey's poor urban districts.

These monumental aspects of the cases make it obvious that a relatively brief chapter can hardly even begin to recount, let alone do justice to, their constitutional, educational, public policy, and fiscal aspects. Over the years, I and others have sought to do that in books, book chapters, articles, reports, and unpublished but widely circulated manuscripts. For those interested in that history, as told from a variety of perspectives, I list a representative sampling of the enormous literature *Robinson/Abbott* has spawned.[9]

In the remainder of this chapter, instead of trying to compress a mountain into a veritable nutshell, I will focus on the most recent developments, beginning with the enactment of New Jersey's current statute—the School Funding Reform Act of 2008—and the court decisions relating to that statute between 2009 and 2011.

The School Funding Reform Act of 2008

There may have been educational reasons why the Corzine administration pressed for a new school funding law in 2006 and 2007. Education certainly was the focus of the administration's rhetoric, but there definitely were fiscal reasons behind that rhetoric.

The Background: Abbott IV and Onward

Statewide school funding in New Jersey was both a mess and very costly. The mess was precipitated by an unexpected and perhaps unique 1997 decision by the New Jersey Supreme Court in *Abbott IV*.[10] This decision struck down the Comprehensive Education Improvement and Funding Act (CEIFA), which had been enacted only six months earlier, but invalidated it only as to the Abbott districts and left it in effect for all other districts.

In prior decisions in *Abbott* and *Robinson*, the court had always struck down the state's school funding laws in their entirety—the Bateman Tanzman Act in 1973, the Public School Education Act in 1990, and the Quality Education Act in 1994.[11] That was true of judicial decisions in other states as well.[12]

It is possible that the court expected the state legislature to respond to *Abbott IV* by abandoning CEIFA and enacting a new statewide law. That would have made sense. A less desirable alternative would have been for the legislature to fully fund for the long term both the Abbott remedies for poor urban districts and CEIFA for all the rest. Inevitably, a dual funding regimen, with most of the state education aid going to poor urban districts, would exacerbate an "us against them" mentality and a political backlash.

For five years after *Abbott IV*, the legislature fully funded CEIFA for the approximately 570 districts not classified as Abbott districts. During those years, full funding of the so-called Abbott remedies was more problematic. The plaintiffs returned to the New Jersey Supreme Court repeatedly, seeking full implementation of their remedies; the court responded with *Abbott V* in May 1998,

Abbott VI in March 2000, *Abbott VII* in May 2000, and *Abbott VIII* in October 2001 and February 2002.[13]

Beginning in March 2002, full funding of both the *Abbott* remedies and of the CEIFA funding formula for other districts was in more serious jeopardy. During that month, the Education Law Center, on behalf of the *Abbott* plaintiffs, agreed with the state on a one-year freeze of further implementation of the *Abbott* remedies at the 2002–03 levels in exchange for increased funding on preschool programs and parity aid. Starting in 2002–03 the state provided all other districts with essentially flat funding.

The state sought a second year freeze of *Abbott* funding, but this time the Education Law Center did not agree. This issue, along with a variety of continuing implementation issues, went to mediation, which resulted in agreement on everything but the funding freeze.

Meanwhile, flat funding of other districts, with only minor adjustments not based on the statutory formula, became the new normal. Thus, every June, the legislature, through the appropriations process, would determine how much state aid to award districts for the following school year. Usually, its calculations ignored such basic facts as whether district enrollments had increased or decreased. Essentially, districts would receive an amount based on what they had received in the prior year with some slight adjustment based on fiscal and political judgments about how much the state could "afford."

According to one expert, Dr. Ernest C. Reock Jr., the consequence was that the non-Abbott districts were shortchanged between 2002–03 and 2005–06 to the tune of several billion dollars, almost $800 million in 2005–06 alone.[14] The problem continued beyond 2005–06, but the Reock study did not. The hardest hit non-Abbott districts, unsurprisingly, were the poor, nonurban districts and the mid-wealth districts.

The fact that during those years Abbott funding was reduced only slightly because of the court's continuing involvement, while the state aid to other districts suffered greatly and somewhat unpredictably, dramatically exacerbated the rift between the poor urban districts, the so-called Abbott districts, and most of the others. It also did not endear the court to many of the state's taxpayers and parents.

That set the stage for the School Funding Reform Act of 2008. Shortly after Governor Jon Corzine took office in January 2006, his administration sought to get a handle on the school funding issue. Given that educational funding is the largest line item in both the state and local budgets, it is a key element in balancing budgets and keeping taxes under control. At the state level, there is an additional factor: how state school aid is distributed has political impact.

The Corzine Administration's Efforts

The Corzine administration seemed to have a real commitment to improving urban education, but it also seemed to give substantial weight to capping total state aid for education and to allocating more state aid to non-Abbott districts. Since all three could not be accommodated without raising taxes, something had to give, and the Abbott districts and their lawyers feared it would be them.

The focus of the districts and their lawyers was on a process the state had initiated in 2002 to "cost out" a thorough and efficient education. The school funding law still partly in effect then—CEIFA—had sought to link the statutory Core Curriculum Content Standards, found to be a constitutionally acceptable definition of a T&E education, with the funding formula, but it failed to do so in an acceptable manner. The costing-out process was launched to cure that problem and pave the way for a new school funding formula. However, nothing resulting from the process was made public until December 2006, almost a year after the Corzine administration had taken office, when a Report on the Cost of Education was issued.

New Jersey was hardly alone in adopting a costing-out approach. During the first decade of the twenty-first century, many states, whether or not they were operating under state court constitutional orders, commissioned costing-out studies. Most of those studies wound up recommending substantial increases in state educational funding. New Jersey's was to the contrary. That may not be surprising, since as a result of the *Abbott* litigation the state's spending levels already were among the highest in the country, substantially above the national average.

The main concern of the Abbott districts, therefore, was that, in the name of objectively and professionally defining the cost of a T&E education, the state would find ways to understate the real costs and thereby reduce its funding levels. Many other districts and education advocates shared that concern.

At statewide public hearings and in public comments relating to the December 2006 report, criticism far outweighed support. Indeed, few spoke in favor of the costing-out study other than NJDOE staff and the paid consultants whose work was at the heart of the project. That set in motion an extended and detailed review and adjustment process, which led to a January 2007 addendum to the report and then a December 2007 final report entitled *A Formula for Success: All Children, All Communities.*[15] This became the basis of a new school funding bill developed by the Corzine administration, which was enacted in January 2008 during a lame duck legislative session as the School Funding Reform Act of 2008 (SFRA).[16]

Within a few months, the state, rather than the Abbott districts as had been the norm, brought the case back to the New Jersey Supreme Court seeking a declaration that SFRA satisfied the constitutional rights of all students and that, therefore, the court's "Abbott remedies" "are no longer necessary." The Education Law Center, on behalf of the Abbott students, opposed the state's motion and made its own motion asking that the Abbott remedies remain in force.

The court heard oral arguments from the parties on September 22, 2008, but concluded that the arguments, and the briefs and affidavits the parties had submitted, did not provide an adequate basis for the justices to resolve the competing constitutional arguments. Instead, in a decision issued on November 18, 2008, *Abbott XIX*, the court remanded the case to a lower court judge sitting as a special master for the supreme court.[17] The assignment to the special master, Judge Doyne, was "to conduct a plenary hearing to develop a full and complete evidential record that addresses the factual contentions raised by the parties and amici curiae before this Court."[18]

Hearings before the Special Master

The hearings were to be conducted on an expedited basis and Judge Doyne was instructed to submit a report on his factual findings and conclusions within sixty days of the completion of the evidentiary hearing. He also was given a somewhat unusual instruction: on the issue of whether SFRA's funding formula guaranteed sufficient resources to enable the Abbott districts to provide their students with a thorough and efficient education based on the Core Curriculum Content Standards, the state had the burden of proof.

Usually, when the constitutionality of a statute is at issue, there is a presumption of validity favoring the state and the burden of proof is placed on the challenging party. Here, however, the court found that the context was different and special. SFRA sought to respond to decades of constitutional rulings about the repeatedly thwarted constitutional rights of students in poor urban districts and to replace remedies imposed by the court in the absence of sufficient legislative remedies. The question before the court, therefore, was whether SFRA's formula should be permitted to replace the court-ordered funding methodology. The court specifically imposed the burden on the state and so advised the special master.

The court also flagged an issue that wound up at the center of the *Abbott XXI* decision in 2011, albeit in a different context—whether the court properly had before it all the state's students or just those in the Abbott districts. In *Abbott XIX*, the state sought to have the court validate SFRA's constitutionality statewide for all students. The court declined to do so because only the Abbott district students were before it as parties. To rule on SFRA's constitutionality for other students would constitute an inappropriate advisory opinion.

It was clear from the court's per curiam[19] opinion in *Abbott XIX* that when the case returned to it from Judge Doyne the central question would be whether the SFRA funding formula, as an alternative to the court's *Abbott* remedies, "can ensure Abbott districts have sufficient resources to enable them to provide a thorough and efficient education, as defined by the CCCS standards."[20] The court made clear that that did not mean SFRA would have to assure the Abbott districts the exact same dollar amount as the court's *Abbott* remedies.

The hearings before Judge Doyne began on February 9, 2009, less than three months after the New Jersey Supreme Court remanded the case to him, and concluded on March 3, 2009. Less than three weeks later on March 21, after hearing testimony from twenty-nine witnesses (eleven presented by the state and eighteen by the plaintiffs), Judge Doyne issued his eighty-three-page Opinion/Recommendations, which was officially filed with the supreme court on March 26. He dealt elaborately with the history of *Abbott* and *Robinson*, with the five-year costing-out process and with the SFRA formula, bringing to bear on the second and third aspects fact and expert testimony. He outlined the state defendants' and plaintiffs' cases, and provided relatively brief legal and general analyses.

Like the supreme court, Judge Doyne saw the issue before him as focused "solely upon the constitutionality of SFRA as it applies to the students in the Abbott districts." He may have inadvertently muddied the analytical waters, however, when he added that "to intelligently analyze and review SFRA, the court is compelled to also observe the full panoply of rights and expectations of all our students."[21]

After all that, Judge Doyne's conclusions were equivocal. Although SFRA was, in his view, "an acceptable structure in an attempt to secure the thorough and efficient education so desperately needed for the development of our youth," it was not a perfect solution and there was no guarantee of its educational success.[22] Indeed, his unease about its effect led to a concrete recommendation at variance with the state's statutory approach and legal argument. Judge Doyne recommended to the supreme court that, at least for the first three years of SFRA's implementation, supplemental funding for the Abbott districts should continue as a "safety net." Without it, Judge Doyne stated that, in his view, SFRA should not be found constitutional. He arrived at that recommendation notwithstanding the state's strongly made argument that continuing Abbott supplemental funding would undermine SFRA's unitary thrust. His bottom line on this point was that "[t]his court is not satisfied elimination of this provision [for supplementary funding] adequately serves the needs of Abbott district students, at least during the transitional period when empirical evidence can be established. At that point, funding will have made the transition from anticipation to reality and analysis can be empirically based."[23]

Arguments before the State Supreme Court

Continuing on an expedited schedule, the New Jersey Supreme Court heard oral argument on April 28, 2009, barely more than a month after it received

Judge Doyne's Opinion/Recommendations. In exactly another month, on May 28, 2009, the supreme court issued its unanimous decision, *Abbott XX*, in an opinion authored by Justice Jaynee LaVecchia.[24] She was joined by Justices Albin, Wallace, Rivera-Soto, and Hoens. As with *Abbott XIX*, Chief Justice Rabner and Justice Long recused themselves.

The court systematically considered the plaintiffs' complaints about SFRA's constitutional infirmities and the state's arguments in justification, all in the context of Judge Doyne's findings and recommendations. Ultimately, the supreme court accepted his bottom line recommendation that SFRA should be found facially constitutional and permitted to go into effect as a unitary statewide school funding formula. However, the court rejected Judge Doyne's recommendation that, because of the uncertainty about how SFRA would work in practice, state supplemental funding of the Abbott districts should be kept in place as a safety net.

At the heart of the court's validation of SFRA were several interrelated factors:

- That the state had demonstrated manifest good faith by basing SFRA on a multiyear professional costing-out process;
- That, in translating the results of the costing-out process into a statutory funding formula, the state had tended to opt for even higher cost factors;
- That SFRA explicitly committed the state to "look back" periodically at its effects on the ground and adjust the formula to ensure that SFRA worked in practice, with the first look-back scheduled for 2010, less than two years from the date of the court's *Abbott XX* decision; and
- That from a jurisprudential or separation-of-powers perspective the court was confronted in *Abbott XX* with a different situation than in most prior stages of the litigation—here the court was not confronted with "legislative inaction or failure to identify and provide realistic education funding support to at-risk children . . . ;" instead, the other branches had acted thoughtfully, responsibly and in good faith, all the more impressive because these are "difficult economic times when there is extreme pressure on scarce State resources."[25]

The New Jersey Supreme Court also was influenced by the state's commitment to fully fund SFRA, especially for the initial years leading up to the 2010 look-back. At oral argument, Attorney General Anne Milgram had suggested, when questioned about the state's long record of failing to fully fund its statutory formulae, that the court build into its decision a requirement of full funding. In fact, the court did precisely that, tying full funding to the statutory look-back requirement in the following clear and unequivocal language:

Our finding of constitutionality is premised on the expectation that the State will continue to provide school funding aid during this and the next

two years at the levels required by SFRA's formula each year. Our holding
further depends on the mandated review of the formula's weights and
other operative parts after three years of implementation. . . . Today's
holding issues in the good faith anticipation of a continued commitment by the Legislature and Executive to address whatever adjustments
are necessary to keep SFRA operating at its optimal level. The three year
look-back, and the State's adjustments based on that review, will provide more information about the efficacy of this funding formula. There
should be no doubt that we would require remediation of any deficiencies of a constitutional dimension, if such problems do emerge. . . . With
that understanding, SFRA may be implemented as it was designed, as a
state-wide unitary system of education funding.[26]

That understanding, and the related notion that a fully funded SFRA formula
would assure "predictability and transparency in budgeting, and accountabil-
ity,"[27] were at the heart of the New Jersey Supreme Court's ruling about SFRA's
facial constitutionality. It appeared to the court and to all the world that New
Jersey's three branches of state government had finally gotten onto the same
page over the extraordinarily longstanding, contentious and expensive issue of
school funding

Unfortunately, any potential for governmental self-congratulation dissi-
pated quickly. SFRA had been implemented by the state in 2008–09, while the
supreme court was considering whether it satisfied constitutional standards,
and, ironically, it was fully funded that year—but only that year.

Budget Issues

In 2009–10, both Governor Jon Corzine, SFRA's main promoter, and his successor, Governor Chris Christie, took substantial bites out of SFRA funding. Corzine
failed to fully fund a statutory phase-in of the SFRA formula to the tune of a $303
million shortfall in state education aid. After Christie was sworn in as governor
in January 2010, he took a significantly larger bite out of state aid, requiring
that districts offset $476 million in state education aid with funds from their
surpluses. Granted this did not require that districts reduce their spending, but
it required them to draw substantially on "rainy-day" funds they had assiduously
set aside for district emergencies.

This reduction was in an executive order accompanying Christie's formal
declaration of a "state of fiscal emergency" on February 11, 2010, just a few weeks
after he was sworn into office.[28] The Perth Amboy school district, an Abbott district, challenged Christie's action in the courts, but a three-judge intermediate
appellate panel upheld his action.[29]

In March 2010, when Christie announced his stripped-down state budget for
2010–11, matters worsened regarding the funding of SFRA. The overall proposed

cut in state education aid amounted to $820 million, with many wealthy districts slated to receive no direct state aid, but with the large and poor urban districts facing by far the largest dollar reductions. As it turned out, Christie's budget proposal wound up understating by half the total state education aid cuts and underfunding of SFRA that actually occurred in 2010–11.

Thus were the seeds planted for the legislative and executive branches to renege on the bargain they ostensibly had struck with the court in connection with the May 2009 *Abbott XX* decision. New Jersey would be propelled to the brink of a constitutional crisis that began to play out with the most recent *Abbott* decision: *Abbott XXI.*

Abbott XXI

After Governor Christie's 2009–10 state aid reduction and his proposed budget for 2010–11, the Education Law Center returned to the New Jersey Supreme Court in June 2010 with a "motion in aid of litigants' rights" seeking to enjoin the state from underfunding SFRA.[30] On June 29, the legislature passed the Appropriations Act for FY 2011 (the 2010–11 school year) formalizing the underfunding of SFRA. Unlike *Abbott XX*, in which the court acted expeditiously, this time around was much slower. It was not until January 5, 2011, more than halfway through the school year, that the court even heard oral argument from the parties.

On January 13, 2011, the court issued an order remanding the matter again to Judge Doyne for an evidentiary hearing on whether "school funding through SFRA, at the current underfunded levels, can provide a constitutional thorough and efficient education for New Jersey school children."[31] Although elsewhere in the order there was reference to the rights of students in Abbott districts, this broader formulation plays into a central argument that emerged in *Abbott XXI*— whether the court's inquiry was limited to the Abbott district students or to all at-risk students throughout the state.

Another issue flagged by the order was which school year's state aid would be the focus of the remand hearing and the supreme court's ultimate disposition. On behalf of the plaintiffs, the Education Law Center had decided not to seek restoration of 100 percent of the funding for the current school year, 2010–11, presumably because that school year would have come close to ending by the time the court rendered its decision. Nonetheless, the court specified in its order the "basis for the record shall be the level of funding provided in the current school year."[32]

Finally, consistent with what it had done regarding SFRA's constitutionality in *Abbott XX*, the court imposed on the state "the burden of demonstrating that the present level of school funding distributed through the SFRA formula can provide for a thorough and efficient education as measured by the comprehensive core curriculum standards in districts with high, medium, and low concentrations of disadvantaged students."[33] This again was seemingly a reference to students beyond the Abbott districts.

The hearings before Judge Doyne began on February 14, 2011, after briefing by the parties partly on the extent to which he could hear evidence about the state's fiscal crisis. The hearings concluded on February 25. Closing arguments were on March 2 and post-trial submissions were transmitted on March 14. Judge Doyne submitted his eighty-nine-page Opinion/Recommendations to the supreme court only eight days later, on March 22.

Obviously, Judge Doyne was no stranger to either the supreme court's expectations of a remand hearing or the subject matter of the February to March 2011 hearing he conducted. To the extent that the state had any influence on Judge Doyne's focus, clearly it was to press ahead with evidence about the fiscal crisis confronting New Jersey. It also sought to raise an old school-funding litigation defense of states: that "money really doesn't matter," that there is no clear and measureable correlation between the amount of money spent and the quality of education afforded students. By contrast, the plaintiffs' focus was on the educational impact of what had turned out to be a huge SFRA funding shortfall—$1.7 billion, or almost 20 percent.

Relatively early in the remand hearing, Judge Doyne took a very unusual step. He opened proceedings on February 16, the third hearing day, by placing on the record his strong concerns about the direction of the state's case and his recommendation that the state's lawyers consider reframing it. In effect, Judge Doyne expressed concern that the state seemed to be attacking SFRA itself, the school funding law it had so ardently defended before the supreme court and before Judge Doyne just a year earlier, on the ground that money did not matter. In a comment directed to the state's chief trial attorney, Judge Doyne remonstrated:

> The state's apparent position appears anomalous to this court. That is, if it's the state's position that there is an insufficient correlation between funding and results, it would appear you're in the wrong court. Now that, of course, is separate and apart from the state coming before this court last year . . . asking for the implementation of SFRA. . . . Separate and apart from the significant complications of SFRA, in its distilled form it is the supposition that educators can quantify moneys needed to deliver a thorough and efficient education. Premised upon that supposition, the state came before the Supreme Court and said, in sum or substance, relieve us from the [parity funding] obligations, because we can now demonstrate to you convincingly that if you spend x number of dollars, we will be able to deliver a thorough and efficient education. So for the state now apparently to take the position that there is an insufficient

correlation between funding and results is not only anomalous, but it's disparate from its prior position before the court. . . . [I]f the state is going to seek to suggest to this court there's an insufficient correlation between funding and results, we can conclude the hearing today.[34]

Judge Doyne went on to say, "So rather than spend the next two, three or four weeks or however long it may be hearing this matter, if the state prefers to simply go before the [supreme] court . . . and say either we cannot defend [SFRA] on the basis that the cuts allow us to provide a thorough and efficient [education], or we're no longer interested in defending SFRA, or take any other position that's not consonant with the remand, let's do so now. . . . I'm not here to explore the wisdom of SFRA. I'm not here to explore whether money is the talisman for all evils."[35]

The state did not seem to take Judge Doyne's admonition to heart, however. Its only witness during the very same session was Professor Eric Hanushek, a veteran expert witness for states defending their school funding laws against attacks of insufficiency and inequality. Hanushek's principal line of defense is that money does not matter or, more precisely, if you spend money in ill-advised ways it will not improve educational results.

Under cross-examination, Hanushek acknowledged that his testimony was not specific to New Jersey and that he had not "studied New Jersey specifically" or "focused on individual schools in New Jersey." Nor was he familiar with the origin and details of the core curriculum content standards, which constitute New Jersey's benchmark of a thorough and efficient education.[36]

Later, in cross-examination, Hanushek was led down a slippery slope. After testifying that a 5 to 10 percent reduction in state education aid, the underfunding range the state had asked him to opine about, would not prevent districts from providing a thorough and efficient education, he conceded that his opinion probably would not change if the state aid reduction was 10 to 20 percent, or even 20 to 30 percent. At and beyond 30 percent, Hanushek acknowledged "he would start getting [queasy]," but even at a 50 percent reduction he did not seem prepared to give an opinion that the district would be disabled from providing a T&E education.[37]

Despite the sternness of Judge Doyne's admonition to the state's lawyers and Professor Hanushek's failure to address the main substance of the remand, the judge's Opinion/Recommendations to the New Jersey Supreme Court were very temperate, almost generous, toward the state's case and Professor Hanushek. Still, Judge Doyne's clear conclusion was that the state had failed to bear its burden, "The Supreme Court directed the remand hearing address whether current levels of funding for FY11, through the SFRA formula, can permit our school districts to provide a thorough and efficient education to the children of our State. Given the proofs adduced . . . , the answer to this limited inquiry can only be 'no.'"[38] Toward the end of his Opinion/Recommendations, Judge Doyne remarked on the "obvious" irony that he had partially addressed earlier. It was the parties' striking flip-flop between *Abbott XX* and *Abbott XXI.*

Comparison with Abbott XX

In *Abbott XX*, ELC had vigorously attacked SFRA's adequacy to satisfy the student plaintiffs' constitutional rights. In contrast, the state had as vigorously defended SFRA, emphasizing that it would provide a professionally developed unitary funding system that would meet the constitutional rights not only of students in the Abbott districts but also of at-risk students throughout the state. As a consequence, the state sought and largely obtained not only the end of the court's *Abbott* remedies but also the elimination of Abbott districts as a separate funding category.

In *Abbott XXI*, by comparison, ELC was seeking full funding of SFRA, presumably on the theory that, whatever its shortcomings, SFRA would be better for ELC's clients if it were fully funded. ELC went even further, though—it sought to speak on behalf of all New Jersey students, or at least all at-risk students, not just those in the former Abbott districts. To do so, it was seeking to have the state fully fund SFRA for all students under its unitary system

As Judge Doyne's earlier discussion made clear, the state's flip-flop in *Abbott XXI* was even more extreme—it seemed to be arguing against SFRA on the grounds that money did not really correlate with educational quality or outcomes, and that, in any event, SFRA was spending too much of it.

Of course, *Abbott XX* was argued and decided during the Corzine administration and *Abbott XXI* was argued and decided during the Christie administration, and therein may lay the difference. Although the national and state fiscal crisis may have worsened after Christie assumed office in January 2010, there certainly was a serious, bona fide crisis in 2008 and 2009 when Corzine was completing his term, and the court noted that in its *Abbott XX* decision.

Governor Christie's Approach and the State Supreme Court

Abbott XXI was argued and decided in a highly charged context for reasons in addition to the fiscal problems confronting New Jersey, though. Early in his term, Christie made clear that changing the character and role of the state supreme court ranked high on his agenda. Although he regularly used *Abbott* and the fiscal crisis as a justification, there always seemed to be deeper philosophical and ideological roots. The phenomenon was by no means limited to New Jersey. Newly elected Republican governors across the country were pushing an agenda that involved reducing government's role and consequent spending, diminishing the power of public employees and their unions, strategically privatizing traditionally public functions such as education, and restricting the ability of courts to interfere with the implementation of those objectives.

In New Jersey, perhaps because of the governor's style and personality, there was a particularly biting edge to Christie's attacks on the state supreme court. For many reasons he presented Abbott as the poster child for everything that was wrong with a runaway, unelected court "making policy." As an opening gambit in his plan to rein in the court, Christie refused to reappoint John Wallace, the only African American justice who had ever served on the court. Clearly, Wallace was being used as a symbol of the lengths to which Christie would go to carry out his plan to reinvent the court and its role in state government. Although Christie regularly characterized Wallace as a part of the runaway judiciary problem, in truth Wallace was very much a centrist on *Abbott* and pretty much everything else that came before the court. He was just in the wrong place at the wrong time.

But Wallace and his treatment at the hands of Christie became a symbol for others in New Jersey. The minority community, and many others, rose up in indignation. After all, here was someone only about two years from mandatory retirement at age seventy, a longtime and, by all accounts, highly competent judge. Had Christie reappointed him to the court to serve until age seventy the governor still would have had the Wallace seat to fill during his first term.

The outcry against Christie's action quickly reached New Jersey's Democrat-dominated state senate, which had to confirm the appointment of John Wallace's successor on the court, Anne Patterson, a respected trial attorney. Senate president Steve Sweeney announced that the senate would not act on the confirmation for twenty-two months, the period during which Wallace would have continued to serve had he been reappointed by Christie.

That left a vacancy on the supreme court, which, by longstanding practice, was filled by the chief justice's elevation of the senior judge on the intermediate appellate court, in this case Judge Edwin Stern. Like Wallace, Stern was soon to turn seventy, at which point he would have to retire from the bench. Nonetheless, another storm developed, this one from within the court. Justice Roberto Rivera-Soto, the court's first and only Hispanic justice, had proven himself to be controversial throughout most of his term. In fact, he was one of only two sitting justices in more than thirty years to be censured by the court, on a complaint filed by the New Jersey Advisory Committee on Judicial Conduct, for using his influence as a justice on behalf of his son in a legal dispute.

Perhaps in the spirit of payback, on December 10, 2010, Rivera-Soto issued an "abstaining opinion" in an otherwise uncontroversial case.[39] He announced that he would be abstaining from all supreme court decisions for an indefinite time because he believed that the temporary assignment of Judge Stern to fill the Wallace vacancy made the court's composition unconstitutional. His

theory was that the assignment was not "necessary," the constitutional standard for when the chief justice could elevate a judge to the supreme court.
Rivera-Soto's action led to calls for his resignation, which went unheeded, and
to consternation within the court.

The plot thickened even further. First, on January 3, 2011, two days before
the supreme court heard the initial oral argument in *Abbott XXI*, Rivera-Soto
sent a letter to the governor indicating he did not wish to be reappointed when
his initial seven-year term on the court expired on September 11, 2011. Second,
on January 12, 2011, Rivera-Soto participated in a decision of the court and wrote
an opinion stating that he had reconsidered his earlier position and would participate in cases where Judge Stern's vote would not affect the outcome. Rivera-
Soto's behavior in *Abbott XXI*, as we will see, may indicate that he modified his
modified position.

The behavior of both Governor Christie and Justice Rivera-Soto, when
added to the parties' flip-flops in connection to SFRA, made for a tumultuous,
tense, and, frankly, peculiar context for the supreme court to address an issue
of great complexity and public importance in *Abbott XXI*. There is still another
dimension to consider—recusal and nonrecusal decisions by three justices and
their impact on the court's composition.

Throughout the most recent stage of the *Abbott* litigation—reflected in the
Abbott XIX, XX, and *XXI* decisions from November 2008 through May 2011, Chief
Justice Stuart Rabner and Associate Justice Virginia Long had recused themselves from participating. Since no reasons need be given, why judges choose
to recuse themselves or to participate often are matters of speculation. In the
case of the chief justice, it is quite clear, however—he was Governor Corzine's
attorney general when SFRA was being formulated.

Justice Long is a less clear case. She recused herself from *Abbott XIX* and
XX and the rumor was that it was because a relative of hers was employed by
an Abbott school district. She seemed to be poised to participate in *Abbott XXI*,
however. In October 2010, it was reported that a supreme court spokesperson
had confirmed her participation.[40] On January 13, 2011, she signed the court's
remand order. The scuttlebutt factory reported that Justice Long's relative no
longer worked for an Abbott district. Between January 13 and the oral argument
on April 28, Justice Long decided to recuse herself after all. Yet again, rumor
offered an explanation—Justice Long's relative was employed by a non-Abbott
school district whose superintendent testified at the remand hearing before
Judge Doyne and the state pressured her to recuse herself. As with all scuttlebutt, this is without documentable basis, which does not mean it is untrue.

As to the court's composition, there was a last recusal issue, but it
related to a justice who chose not to recuse herself—Justice Helen Hoens. The
issue regarding her participation related to her husband's position. Robert

Schwaneberg was a longtime political and legal reporter for the *Star-Ledger* until the fall of 2008. He then became a health care policy adviser on Governor Christie's staff serving at the governor's pleasure. Justice Hoens would be up for renomination by Governor Christie in October 2013, toward the end of his term, adding to her vulnerability.

In any event, the result was that a court under siege had to confront a case of momentous importance with an odd complement of judges. There were five in total, a quorum under the court's rules. Four were justices and the fifth was a lower court judge, the constitutionality of whose elevation had been challenged by one of the four sitting justices. Without Judge Stern, the court would have lacked a quorum. The oddity of the situation is compounded by the fact that one of the four justices had made himself a lame duck and had suggested that his participation in cases coming before the court would be unpredictable. Indeed, one of his stated positions was that he would not participate in any case where Stern's vote could be decisive. Of course, that was exactly the situation in *Abbott XXI*.

The oral reargument of the case on April 28 shed some interesting light on the court's approach. A few exchanges between the court and the parties' lawyers were especially revealing. The argument began with David Sciarra, ELC executive director, arguing on behalf of the plaintiff children. Justice LaVecchia's first question zeroed in on what became a central issue. She asked exactly which children Sciarra and ELC represented. Although he tried to claim that he had come to represent all the state's children, or at least all its at-risk children, under SFRA, his argument never took off. LaVecchia went on to other matters, but the point was made.

One might have expected the state's lawyer to seize on that point as a way to reduce the state's potential liability from $1.6 or 1.7 billion, the cost of fully funding SFRA for all students, to less than a third of that amount, the cost of fully funding only the former Abbott districts. But Peter Verniero, a former New Jersey Supreme Court justice who had been retained to argue on behalf of the state, made no mention of Justice LaVecchia's point. Instead, he focused on two themes—Professor Hanushek's theory that money does not really matter and the budget crisis trumping the constitutional rights of students. On the latter theme, the legal argument was that the New Jersey Constitution's appropriations clause, which vested authority over funding in the legislature, prevails over the education clause.[41]

Justice Barry Albin pressed Verniero on that, however. The justice asked whether a fiscal crisis could justify the state in refusing to provide free legal services to some impecunious criminal defendants. Verniero conceded that it could not—another important point made.

This set the stage for the latest—but almost certainly not last—chapter in this Russian novel of a lawsuit. It could well be the most dramatic, however, although the 1976 denouement of the *Robinson v. Cahill* phase of this litigation could be a serious contender.

As described previously, in *Robinson VI*, the New Jersey Supreme Court found the Public School Education Act of 1975 facially constitutional notwithstanding serious challenges to it by the plaintiff students (sound familiar?).[42] Then the trouble began in earnest when the legislature failed to appropriate any funds for its new and constitutionally validated statute. It took a full-blown constitutional crisis and a court injunction against spending any public funds on the public schools to break the logjam and produce the state income tax.

The *Abbott XXI* scene was staged on an equally dark and foreboding set. Governor Christie was persistently railing against the court's activism and threatening dire consequences if it continued, including that he might simply ignore the court's decision in *Abbott XXI* if he did not agree with it. The court was riven from within as it had never been previously. The public sentiment was decidedly antitax and more than a little hostile to spending more of "our" tax dollars on "their" children.

Members of the Court

Into this maelstrom came four justices and a judge missing their chief justice and their staunchest justice at the progressive end of an increasingly narrow spectrum of judicial opinion. Of those sitting, Albin seemed to be most likely, and Rivera-Soto least likely, to support the plaintiffs' position. LaVecchia, Stern, and Hoens seemed in between, with their precise locations subject to debate and difference of opinion. To the extent any consensus emerged, it was to place LaVecchia and Stern somewhat closer to Albin than to Rivera-Soto on the issues involved in *Abbott XXI*, and Hoens closer to Rivera-Soto.

The difficulty of predicting votes was compounded by the fact that *Abbott XXI* did not involve a classic liberal-conservative dichotomy. In a real sense, it was ELC that was asking the court to engage in strict construction, simply to enforce a recent legislative enactment according to its explicit terms, and it was the state that was asking for judicial policy making, to decide how much less than full funding of the statute would be acceptable.

Those who support the idea of a strong and independent judiciary were hoping against hope that the court could find a way to arrive at a unanimous decision. This was especially important because of the court's depleted ranks. The court's viability as an important, durable and positive force in New Jersey seemed to hang in the balance.

In the words of the old saw hope for the best and expect the worst, the court's fragmentation in *Abbott XXI* came close to the worst result. Justice LaVecchia wrote a "majority" opinion, but actually only Judge Stern joined in it. Justice Albin concurred in the judgment but did not join in LaVecchia's opinion and wrote his own going further than she had. Justices Hoens and Rivera-Soto each wrote a dissenting opinion and joined in the other's.

The final tally was 3–2, with Judge Stern providing the deciding vote. Rivera-Soto, who had taken the position that he would not vote in a case where Stern's vote was decisive, changed his position and voted in *Abbott XXI*. This actually was the most divided supreme court in the thirty-one-year history of the *Abbott* litigation, in sharp contrast to the norm.

Between *Abbott I* in 1985 and *Abbott XXI*, the court issued eleven decisions and ten published orders.[43] Of the eleven decisions, eight were unanimous, one had a single dissenting justice,[44] one had a justice partly dissenting and partly concurring and another dissenting,[45] and only the most recent decision had two justices (of the five who participated) dissenting.

The Opinions

What remains is to understand what the justices said in their conflicting opinions and where we go from here.

The key opinion is Justice LaVecchia's. That there were only three jurists (two justices and a judge) in the majority may weaken the precedential weight of *Abbott XXI*, but whatever precedent it set has to be found in the LaVecchia opinion.

Having said that, the LaVecchia opinion is surprising, not so much for the substance of its legal ruling as for its tone. It expresses anger and frustration at the executive and legislative branches, but especially at the executive. At points, it is sharp and derisive. What is surprising is not that a justice of the New Jersey Supreme Court could feel that way and write an opinion accordingly, but that Justice LaVecchia could. For much of her tenure on the court, as a political independent she seemed to be center-right on a decidedly liberal court, at least on social issues. Beyond that, she seemed supportive of executive agencies almost to a fault. Court pundits tended to attribute that to her legal career before she was named to the bench.

Between LaVecchia's graduation from Rutgers School of Law-Newark in 1979 and her appointment to the New Jersey Supreme Court in 2000, she spent the great bulk of the intervening years working in various capacities in the state's executive branch. She went from stints as a deputy attorney general and assistant and deputy counsel to Governor Thomas Kean to being director and chief administrative law judge for the Office of Administrative Law, director of the Division of Law in the Department of Law and Public Safety, and New Jersey commissioner of banking and insurance. Given this impressive record of accomplishment, I suppose one could excuse LaVecchia if she seemed partial to the executive branch earlier in her career on the bench.

But any such perceived partiality has been extinguished by her opinion in *Abbott XXI*. Justice LaVecchia repeatedly criticized the other branches of government in the strongest terms for their failure to honor a bargain they had struck with the court in *Abbott XX*. Perhaps the most passionate statement appeared deep in the opinion when she posed a rhetorical question: "To state the question is to present its answer: how is it that children of the plaintiff class of Abbott schoolchildren, who have been designated victims of constitutional deprivation and who have secured judicial orders granting them specific, definite, and certain relief, must now come begging to the Governor and the Legislature for the full measure of their education funding? And, how can it be acceptable that we come to that state of affairs because the State abandoned its promise? The State's position is simply untenable."[46]

Elsewhere Justice LaVecchia peppered her opinion with references to the state's "reneging on the representations it made," "breach[ing] the very premise underlying the grant of relief it secured with *Abbott XX*,"[47] failing to "honor its commitment,"[48] making "a conscious and calculated decision to underfund the SFRA formula" thereby "directly contraven[ing] the representations made by the State when procuring relief from prior judicial remedial orders,"[49] "breach[ing] the *Abbott XX* judgment that carried ongoing obligations owed by the State to the Abbott plaintiff class,"[50] and "notwithstanding its promises that SFRA funding would replace the parity funding remedy, . . . not deliver[ing] the quid pro quo."[51]

The LaVecchia opinion also described in detail what the justice characterized as then Attorney General Anne Milgram's "rare appearance on behalf of the state" in the *Abbott XX* oral argument. Milgram "made representations that were both remarkable and singularly persuasive, for as our ruling stated, the *Abbott XX* decision was, in no small way, a matter of trust between the branches of government."[52] Most dramatically, when the attorney general was pressed by the justices for assurance that SFRA, if approved by the court, would be fully funded and periodically adjusted as necessary, she provided repeated assurance. She seemed to base that on the fact that SFRA reflected a complete partnership between the state department of education on behalf of the executive branch and the legislature. To underscore her assurance to the court, the attorney general said that, "[I]f the Court is concerned about the Abbott School Districts under this formula, say that the formula is constitutional to the extent it is always fully funded as to the Abbott School Districts. That's a reasonable way for the Court to have the assurances that you're looking for about what's going to happen in the future."[53]

Lest that statement at oral argument leave any doubt about the state's intention, Attorney General Milgram reiterated the point even more strongly: "The budget is the wors[t,] I think[,] it's probably been in the State of New Jersey for decades. We are in dire fiscal circumstances, and it is funded. This school funding formula is funded. And if you want the assurance to make sure that it's funded next year related to the Abbotts then find that for it to be constitutional it has to be fully funded."[54]

Justice LaVecchia's strongly critical statements about the other branches were embedded in a sequence of points that anticipated some of the key substantive elements of her opinion. The sequence went as follows:

- The state had explicitly represented, indeed had persuaded the court to accept its representations, that SFRA would be fully funded.[55]
- The state's failure to underfund SFRA was undisputed.[56]
- The state's decision to underfund was "conscious and calculated."[57]
- By underfunding SFRA, the state had violated both its understanding with the court—"a matter of trust between the branches of government"[58]—and the *Abbott XX* judgment.
- "Like anyone else, the State is not free to walk away from judicial orders enforcing constitutional obligations."[59]

The tone of LaVecchia's opinion and the sense it conveyed that she and the court felt victimized by the other branches were undoubtedly important. However, in the big scheme of things, they are not as important as the substance of her legal analysis and conclusions. Indeed, one could read her opinion to suggest that a third element—pragmatic political considerations—may have played a role. After all, she may well have wanted to balance a number of potentially conflicting pressures on the court. To name some of the most important:

- Adhering to the court's multidecade jurisprudence in *Robinson* and *Abbott* anchored on the fundamental constitutional rights of students in New Jersey's poor urban school districts;
- The ongoing viability of the court as an independent and influential voice on the state's major legal and policy issues, but within a system that recognized separation of governmental powers;
- The real world and political implications of the state's fiscal crisis;
- The adequacy of financial support for the court system over which the other branches had substantial control;
- The morale of judges and court personnel; and
- The life prospects of hundreds of thousands of at-risk students in New Jersey's public schools.

Looking at only the bottom line of the LaVecchia opinion for the moment, it came impressively close to striking a balance among many of these pressures. It endorsed the ongoing constitutional rights of students, and a fully funded SFRA as a plausible way to satisfy them, but only for students in the former Abbott districts. That reduced the price tag of the decision from as much as $1.7 billion to less than $500 million, almost precisely the amount of an unexpected state revenue excess, and reflected an awareness of the state's ongoing budgetary problems.

It emphasized that the court was merely enforcing an explicit deal it had struck in *Abbott XX* with the other branches—namely that SFRA's constitutionality was expressly conditioned on it being fully funded for its first three years (through 2010–11) at which point the other branches would take a careful look at whether SFRA was functioning as promised and, to the extent it was not, would make all necessary adjustments. This was deference to the other branches, not usurpation of their authority, as the court itself recognized: "[O]ur holding in Abbott XX was a good-faith demonstration of deference to the political branches' authority." But the court went on to caution that it was "not an invitation to retreat from the hard-won progress that our state had made toward guaranteeing the children in Abbott districts the promise of educational opportunity."[60]

Clearly, the so-called three-year look-back was considered to be far more than a bureaucratic checkoff. The court was led to believe that it would be a rigorous review of how SFRA was operating in practice, not just in theory, and that appropriate statutory adjustments would be made to components of the formula if the reexamination showed they were necessary. Said Justice LaVecchia, "That point was critical to this court's extension of trust and expectation of good faith and commitment from the other two branches of government."[61] Of course, the expectation was that the review would be of a fully funded SFRA; without full funding the look-back could not completely serve its intended purpose, and a look back in 2010 seemed beside the point to the plaintiffs.

Still, after ordering that the Abbott districts be fully funded under SFRA in FY 2012, Justice LaVecchia further ordered that "whether or not the formula is fully funded on a statewide basis, the State nevertheless must undertake a look-back analysis that is meaningful and relevant for the Abbott districts so that SFRA continues to operate optimally and as intended in future years for pupils in those districts."[62]

How did she reach that bottom line? The main doctrinal issue the court had to address related to the state's argument that the New Jersey constitution's appropriations clause gave the legislature the power to override statutory rights such as those provided by SFRA. To a degree, the court agreed, but only as to students residing outside of the former Abbott districts. Although those students have a right under the state constitution's education clause to a "thorough and efficient" education, the court had never found that that right was violated by the prior school funding law, CEIFA, and SFRA gave them a statutory claim not directly linked to an underlying constitutional claim.

By contrast, throughout the long history of the *Abbott* litigation the court had found that the constitutional rights of students in the Abbott districts had been violated repeatedly by the state's school funding statutes. As a result, the court had to put in place the parity remedies until the other branches met their obligations. In *Abbott XX*, the court found for the first time that the other branches had enacted a statute that was at least facially constitutional, and it ordered that SFRA be permitted to go into effect in substitution for the court's constitutional parity remedies.[63] Consequently, SFRA involved a direct linkage between the statutory funding formula and the underlying constitutional rights of those Abbott district students. In a much earlier stage of the *Abbott* litigation, the court had said that if there were a conflict between the appropriations clause and the education clause the latter would prevail. When presented with that issue in *Abbott XXI*, Justice LaVecchia's opinion adhered to that view.

The second step in the doctrinal analysis was to accept Judge Doyne's Opinion/Recommendations that an underfunded SFRA did not enable a range of districts to "properly deliver the CCCS to all students."[64] This was especially true of districts with a high concentration of at-risk students. Said Justice LaVecchia, "It reveals that the cuts to Abbott districts, which are all high concentration [of at-risk student] districts, were not of a de minimus or inconsequential nature that could, or should, be greeted by this Court with indulgence. Nor, based on the State's [un]equivocal representations about future levels of funding made to us at argument, can we view this as an aberrational or temporary alteration in the State's responsibilities."[65]

The court's adoption of Judge Doyne's conclusions was made easier by the fact that the court had imposed upon the state the burden of proving that underfunding of SFRA did not prevent the Abbott districts from providing their students with educational opportunities sufficient to enable them to meet the CCCS. Indeed, a doctrinal purist might argue that the remand to Judge Doyne for that purpose was not even necessary since the acknowledged underfunding of SFRA, and the state's failure to conduct a careful review of the act's operation, violated explicit conditions of SFRA's constitutionality and justified the court in vacating its holding of facial constitutionality in *Abbott XX*. Justice LaVecchia recognized toward the end of her opinion that this might have led to a choice for the state: either "provide the Abbott districts with the full funding promised by SFRA, or return to the parity remedy that the previous remedial orders required." She quickly rejected giving the state that choice, however, because neither of the parties sought to return to the parity remedy and the court had no "independent interest in perpetuating it."[66]

Justice LaVecchia gave another state argument the short shrift it deserved. The state asserted that available funding could have been used more effectively and efficiently by school districts both with the tools they already had and with specific educational reforms, such as those relating to tenure laws, teacher evaluation, and collective bargaining. The court dismissed the former as a "broad brush attempt at disparagement [that] is unpersuasive," adding that"we cannot help but note that a significant portion of the Abbott SFRA funds go to districts that remain under State supervision. The State should tend its own house."[67] As to the latter—an array of future educational policy reforms—the opinion had this to say:

> While there may be virtue in future educational policy reforms, the debate regarding how best to transform the educational system must be reserved for a different forum. The State's presentation of such arguments in connection with the instant matter is simultaneously premature and laggard. In one respect, the State cannot transform its defense to this motion . . . into a vehicle to obtain an indication of some judicial approval for collateral labor law and education policy reforms that are, as-yet, unadopted by the Legislature. Nor can the State assert that districts should have mitigated the impact of budget reductions somehow before those initiatives were legislatively obtained. Unless and until the State achieves the legislative reforms it prefers, and puts these tools in the hands of districts, arguments attacking collective bargaining agreements or targeting interest groups in the education community, do not advance the State's position in this matter.[68]

Justice LaVecchia finished hammering the nail into the coffin of the state's "efficiency" argument by pointing out that underfunding of SFRA contributes greatly to inefficiency by eliminating any predictability, certainty, and transparency in the funding of school districts and returns New Jersey "to the structureless situations of the past where school districts had no way to plan because they could not anticipate in advance what the State would choose to fund for education from year to year."[69]

The other opinions in *Abbott XXI* require much less attention than Justice LaVecchia's. Justice Albin chose to concur in the judgment and remedy but not join in the LaVecchia opinion. Instead, he wrote his own concurring opinion, which may reflect good public policy, but not a sufficiently strong doctrinal basis to justify imposing that policy through a court order.

Justice Albin's position was that at-risk students in all 205 school districts spending below what SFRA had denominated the adequacy level were entitled to a remedy from the court because Judge Doyne had found that their constitutional rights were violated by SFRA's underfunding. Those 205 districts included 18 of the 31 former Abbott districts (the other 13 were already spending above SFRA's adequacy level). Although most or all of the hundreds of remaining New Jersey districts had at-risk students in their schools, Justice Albin conceded that those students were not entitled to a constitutional remedy in *Abbott XXI* because there was no finding that their constitutional rights had been violated by SFRA's underfunding.

Justice Albin's reasoning was as follows:

- By upholding SFRA's constitutionality in *Abbott XX*, the New Jersey Supreme Court may have implicitly recognized that all at-risk students in the State had a constitutional right to a fully funded SFRA.
- In any event, the supreme court's January 13, 2011, remand order empowered Judge Doyne to determine whether, notwithstanding the State's underfunding of SFRA, the state could prove that the constitutional mandate of a thorough and efficient education was still being provided by districts with high, medium and low concentrations of disadvantaged children.
- This assignment to Judge Doyne clearly indicated that the court had in mind constitutional rights of students beyond those in the Abbott districts.
- Judge Doyne's Opinion/Recommendations concluded with a finding that SFRA's underfunding denied at-risk students in at least the 205 districts spending below the adequacy level their constitutional rights.
- In *Abbott XXI*, a majority of the court accepted that finding, thereby investing all those at-risk students with a constitutional right that should entitle them to the full funding remedy.

Justice Albin's argument seemed to turn upon his understanding that the supreme court had sought findings and conclusions from Judge Doyne about the statewide constitutionality of SFRA. According to Albin, Doyne responded by making "factfindings . . . supported by credible evidence in the record," which indicated that, "the State is in violation of its constitutional obligation to provide a thorough and efficient education to the at-risk students in 205 school districts statewide."[70]

Because Doyne's fact-findings satisfied the "credible evidence" standard, the supreme court had to defer to them. The implication is that, as a consequence, they became the supreme court's findings and the basis for Albin's conclusion that the court had found a constitutional violation that reached beyond the Abbott districts.

That seems to invest Judge Doyne and his findings with too much doctrinal heft. Despite the loose language of the remand order, it is hard to imagine that the court really intended to expand the plaintiff class beyond its historical scope. If that was its intention, it should have been much clearer and more explicit about it.

A related issue is whether the Education Law Center could be the lawyer for those 187 additional districts and their at-risk students without the benefit of any specific undertaking to create a lawyer-client relationship. Justice Albin tried to obviate that difficulty by referring to ELC as the "equitable representative of all at-risk children in the State."[71]

On balance, Justice LaVecchia seems to get the better of the doctrinal exchange with Justice Albin. On the policy level, though, LaVecchia's result is troublesome because it resurrects the contentious bifurcated funding system that distinguishes between Abbott districts and all others. It also undermines SFRA's laudable goal of directing attention to the educational needs of at-risk students in districts throughout the state.

Of course, that may actually be more a political problem than a problem of constitutional policy, and, as a political problem, it may be better suited to action by the elected branches. Indeed, the legislature responded to the court's decision in *Abbott XXI* by legislatively extending the judicial remedy to include other at-risk students.

As to constitutional policy, to recognize the educational rights of all at-risk students does not dictate who should fund the satisfaction of those rights. Imagine a handful of at-risk students in the state's wealthiest school district. That they should receive educational programs and resources sufficient to meet their needs is clear; that the state should provide a substantial part of the necessary funding, given our shared state-local funding system, is less so. Nothing precludes the state from doing so unless that disables it from providing necessary funding to at-risk students in poor districts, but under our system there is certainly no constitutional requirement for the state to provide funding if the local district can do so.

Justices Hoens and Rivera-Soto wrote separate dissenting opinions, but each also joined in the other's opinion. The Hoens dissent focused on three reasons the plaintiffs' motion should be dismissed. Two were relatively narrow and technical (the standards for granting plaintiffs' motion and the sufficiency of support in the record for Judge Doyne's findings on remand). The third was potentially all encompassing (the overriding impact of the state's fiscal crisis), but it actually was part of the first narrower ground.

Justice Hoens's first reason was that the plaintiffs had failed to satisfy the standards for the granting of a motion in aid of litigants' rights: (1) that the other party has been the subject of a court order, (2) with which it failed to comply, (3) although it was fully capable of doing so. She expressed doubt that any of the standards had been satisfied. In her view, a view sharply at variance with the three jurists in the majority including Justice LaVecchia who had written the court's *Abbott XX* opinion for a unanimous court, the court had not explicitly ordered full funding of SFRA in that decision. Instead, said Justice Hoens, *Abbott XX* only referred to "anticipated future funding" of the SFRA formula and this fell short of a constitutional full funding mandate.[72] Presumably, the *Abbott XX* language to which she was referring was the following: "Our finding of constitutionality is premised on the expectation that the State will continue to provide school funding aid during this and the next two years at the levels required by SFRA's formula each year."[73]

Because of Justice Hoens's reading of that language, she concluded that there was no court order with which the state had failed to comply. In any event, even if there had been a full funding order with which the state had failed to comply, there was no proof that the state's failure was willful in the sense that it was fully capable of compliance. Here Justice Hoens brings to bear her all-encompassing point—that New Jersey's "unprecedented and unforeseen fiscal calamity" was a justification for the elected branches "to make hard choices requiring reductions of funding affecting numerous and diverse interests, including those of constitutional dimension."[74] In effect, the fiscal calamity had rendered the state incapable of complying with a full funding order. In other words, the fiscal crisis trumped the vindication of constitutional rights and the court had no business impinging upon the appropriations decisions made by the elected branches.

This point is at the heart of the difference between majority and dissenters in *Abbott XXI*. For the majority, the court continues in its role as last-resort guarantor of constitutional rights even when satisfying those rights is costly, inconvenient, or politically difficult. For the dissenters, the court's role is to defer to the other branches over matters relating to the appropriations clause, at least where those branches can justify their actions based on the existence of a fiscal crisis.

The final opinion in *Abbott XXI* is Justice Rivera-Soto's eccentric dissent in which Justice Hoens joined. The great bulk of this dissent is devoted to a "procedural concern"—namely, that when the court decides a "dispositive" motion, it must have a minimum of four affirmative votes even if the court is properly functioning with a five-judge quorum. The consequence of that procedural requirement, says Justice Rivera-Soto, is that the motion in aid of litigants' rights granted by the majority in *Abbott XXI* was procedurally flawed because it only garnered three votes.[75]

Of course, the justice derived that procedural "rule of practice in fact" from putting the clerk of the supreme court, and presumably others including Rivera-Soto's law clerks, through an exhaustive tabulation exercise that involved reviewing 38,170 motions decided by the court between June 24, 1987, and April 11, 2011, to determine what the justices' vote breakdown was on each.[76] As Justice LaVecchia pointed out trenchantly in her opinion, the fact that Justices Rivera-Soto and Hoens, just two weeks before *Abbott XXI*, had joined together to form two thirds of a three-judge majority to decide a case did not seem to faze them.

Rivera-Soto's dissent complained about the majority's departure from another "salutary" and almost universal procedural practice—of deciding "contentious cases" by unanimous vote.[77] Of course, consensus is desirable and to be sought whenever possible, but to intimate that a single recalcitrant justice can effectively veto a decision of the court's majority in an important case seems incompatible with long-standing judicial practice and sound constitutional policy.

Although most of Rivera-Soto's dissenting opinion was focused on this sort of procedural and numerical matter, he occasionally expressed his views about the substance of *Abbott XXI* and about the court's jurisprudence generally. Clearly, he was partial to the state's position. He referred to the court's *Abbott* decisions, at least the more recent ones, as reflecting a "fundamentally flawed and misguided approach." By contrast, SFRA was "reasoned, thoughtful and informed"[78] and "represented a sea change in how New Jersey endeavored to provide the constitutionally required 'thorough and efficient system of free public schools.'"[79]

Justice Rivera-Soto's animus toward the court emerged most clearly in the last paragraph of his dissenting opinion when he railed against the majority's "unseemly power grab under the guise of unnecessary constitutional adjudication. . . . [T]his Court usurps [the political branches'] choice and errs grievously in employing a procedurally suspect means to ramrod a billion dollar remedy this State can ill-afford."[80]

Abbott XXI clearly provoked strong, and strongly opposed, views within the New Jersey Supreme Court. The last question to be addressed in this chapter is how the other two branches of state government, and the public at large, will react. Potentially, as Rivera-Soto's rhetoric suggests, that is quite literally a billion-dollar question, not only in the immediate aftermath of *Abbott XXI*, but also in the longer term.

Beyond the Courts

Under the Christie administration, the executive branch often seems to start and end with the governor himself, and Governor Christie has hardly been a shrinking violet when it comes to *Abbott* and school funding. As noted earlier, before the court decided *Abbott XXI*, the governor threatened to ignore the decision if he disagreed with it. He backed away from this threat, and after the decision was announced he said he would defer to the legislature. In a press release, after acknowledging his obligation to "comply with the New Jersey Constitution as interpreted by the New Jersey Supreme Court," Governor Christie said, "it is now up to the Legislature to determine how the State is best able to fund the additional $500 million in aid to the Abbott districts specifically ordered in footnote twenty three by the Court's majority while also meeting the State's other funding priorities as I proposed them." In a concluding reminder, though, the governor reiterated, "I do not believe raising taxes is the answer."[81]

The legislature's action may have surprised the governor, however. Unlike its complicity with the governor on other controversial issues, the Democrat-controlled legislature seems to be charting a different course on the budget and school funding.[82] On June 29, just before the budget deadline, the legislature adopted a package of bills—the annual appropriations act and two bills relating to school funding—and sent them to the governor for action. The appropriations act contemplated a state budget of $30.6 billion, about $1.2 billion more than the governor's February 22 proposal, with $1.1 billion in additional state education aid and the restoration of other cuts mainly in programs for low-income New Jerseyans.[83] Under the legislative appropriations approach, the state would have made good on its constitutional obligation to students in the Abbott districts, as well as provide the funding necessary to bring all districts to SFRA's adequacy level. The other two bills, designed to operate in tandem, would have reestablished the "millionaires' tax" and used the estimated proceeds of $458 million to fully fund SFRA for all districts.[84]

Needless to say, this was not the last word on the subject. The following day, June 30, Governor Christie exercised his line item veto power to eliminate almost $1 billion from the appropriations bill—reducing it to $29.7 billion, only slightly more than his original budget proposal. He also flatly vetoed the millionaires' tax bill.

When the dust settled, at least for the time being, there was about $850 million in additional state education aid, but less than one-third of it distributed based on SFRA. As a result of *Abbott XXI*, the former Abbott districts were to receive an additional $446.9 million. Another $400 million would be distributed to other districts, $250 million as proposed in Christie's original budget proposal and an additional $150 million added on June 30. The $150 million would be spread among all the non-Abbott districts, with each getting an amount equal to roughly one percent of its overall budget.

The Christie line item veto cuts, not only to education but also to other core services for low-income residents, provoked outrage and bitterness across a broad spectrum. The strongest expression of it was from the senate president, Steve Sweeney, a Democrat. He used derogatory language about Governor Christie of the sort seldom heard or read publicly about a chief executive of New Jersey, referring to Christie as "cruel," "vindictive," "mean-spirited," and acting "in bad faith." The tirade, reported in the *Star-Ledger*, continued with Christie characterized as a "bully," a "punk," a "rotten bastard," and even a "rotten prick."[85]

Clearly, this is far beyond the usual partisan wrangling; it is, as the title of the *Star-Ledger* article suggests, personal. Less than a week earlier, Sweeney and the Democratic legislative leadership had gone out on a limb with their constituents by supporting Christie's pension and health reform plan. Now, instead of responding to the Democrats' budget initiatives in a spirit of cooperation, the governor had not only sawed off the limb but had conceivably chopped down the whole tree.

Strong criticism of the governor was not in short supply from other quarters, though. His sharp cuts to the state's struggling cities, to health care for the working poor, to women's health care, to AIDS funding, to mental health services, to legal services for the poor, to after-school programs, to agencies serving sexually and physically abused children, and even to the legislature provoked outrage and disappointment. Senator Loretta Weinberg, another legislative adversary of Christie, said his cuts were "cynical and overtly political," and that "[t]he only people that benefit in Chris Christie's new normal are economically well-off, white and male."[86]

Consternation extended in multiple directions: to the public higher education community where deep cuts, especially to tuition grants for low-income students, were said to threaten college opportunity and affordability; to the State League of Municipalities where Christie's budget cuts would harm local efforts to provide local property tax relief; and to individual urban mayors because a $159-million program of transitional aid to the poorest cities was virtually eliminated, along with $50 million in special funding for cash-strapped police departments that had been added by the Democrats.[87]

The depth and extent of the reactions against Christie's vetoes may actually have galvanized the Democratic majority in both legislative houses to rally behind its core constituencies and to take on the governor seriously. The immediate battleground was the legislature's post–July 1 session in which the Democratic senators sought to override thirty-nine Christie cuts. Because that requires a two-thirds vote in the forty-member senate, twenty-seven was the magic number. With twenty-four Democratic senators, that meant at least three Republican senators would have to join a unified Democratic voting bloc; on vote after vote, none did.[88]

The Republican senators' refusal to break ranks in the effort to override the governor's vetoes did not go unnoticed by many media editorial voices, which, overwhelmingly, reacted negatively.[89] Moreover, Christie's cuts in state aid to urban districts not only put greater pressure on overburdened local property ratables but also jeopardized their credit ratings.[90]

The longer-term battleground became the November 2011 election, in which the entire legislature was up for reelection under a redistricting map proposed by the Democratic Party.[91] Clearly, the Democrats banked on a combination of that map and the effects of Christie's draconian budget cuts, adversely affecting suburban as well as urban areas, to propel them to a resounding victory in November and extend their already substantial margins in both legislative houses to the point where they hoped to achieve a veto-proof majority. But the Republican Party, led by a still relatively popular

Governor Christie, hoped to cut into, if not reverse, the large Democratic majorities in both legislative houses.

What occurred was a Democratic victory, but hardly one of epic proportions. The Democrats added one seat in the state assembly, extending their already substantial majority to forty-eight of the eighty seats. That constituted exactly 60 percent. In the state senate the party breakdown remained unchanged with the Democrats holding twenty-four of the forty seats, also exactly 60 percent. In both houses, the Democratic majority fell short of the two thirds necessary to override gubernatorial vetoes. These results, nonetheless, prompted the Democratic Party leadership to claim victory in very strong terms. The state party chair, Assemblyman John Wisniewski, proclaimed that the still relatively popular governor was "all coat and no tails." Wisnieski also predicted, "It's going to be a Democratic agenda. . . . The governor needs to work with us."[92]

What has happened since is a complicated political minuet with Governor Christie and Senator Sweeney collaborating more often than one might have predicted given the extremely harsh words they exchanged publicly. The parties remained sharply at odds, however, on many major issues, such as tax policy and education funding. Even after *Abbott XXI*, full funding of SFRA by the state has not materialized, and embedded in the heated debate about the fiscal year 2013 budget is a gubernatorial effort to effectively alter important elements of SFRA without the benefit of legislative action.

The details of this minuet and how it will wind up when the music ends are beyond the scope of this chapter. But they will have much to say about the fate of New Jersey's extraordinary effort to equalize educational opportunities, especially of poor, minority children in the state's hard-pressed cities.

Considering the Court

This chapter has to end where it began, with a focus on the New Jersey Supreme Court. For the moment at least, the court seems to have escaped one of the most powerful and threatening weapons aimed at it and its seminal role in the state's governance. Since the 1947 constitution intentionally reconstituted it as a powerful, independent branch of government, the New Jersey Supreme Court has been a force with which to be reckoned.

After the court's extraordinary four-decade-long commitment to *Robinson v. Cahill* and *Abbott v. Burke*, in the spring of 2011 it seemed that *Abbott XXI* might signal the court's swan song—its retreat as a major governmental force. A depleted and divided five-judge court managed to defy the odds, however, and preserve its important governmental role at least for the foreseeable future. With all the controversy provoked by the majority decision in *Abbott XXI* and its impact on the state budget, the court seems to have receded from the limelight. A belligerent governor backed away from his threats to ignore the court's decision if he did not agree with it, and both the governor and the legislature fully implemented the court's specific fiscal order to the tune of almost $450 million without a quibble or complaint. Beyond that, the governor has even seemed to soft-pedal his vow to refashion the court in his preferred image.

There may be several reasons for the governor's more temperate tone about the court's composition. First, he may have decided that time is on his side since he gets to appoint or reappoint a majority of the seven justices during his initial term. Still, the right to appoint doesn't assure that appointees will be confirmed, especially if the November 2011 elections and the 2012 budget wars have emboldened the senate Democrats. The long delay in the confirmation of Justice Anne Patterson may be proof positive of that.[93] But, even more to the point, the governor's effort in the spring of 2012 to add two justices—one the first Asian nominee and the other the first openly gay nominee—was stymied by the Democratic state senate in a down and dirty political fight.[94] Eventually, the two vacancies on the seven-member court will have to be filled, and whether the governor and the Democratic legislative leadership can find a way to compromise about that is likely to be a major ongoing story.

Second, we know from judicial history in New Jersey and the nation that appointees do not always perform as the appointing authority expected. One only has to invoke the phrase "the Warren Court" to make that point dramatically.[95]

If an independent, assertive judiciary is still alive in New Jersey, as it very much seems to be, much of the recent credit has to go to Justice Jaynee LaVecchia, who spoke for the court in *Abbott XX* and *XXI*, on behalf of a unanimous court in the former and a sharply divided and internally splintered court in the latter. Justice LaVecchia and her colleagues have managed to keep the court on its courageous path of being the "last-resort guarantor of the Constitution's command" in New Jersey through an extremely difficult time.[96]

Although further challenges surely await, this is encouraging evidence for those who value a strong and independent judiciary that its unique role in New Jersey and its ability to shake the nation since 1947 can survive the vicissitudes of the day.

NOTES

1. *Robinson v. Cahill*, 69 N.J. 449 (1976).
2. *Robinson v. Cahill*, 70 N.J. 155 (1976).
3. *Abbott v. Burke*, 206 N.J. 332, 383–384 (2011). In a footnote to the quoted text, Judge Doyne cited all the supreme court opinions in *Abbott*, as well as five additional ones in *Robinson*. In both *Robinson* and *Abbott*, the supreme court also issued a number of important published orders that Judge Doyne did not list.

4. 31 A. 1017 (N.J. 1895).

5. Compare *Robinson v. Cahill*, 62 N.J. 473 (1973), with *Robinson v. Cahill*, 118 N.J. Super. 223 (Law Div. 1972).

6. New Jersey Constitution, article VIII, sec. 4, par. 1.

7. Paul L. Tractenberg, "Beyond Educational Adequacy: Looking Backward and Forward Through the Lens of New Jersey," *Stanford Journal of Civil Rights & Civil Liberties* 4 (2008): 411.

8. Guinness World Records actually has a category of "Longest running civil court case by an individual" in which it lists an obscure case—*Martin v. Sample*—as "still active" since it was filed on December 14, 1972. The problem is that the mainstream legal reference sites show nothing for the case since 1982, raising a serious question of what Guinness means by "still active." "Longest Running Civil Court Case by an Individual," *Guinness Book of World Records* (June 2012), http://www.guinnessworldrecords.com/records-1/longest-running-civil-court-case-by-an-individual/.

9. See, for example, Deborah Yaffe, *Other People's Children* (New Brunswick, NJ: Rutgers University Press, 2007); Gordon MacInnes, *In Plain Sight: Simple, Difficult Lessons from New Jersey's Expensive Effort to Close the Achievement Gap* (New York: Century Foundation, 2009); Richard Lehne, *The Quest for Justice: The Politics of School Finance Reform* (New York: Longman, 1978); Barry Gold, *Still Separate and Unequal: Segregation and the Future of Urban School Reform* (New York: Teachers College Press, 2007); Paul L. Tractenberg, "Robinson v. Cahill: The 'Thorough and Efficient' Clause," *Law and Contemporary Problems* 38 (1974): 312; Paul L. Tractenberg, "The Evolution and Implementation of Educational Rights under the New Jersey Constitution of 1947," *Rutgers Law Journal* 29 (1998): 827.

10. *Abbott v. Burke*, 149 N.J. 145. (1997) (invalidating in part New Jersey Statutes Annotated §§ 18A:7F-1–34 [West 2012]).

11. *Robinson v. Cahill*, 62 N.J. 473 (1973) (invalidating New Jersey Statutes Annotated, sec. 18A:58–1–5.6 (West 2012) (repealed 1975)); *Abbott v. Burke*, 119 N.J. 287 (1990) (invalidating New Jersey Statutes Annotated, sec. 18A:7A-1–2 (West 2012) (repealed 1996)); *Abbott v. Burke*, 136 N.J. 444 (1994) (invalidating New Jersey Statutes Annotated, sec. 18A:7D-1–4 (West 2012) (repealed 1996)).

12. See, for example, *Rose v. Council for Better Education*, 790 S.W.2d 186 (Ky. 1989); *Campaign for Fiscal Equity v. State of New York*, 100 N.Y.2d 893 (2003).

13. *Abbott v. Burke*, 153 N.J. 480 (1998) (providing for whole school reform, full-day kindergarten, preschool for all three- and four-year-olds, a state-funded facilities program, and an assortment of supplemental programs including health and social services, increased security, technology, alternative education, school-to-work, after-school and summer school programs); *Abbott v. Burke*, 163 N.J. 95 (2000) (ordering the state to overhaul and implement the preschool program as directed in *Abbott V*); *Abbott v. Burke*, 164 N.J. 84 (2000) (reaffirming that *Abbott V* required the state to fully fund the school facilities program); *Abbott v. Burke*, 170 N.J. 537, 540 (2002) (directing timely state decisions about preschool plans and budgets, and dealing with an administrative appeals process to resolve disputes between districts and the NJDOE over plans and budgets); *Abbott v. Burke*, 170 N.J. at 544–545 (further clarifying requirements for state implementation of the *Abbott V* preschool mandate).

14. Ernest C. Reock Jr., "Estimated Financial Impact of the 'Freeze' of State Aid on New Jersey School Districts, 2002–03 to 2005–06," *Institute on Education Law and Policy* (January 2007), ielp.rutgers.edu/docs/CEIFA_Reock_Final.pdf.

15. "A Formula for Success: All Children, All Communities," *New Jersey State Department of Education* (December 2007): www.nj.gov/education/sff/reports/AllChildrenAllCommunities.pdf.

16. New Jersey Statutes Annotated, sec. 18A:7F-43 (West 2012).

17. *Abbott v. Burke*, 196 N.J. 544 (2008).

18. Ibid. (court order). As was true of most stages of the *Abbott* and *Robinson* litigation, a substantial number of amici curiae, or friends of the court, submitted legal briefs to the court and occasionally were permitted to present oral arguments. For example, in connection with *Abbott XIX*, there were briefs submitted to the court on behalf of twenty-nine amici, including a majority of the Abbott districts and many of the state's leading educational advocacy and civic organizations.

19. A per curiam opinion is issued by an appellate court collectively and anonymously, that is, without a judge or justice being identified as its author. In *Abbott XIX*, the per curiam opinion represented the unanimous decision of the five sitting justices. Chief Justice Rabner and Associate Justice Long had recused themselves from participating.

20. Abbott v. Burke, 196 N.J. 544, 565 (2008).

21. *Abbott v. Burke*, 199 N.J. 140, 240 (2009) (Doyne, J., Opinion/Recommendations to the Supreme Court).

22. Ibid. at 250.

23. Ibid. at 249.

24. *Abbott v. Burke*, 199 N.J. 140 (2009).

25. Ibid. at 172.

26. Ibid. at 146–147.

27. Ibid. at 173.

28. N.J. Exec. Order No. 14 (Feb. 11, 2010), www.nj.gov/infobank/circular/eocc14.pdf.

29. *Perth Amboy Bd. of Ed. v. Christie*, 413 N.J. Super 590 (App. Div. 2010).

30. This was the customary vehicle the Education Law Center used to bring *Abbott* back before the New Jersey Supreme Court directly. *See* N.J. Ct. R. 1:10–3, 2:8–1.

31. *Abbott v. Burke*, 206 N.J. 332, 356–357 (2011).

32. Ibid.

33. Ibid. at 357.

34. Transcript of Proceedings at 5–7 (limited remand by N.J. Supreme Court by unpublished order on January 13, 2011), *see Abbott v. Burke*, 206 N.J. 332, 356 (2011).

35. Ibid. at 7–8.

36. Ibid. at 64 and 76.

37. Ibid. at 79.

38. *Abbott v. Burke*, 206 N.J. 332, 463 (2011) (Doyne, J., Opinion/Recommendations to the Supreme Court).

39. For a description of Rivera-Soto's behavior in this regard, see Tom Hester, "N.J. Supreme Court Justice Rivera-Soto Abstaining from Decisions in Protest," *New Jersey NewsRoom* (December 10, 2010), http://www.newjerseynewsroom.com/state/nj-supreme -court-justice-rivera-soto-abstaining-from-decisions-in-protest.

40. John Mooney, "As Abbott Returns to Supreme Court, Familiar Faces Play Pivotal Roles," NJ Spotlight (April 2011), http://www.njspotlight.com/stories/11/0421/0059/.

41. New Jersey Constitution, article VIII, sec. 2, par. 2. and sec. 4, par. 1.

42. *Robinson v. Cahill*, 70 N.J. 155 (1976).

43. The orders were issued between June 2002 (*Abbott IX*) and February 2008 (*Abbott XVIII*); they included three of the four single-justice dissents and one of the two two-justice dissents.

44. *Abbott v. Burke*, 149 N.J. 145 (1997) (Garibaldi, J., dissenting).
45. *Abbott v. Burke*, 170 N.J. 537 (2002) (LaVecchia, J., concurring in part and dissenting in part; Stein, J., dissenting).
46. *Abbott v. Burke*, 206 N.J. 332, 363 (2011).
47. Ibid. at 341.
48. Ibid. at 356.
49. Ibid. at 359.
50. Ibid. at 360.
51. Ibid. at 361.
52. Ibid. at 352.
53. Ibid. at 353.
54. Ibid.
55. Ibid. at 359.
56. Ibid.
57. Ibid.
58. Ibid. at 352.
59. Ibid. at 342.
60. Ibid. at 355.
61. Ibid. at 354.
62. Ibid. at 376.
63. There was something of a parallel in the *Robinson* phase of the litigation when, in 1976, the court ruled that the Public School Education Act of 1975 was facially constitutional and permitted it to go into effect. See *Robinson v. Cahill*, 70 N.J. 155 (1976).
64. *Abbott v. Burke*, 206 N.J. 332, 358 (2011).
65. Ibid. at 360 (presumably, the last sentence refers to the occasional one-year freezes the court had permitted when the state argued that there were temporary circumstances justifying flexibility).
66. Ibid. at 369.
67. Ibid. at 367.
68. Ibid.
69. Ibid. at 368.
70. Ibid. at 477 (Albin, J., concurring).
71. Ibid. at 482.
72. Ibid. at 493 (Hoens, J. dissenting).
73. *Abbott v. Burke*, 199 N.J. 140, 147 (2009).
74. *Abbott*, 206 N.J. at 495 (Hoens, J., dissenting).
75. By the way, an odd aside in Rivera-Soto's dissenting opinion was his renumbering of the published Abbott opinions and orders to conclude that *Abbott XXI* actually was *Abbott XXII*. Compare *Abbott v. Burke*, 206 N.J. 332, 483 (2011) (Rivera-Soto, J., dissenting), with "Abbott Decisions," *Education Law Center* (May 2011), http://www.edlawcenter.org/cases/abbott-v-burke/abbott-decisions.html.
76. Apparently, Justice Rivera-Soto would have preferred to review motions decided by the court from the start—1947—but since the earlier data were not available electronically and the task of compiling information for the forty years prior to June 24, 1987, would have been "overwhelming," he decided that a sample size spanning almost twenty-four years would suffice. See *Abbott*, 206 N.J. at 483 (Rivera-Soto, J., dissenting).
77. Ibid. Perhaps the justice should urge this approach on the U.S. Supreme Court. See, for example, *San Antonio v. Rodriguez*, 411 U.S. 1 (1973); *Bush v. Gore*, 531 U.S. 98 (2000);

Citizens United v. Federal Election Commission, 558 U.S. 310 (2010); *National Federation of Independent Business v. Sebelius*, 132 S.Ct. 2566 (2012) (all cases decided 5–4).

78. *Abbott*, 206 N.J. at 485.
79. Ibid. at 484–485.
80. Ibid. at 491.
81. Chris Christie, "Governor Chris Christie on the New Jersey Supreme Court's Abbott Decision," *State of New Jersey* (May 24, 2011), http://www.state.nj.us/governor/news/news/552011/approved/20110524a.html.
82. See Jarrett Renshaw, "Christie, Top Lawmakers Reach Deal on Overhauling NJ Pension and Health Benefits," *Northjersey.com*, June 15, 2011, http://www.northjersey.com/news/061511_Deal_reached_on_overhauling_pension_and_health_benefits.html; Chris Megerian, "N.J. Assembly Passes Landmark Employee Benefits Overhaul," June 24, 2011, http://www.nj.com/politics/index.ssf/2011/06/assembly_passes_landmark _emplo.html.
83. S-4000, 214th Leg. (N.J. 2011); A-4200, 214th Leg. (N.J. 2011).
84. S-2969, 214th Leg. (N.J. 2011); A-4202, 214th Leg (N.J. 2011); S-2970, 214th Leg. (N.J. 2011); A-4203, 214th Leg. (N.J. 2011).
85. Tom Moran, "Sweeney Unleashes His Fury as N.J. Budget Battle Turns Personal," *Newark Star-Ledger*, July 3, 2011, http://blog.nj.com/njv_tom_moran/2011/07/democrats_cry _foul_at_gov_chri.html
86. Jarrett Renshaw, "Outrage and Disappointment Follow Gov. Christie's Line-item Veto of Democrats' $30.6B Budget," *Newark Star-Ledger*, July 2, 2011, http://www.nj.com/news/index.ssf/2011/07/outrage_and_disappointment_fol.html.
87. Jarrett Renshaw, "N.J. Cities Likely to Suffer Most from Gov. Christie Budget Cuts," *Newark Star-Ledger*, July 1, 2011, http://www.nj.com/news/index.ssf/2011/07/nj_cities _likely_to_suffer_mos.html.
88. State Senator Jennifer Beck was the lone departure when she voted with the Democrats to restore funding for family planning clinics. Michael Symons, "Family-Planning Veto Override Unlikely, As Six GOP Backers Back Off," *Asbury Park Press*, August 3, 2010, http://blogs.app.com/capitolquickies/2010/08/03/family-planning-veto-override-unlikely -as-six-gop-backers-back-off/.
89. See, for example, Irwin Stoolmacher, "N.J. Budget, Public Worker Benefit Changes Leaves Burden Unbalanced," *Times of Trenton*, July 8, 2011, http://www.nj.com/times-opinion/index.ssf/2011/07/opinion_nj_budget_public_worke.html; Mary E. Forsberg, "Gov. Chris Christie's Budget Cuts Harm N.J.'S Most Vulnerable While He Protects Millionaires," *Times of Trenton*, July 6, 2011, http://www.nj.com/times-opinion/index.ssf/2011/07/opinion _gov_chris_christies_bu.html; Barbara Buono, "N.J. Budget Cuts Target Resources for the Neediest Residents," *Times of Trenton*, July 27, 2011, http://www.nj.com/times -opinion/index.ssf/2011/07/opinion_nj_budget_cuts_target.html.
90. Elise Young, "Christie's Cuts in Aid Imperil Moody's Ratings for Six Cities," *Bloomberg*, July 13, 2011, http://www.bloomberg.com/news/2011–07–13/christie-s-cuts-in -aid-imperil-moody-s-ratings-for-six-cities.html.
91. Mark J. Magyar, "Redistricting Map Preserves the Incumbent Advantage," *NJSpotlight*, April 4, 2011, http://www.njspotlight.com/stories/11/0404/0207/.
92. Chris Megerian and Matt Friedman, "N.J. Legislative Election Results: Democrats Fend Off GOP Funding, Christie Campaigning," *Newark Star-Ledger*, November 9, 2011, http://www.nj.com/news/index.ssf/2011/11/nj_legislative_elections_resul.html.
93. In an unprecedented move, Governor Christie nominated Anne Patterson, an attorney in private practice, to replace Justice John Wallace, who became the first sitting justice denied tenure. Claire Heininger and Lisa Fleisher, "Gov. Chris Christie Nominates

Lawyer Anne M. Patterson to N.J. Supreme Court," *Newark Star-Ledger*, May 3, 2010, http://www.nj.com/news/index.ssf/2010/05/gov_chris_christie_nominates_1.html.

94. MaryAnn Spoto, "What Price Is N.J.'s Judiciary System Paying for Gov. Christie's Battle with Senate Dems?" *Newark Star-Ledger*, June 11, 2012, http://www.nj.com/news/index.ssf/2012/06/what_price_is_njs_judiciary_sy.html.

95. Observers believed that former Chief Justice Poritz would be a more conservative legal thinker than was displayed during her time on the court. See Virginia A. Long "The Purple Thread: Social Justice as a Recurring Theme in the Decisions of the Poritz Court," *Rutgers Law Review* 59 (2007): 535.

96. *Robinson v. Cahill*, 69 N.J. 133, 154 (1975).

Conclusion

New Jersey's 1947 Constitution and the Creation of a Modern State Supreme Court

JOHN B. WEFING

The year 1947 marked a watershed for New Jersey and its court system. The creaky century-old state constitution was radically rewritten and a new, modernized judicial system was the capstone. The resulting New Jersey Supreme Court had the independence and structure to become one of the nation's leading state supreme courts, widely considered strong and highly effective, if more activist than some favor.

The 1947 constitution, New Jersey's third, represented a major departure from the first two, the constitutions of 1776 and 1844. The first was only a few pages long and was adopted shortly after the Continental Congress had urged the thirteen colonies to promulgate constitutions.

> With reports that General William Howe was landing with his troops at Sandy Hook and with British invasion imminent, New Jersey's first constitution was drawn with understandable haste. On June 24, the Provincial Congress of New Jersey appointed a special committee of ten to meet at Burlington and draft the document. Two days later it was completed, and on July 2, 1776, two days before the Declaration of Independence was signed, New Jersey, with the acceptance of the draft by the Provincial Congress, became the third colony to adopt a constitution.[1]

The 1776 constitution vested most of the governmental power in the legislature. Although it provided for a court of appeals and other judicial officers, the judiciary had little independence or authority.[2] Indeed, separation of powers was honored in the breach since the court of appeals consisted of the governor and members of the legislative council.[3]

During New Jersey's early state constitutional history, judges, other than members of the court of appeals, were appointed by the legislative council and the general assembly and commissioned by the governor.[4] However, when Andrew Jackson was elected president in 1829, a national movement developed in support of the popular election of judges. One characteristic of the Jacksonian revolt was faith in the wisdom of the common man and, as New Jersey Chief Justice Arthur T. Vanderbilt said more than a century later, this "resulted in the antiprofessionalism of the period, with devastating effects on the bar. . . . The new notions of equality in fact were applied in the selection of judges, resulting in an inferior judiciary in the second half of the nineteenth century."[5]

Many states changed their systems in response and adopted procedures that included election of judges. Showing early independence and resistance to national trends, though, New Jersey largely continued to appoint its judges, even after it adopted its second constitution in 1844. The one exception—local justices of the peace—was described rather unflatteringly by Chief Justice Vanderbilt, as quoted by former governor and Supreme Court Chief Justice Richard J. Hughes, in *In re Yengo:*

> One of the ways in which our second Constitution, that of 1844, reflected the democratic revolt of the Jacksonian era was in providing for the popular election of justices of the peace by townships and in the cities by wards. Such elections, here and elsewhere throughout the country generally, reflected the popular demand of the period for the direct election of judges who would be "close to the people," and no thought was given to imposing any standards of qualifications for the office. Thus the New Jersey Constitution of 1844 put the justice of the peace in local politics with the undesirable results that inevitably flow from mixing judicial work and politics. The election of a justice of the peace as a prank of his neighbors was not unknown and the office shrank in dignity and usefulness.[6]

Between 1776 and 1844 there were periodic efforts to revise New Jersey's state constitution—in 1790, 1797, 1819, 1827, and 1840.[7] It was not until September 2, 1844, however, that a second New Jersey constitution became effective. This constitution continued to give most of the power to the legislature and provided for a complex and convoluted state court system: "The Judicial power shall be vested in a Court of Errors and Appeals in the last resort in all causes, as heretofore; a Court for the trial of impeachments; a Court of Chancery; a Prerogative Court; a Supreme Court; Circuit Courts, and such inferior Courts as now exist, and as may be hereafter ordained and established by law; which Inferior Courts the Legislature may alter or abolish, as the public good shall require."[8]

In the following century, the state's courts became more, not less, complex and convoluted. By 1947, there were seventeen different classes of courts operating in New Jersey. The system was likened by some to the labyrinth of the early English courts so often described by Charles Dickens.

Although an important set of state constitutional amendments was adopted in 1875, they did nothing to rationalize New Jersey's courts.[9] They did, however, include the education clause, which was continued in the 1947 constitution and became the basis for the important school funding cases discussed by Paul Tractenberg in chapter 10. That clause mandated: "The Legislature shall provide for the maintenance and support of a thorough and efficient system of free public schools for the instruction of all the children in the State between the ages of five and eighteen years."[10]

In 1947, New Jersey not only had far too many classes of courts, it also had an unwieldy highest court, the court of errors and appeals. That court consisted of sixteen members: the chancellor, the nine justices of the supreme court, and six lay members who were usually lawyers but did not have to be.[11] Many judicial publications of the time sharply criticized this court and the system it sat atop because it was unwieldy. Most of the court's members had other functions and did not work full-time in their capacity as members; their appointments were highly political. A notable example of political influence was the appointment of Frank Hague Jr. to the court. Hague was not a well-regarded attorney and apparently was appointed only because he was the son of Mayor Frank Hague of Jersey City, the powerful Hudson County political boss. A. Harry Moore, the governor at the time, freely admitted that he had appointed Hague Jr. to the state's highest court to make his father happy.

Earlier in the 1940s, there had been a number of failed attempts to change the 1844 constitution. A proposal to have a constitutional convention was finally placed on the ballot in 1944. Mayor Hague, who objected to a number of the proposed constitutional provisions, adamantly opposed the constitution. "He took out full-page advertisements in the state newspapers and covered highway billboards throughout New Jersey with messages proclaiming that the new constitution would take away the rights of such groups as farmers, veterans, sportsmen, women, and civil service employees."[12]

As a result of opposition voiced by Mayor Hague and many New Jersey judges and lawyers, the proposed new constitution was defeated. Nonetheless, when Governor Alfred E. Driscoll was elected in 1946, he was convinced of the need for reform and used his inaugural address in 1947 to call for a constitutional convention to radically change the constitution and particularly to reorganize the judicial system. Throughout the struggle, Driscoll fought hard to ensure a strengthened executive and a streamlined judiciary.

At that time, Arthur T. Vanderbilt was a leading legal figure in New Jersey. In addition to being a well-regarded attorney, he also served as Republican leader of Essex County, and he had been dean of the New York University School of Law and president of the American Bar Association. During his service as ABA president, one of Vanderbilt's primary tasks had been the improvement of judicial administration. Not surprisingly, he was one of the leading voices in New Jersey advocating for a streamlined judicial article within the constitution.[13] Other leading lawyers and scholars also had come to recognize the need for reform, but many entrenched interests, including many sitting judges, continued to oppose change.

While Vanderbilt did not attend the constitutional convention, his views were communicated by close associates like Frank Sommer, a mentor of Vanderbilt, who chaired the judiciary committee that drafted the article on the judiciary, and Nathan Jacobs, who had worked in Vanderbilt's law office and was vice chair of the judiciary committee. By this time, Mayor Hague was beginning to lose some of his power, and, after assuring himself that some of his deepest concerns were protected in the new constitution, he wound up supporting it.[14]

The constitution that emerged from the convention gained bipartisan support and was adopted overwhelmingly by the voters at the November 1947 general election. The new constitution, which was to become effective in 1948, dramatically increased the powers of both the executive and judicial branches of government. The governor was empowered to appoint the attorney general, all judges, prosecutors, and other important governmental officials. Additionally, the governor's term was increased from three to four years; unlike the 1844 constitution, the proposed new constitution enabled the governor to serve a second four-year term immediately. Finally, the governor was given line item veto power over the budget.

The new constitution totally overhauled the judicial system with a strong seven-member supreme court, headed by a strong chief justice, at its apex. The chief justice was given control over the administration of the entire court system. The number of courts was reduced, with the superior court becoming the primary trial and appellate court. Although some courts, such as the county and juvenile and domestic relations courts, survived the streamlining of the judiciary for a time, they were merged into the superior court by subsequent constitutional amendments. Now, except for local municipal court judges and state supreme court justices, all state judges are part of the superior court. The chief justice's extensive powers include determining, after judges are appointed to the superior court, where they should be assigned within that court. That includes naming those who will serve as appellate division judges and as assignment and presiding judges.

This assignment power is significant. A strong, capable, and careful chief justice could ensure that the best judges were appointed to the most important posts within the judicial system. One of the first things that Vanderbilt did after his appointment as the first chief justice under the 1947 constitution was to require that all judges produce a weekly report of their activities. While this antagonized some of the judges, it had the effect of making judges more efficient.

Under the 1947 constitution, all New Jersey judges, including justices of the state supreme court, are appointed to seven-year terms by the governor, with the advice and consent of the state senate. If they are reappointed, they achieve tenured status, which means they can serve until the age of seventy, the constitutionally mandated retirement age.

In many other states judges are elected in whole or in part.[15] In New Jersey, however, the electorate's role regarding the judiciary is limited to electing the governor and members of the senate who appoint and confirm judges.[16]

A number of New Jersey's governors have agreed to refer all candidates being considered for judicial appointment to the New Jersey Bar Association for review. That tradition was started by Governor Richard J. Hughes in the 1960s. However, the governor is required neither to use that process nor to follow the bar association's recommendation. Governor Christine Todd Whitman, who served in the 1990s, rejected the bar association's recommendation that one of her supreme court appointees was unqualified and appointed him anyway.[17] Subsequently, other governors utilized the review process, and even Governor Whitman several times used negative recommendations to justify not reappointing superior court judges.

In 2006, Governor Jon Corzine added to the bar review process by Executive Order #36. It created a Judicial Advisory Panel with five retired judges and two members of the public to vet potential appointees to the superior court and subsequently those names were sent to the bar association for its review. However, the order specifically reserved the final decision-making power to the governor: "Consistent with Article VI, Section VI, Par. 1, of the New Jersey Constitution, the Governor retains sole authority to determine whom to nominate to all judicial positions." In 2010, Governor Christopher Christie modified that order to change the advisory body's composition to three retired judges and four members of the public, but final decision-making power remained with the governor.[18]

Another factor involved in the appointment of judges and justices is senatorial courtesy. By tradition, a senator from the county where the nominee lives can block the appointment. This practice has often been roundly criticized, although an argument can be made that a senator from the same county as the judicial nominee may have particularly relevant knowledge about that person's qualifications. Unfortunately, senatorial courtesy is more often used as a bargaining chip to exact some accommodation from the governor or as a means of promoting someone else for appointment to the position.[19]

A final aspect of the appointment process, which may be virtually unique to New Jersey, is the tradition—unwritten but strictly adhered to—of achieving political balance on the supreme court.[20] Since there are seven justices, political balance has typically meant there had to be four justices from one of the two major parties and three from the other. Achieving balance gets more complicated when a justice is an independent, as happened not long ago when the supreme court was composed of four Democrats, two Republicans, and one independent. The complication may have been more theoretical than real, however, since the independent had served in high-level appointive positions in Republican gubernatorial administrations.

More recently, in 2010, when Governor Christie decide not to reappoint Justice John Wallace and the president of the state senate refused to hold confirmation hearings on Governor Christie's nominee, the court ended up with three Democrats, two Republicans, and one independent. Christie's nominee to replace Justice Wallace was a Republican. Eventually the chief justice assigned the presiding judge for administration of the appellate division to serve temporarily on the supreme court.[21]

This tradition of bipartisanship in New Jersey actually long predates the 1947 constitution. Arthur T. Vanderbilt, in *The Challenge of Law Reform,* published in 1955, wrote, "There is another principle of judicial selection the wisdom of which cannot be stressed too strongly. I refer to a bipartisan judiciary . . . such as New Jersey has enjoyed for a century as a matter of unbroken tradition without constitutional or statutory compulsion."[22]

Vanderbilt, a longtime Republican leader of Essex County, demonstrated his awareness of political pressures in his next comment: "A bipartisan system insures that at least half the judges will not be appointed for political considerations, but rather because they are competent lawyers with judicial temperament." He went on to observe that "the decisions of a bipartisan court in cases which are of political importance have more weight with the profession and the public, especially if the decisions are unanimous or predominantly so, than would the decisions of a court chosen exclusively from one political party." He concluded by saying, "Paradoxically though it may sound, a bipartisan judiciary is the only way in this country to achieve a nonpartisan judiciary, and who would deny that all justices should be nonpartisan?"[23]

In his first yearly assignment of superior court judges, Chief Justice Vanderbilt also discussed the importance of the bipartisan nature of the courts. He said, "I have tried throughout to give effect to the recognized tradition in this State for bipartisan courts. Thus I have appointed three Democrats and three Republicans in the appellate division."[24]

The trial courts in New Jersey are also kept politically balanced, with a more or less equal number of Democrats and Republicans serving at the same time.[25] While this doctrine has been primarily based on tradition, for many years there was a statute regarding the old county courts, which provided in part that "all appointments to such judgeships shall be made in such manner that the appointees shall be, as nearly as possible, in equal numbers, members of different political parties, so as to constitute the county court in any such county bipartisan in character."[26] That provision was repealed when the county courts were merged into the superior court.[27]

New Jersey's governors have taken the appointment of state supreme court chief justices and associate justices very seriously and have generally appointed highly qualified individuals. Unlike the practice in many states where high court judges routinely come from the ranks of the trial or appellate judges, appointees to the New Jersey Supreme Court frequently have had no prior judicial experience, but they have served in important legal positions such as attorney general or counsel to the governor or been prominent members of the bar. The overwhelming view over the past six and a half decades has been that New Jersey has been well served by the quality and diversity of its judiciary and especially its highest court.

Governor Alfred Driscoll set a very high standard when he appointed Arthur T. Vanderbilt as the first chief justice of the newly established New Jersey Supreme Court. Vanderbilt's standing in the national legal community was attested to by the fact that President Dwight D. Eisenhower seriously considered appointing him chief justice of the United States Supreme Court. Instead, Eisenhower appointed Earl Warren. Neither Warren nor Vanderbilt had prior judicial experience.

Also attesting to the national stature of the New Jersey Supreme Court in its early years was Eisenhower's choice of William J. Brennan as an associate justice of the U.S. Supreme Court in 1956, after he had served five years on New Jersey's high court. Brennan came to the attention of Eisenhower's chief legal adviser, U.S. Attorney General Herbert Brownell, when Brennan gave a speech as a substitute for Vanderbilt.[28] Brennan became one of the Court's most influential justices.

Meanwhile, as New Jersey's chief justice, Vanderbilt left an indelible mark on the state's jurisprudence and the judicial role. In a major decision that was seriously considered for inclusion in this book, *Winberry v. Salisbury,*[29] Vanderbilt's opinion enabled the supreme court to exercise control over the rules of court procedure free of legislative constraints. The issue before the court in *Winberry* turned on the interpretation of a provision in the 1947 constitution to the effect that "[t]he Supreme Court shall make rules governing the administration of all courts in the State and, *subject to the law,* the practice and procedure in all such courts."[30]

During the drafting of the 1947 constitution, Vanderbilt had written to the committee responsible for the judicial article to oppose that language because it would make the rules of practice and procedure in the courts subject to the overriding will of the legislature. Despite his objection, the language remained intact. Nonetheless, when that very language came before the court

in *Winberry* just a few years later, Vanderbilt found an interpretive way to obviate his earlier objection. He and the court found that the phrase "subject to
the law" applied only to substantive and not procedural law. This arguably
manipulative construction permitted the court to adopt its own rules of procedure and assert its independence from the legislature.[31]

Starting with Vanderbilt, who served between 1948 and 1957, the New Jersey Supreme Court has had a series of extremely capable, intelligent, and assertive chief justices, well served by highly qualified associate justices. Without
exception, the chief justices had significant standing and influence prior to
ascending to their high court positions. As a consequence, they were cowed
by neither the other branches of state government nor by the justices of the
U.S. Supreme Court. In short, they were ready to use the state court's power to
achieve their desired goals regardless of what others thought. Ultimately, they
were confident of the correctness of their positions.[32]

Of the seven chief justices who followed Vanderbilt, his immediate successor was one of the strongest and most assertive. Joseph Weintraub, who
served from 1957 to 1973, was scholarly and proud of his intellect. He had graduated from Cornell as a member of Phi Beta Kappa and won special honors at
Cornell Law School, where he was editor-in-chief of the *Cornell Law Quarterly*.
He was counsel to Governor Robert B. Meyner at the same time that he served
on the Waterfront Commission of New York Harbor. After only seven months
on the superior court, he was appointed to the state supreme court.

Coincidentally, Weintraub had been a high school classmate of Justice
Brennan, but their judicial philosophies and views were hardly the same.
While many of Weintraub's decisions were quite liberal, his criminal law and
procedure decisions were another matter. In general, he believed that evidence that clearly demonstrated the guilt of a defendant should be admissible.
Therefore, he took a very negative view toward the exclusionary rule and the
decisions of the Warren Court expanding defendants' rights particularly under
the Fourth Amendment.[33] That brought him into periodic conflict with the
Warren Court's criminal law and procedure jurisprudence and with his former
high school classmate. Weintraub seemed almost to take pleasure in criticizing the Warren Court's decisions, and he certainly manifested a belief that his
views were as worthy as those of his former classmate William Brennan.[34]

The third chief justice, Pierre Garvin, was tragically short-lived. Appointed
by Governor William Cahill in 1973 to succeed Weintraub, Garvin unfortunately
became ill and died shortly after his appointment. He had been Cahill's chief
counsel and did not have prior judicial experience. At the time of Garvin's
appointment, Cahill was a lame duck, having lost the nomination of his own
party. After Garvin's death, Cahill appointed his predecessor as governor,

Richard J. Hughes, as chief justice, despite the fact that Hughes was a Democrat and Cahill a Republican.[35]

Hughes had an illustrious, perhaps unprecedented career in New Jersey state government. Early on, he served for ten years as a trial judge, an assignment judge, and an appellate division judge. He then left the judiciary to go into private practice to provide for his large family. After his stint in private practice, he was convinced to run for governor and was twice elected. In 1973, a few years after his eight-year governorship ended, Hughes was chosen as New Jersey's fourth chief justice under the 1947 constitution.

Hughes led the court until 1979, proving to be a great conciliator. He also wrote some of the decisions in the long-running series of cases dealing with school funding, the subject of chapter 10 of this book, as well as the court's unanimous opinion in the nation's first right-to-die case, *In re Quinlan*, the subject of chapter 4, co-authored by Professor Robert Olick and Judge Paul Armstrong.

The fifth chief justice, Robert Wilentz, served from 1979 until 1996, the longest tenure of any modern chief justice. He came from a prominent New Jersey legal family. His father, David Wilentz, had been the state's attorney general and prosecuted Bruno Hauptmann in the famous Lindbergh kidnapping case. Subsequently, David Wilentz founded and led a major New Jersey law firm and was longtime Democratic leader of Middlesex County. Robert Wilentz had studied at Princeton before going into military service. Afterward he completed his undergraduate studies at Harvard and then went to Columbia Law School. He worked in the family firm and spent two terms in the New Jersey Assembly before being appointed to the state supreme court (without prior judicial experience) by Governor Brendan Byrne, a Democrat. Wilentz was reappointed by a Republican governor, Thomas Kean. Kean's appointment of a member of the other political party was consistent with New Jersey's unwritten practice designed to cultivate judicial independence. Kean believed it was right to reappoint a competent chief justice despite the fact that he disagreed with Wilentz about a number of cases decided by the Wilentz court—particularly the *Mount Laurel* cases, the focus of Robert Holmes's chapter 3.

Some members of the senate were not so willing to accept the concept of judicial independence and tried to block Kean's reappointment of Wilentz. However, in public deference to the concept of judicial independence, most of the senators who opposed the reappointment relied upon the fact that Wilentz was primarily living in New York City and only had a summer home in New Jersey. Most commentators, however, believed that the real reason for their opposition was the unpopular decisions the court had made. It was a difficult battle and ultimately Wilentz received twenty-one votes—the bare minimum necessary for reappointment. Governor and retired Chief Justice Hughes joined Governor Kean in fighting for the reappointment.

The sixth chief justice was Deborah T. Poritz, who served for ten years beginning in 1996. Law was a second career for her; she had been an English professor before attending the University of Pennsylvania Law School. She used that professional training and her second career to achieve a number of important New Jersey firsts. She was the first woman to serve as chief counsel to the governor (to Governor Thomas Kean), as attorney general of the state, and as chief justice. Like all but one of her seven fellow chief justices, Poritz came to the position with no significant judicial experience. During her decade-long tenure, the court continued to be perceived as generally liberal and activist in its approach.

The seventh chief justice was James Zazzali, who had been serving as an associate justice and was primarily a one-year holdover chief justice until he reached the mandatory retirement age of seventy. He served from 2006 to 2007. Like other New Jersey chief justices, though, Zazzali had a distinguished legal and public service career. A Georgetown Law School graduate, he served in numerous governmental posts including attorney general and chair of the state commission of investigation. It was widely believed that Governor Jon Corzine appointed Zazzali to a one-year term because he planned to appoint his then attorney general, Stuart Rabner, as the chief justice, but wanted him to serve for another year as attorney general before joining the court.

In fact, Stuart Rabner was appointed in 2007 to succeed Zazzali as the eighth chief justice. After graduating from Princeton summa cum laude and Harvard Law School cum laude and clerking for U.S. District Judge Dickinson Debevoise, Rabner served as an assistant U.S. attorney, counsel to the governor, and attorney general of the state. His baptism by fire came in 2009 when he had to deal with the crisis of confidence among the state's judges caused by Governor Christie's effort to reshape the judiciary starting with the supreme court.

A review of New Jersey's chief justices demonstrates that, although one or two had significant judicial experience, there was a much stronger connection between high-level government service, especially in the executive branch, and appointment to the position. Four of the eight chief justices had been counsel to the governor, three had been attorney general, one had been governor, one had been a legislator, and one had been chair of the state commission of investigation.

After the new constitution was adopted in 1947, the *Journal of the American Judicature Society* said, "[T]he People of New Jersey are exchanging America's worst court system for America's best."[36] The new structure, together with the method of appointment and commitment to judicial independence, were instrumental in allowing the court to operate in an independent manner without fear or hesitation.

One example of the unusual power granted to the New Jersey Supreme Court is the chief justice's role in the process of reapportioning the legislature. In most states, reapportionment is handled directly by the legislature. New Jersey, however, provides for a commission composed of five Republicans and five Democrats. If they cannot agree on a plan, and most often they cannot, the chief justice selects a tiebreaker who is supposed to be independent.[37] In the last two reapportionment proceedings, some asserted that the chief justice had selected a tiebreaker who would likely support the Democratic approach. While there is no direct support for that assertion, the Democrats did gain seats after these reapportionments. This type of semipolitical role may have made the New Jersey Supreme Court more political and in part led to the actions of Governor Christie.[38] In 2011, the chief justice chose Alan Rosenthal, a respected academic, as the tiebreaker. The chief justice had requested both the Democrats and the Republicans to submit a list of preferred possibilities. Both lists had included Professor Rosenthal.

Nonetheless, since the 1947 constitution went into effect, the state supreme court has received praise from many commentators. As Gerald Russell wrote, "The New Jersey Supreme Court has built a reputation as an intellectually rigorous and forcefully progressive state Supreme Court."[39] Professors G. Alan Tarr and Mary Porter, in their book about state supreme courts, said, "The New Jersey Supreme Court has assumed a role of leadership in the development of legal doctrine, thereby earning for itself a national reputation for activism and liberal reformism."[40]

Kevin Mulcahy, writing about California and New Jersey, said, "This comment discusses why the New Jersey court receives praise as an activist tribunal and why California's reputation has changed from progressive to stagnant. More importantly, this comment discusses what steps California, and other jurisdictions, should take to model the New Jersey court and attain a similar activist reputation."[41]

Despite Mulcahy's criticism of the California Supreme Court, it still ranks first in a number of studies of the most influential courts as determined by citations to its opinions. For example, in their statistical study, Jake Dear and Edward Jessen conclude that California leads the states in that regard. New Jersey also ranks high, third among state courts (after California and Washington) whose decisions have been followed at least three times by out-of-state courts and fourth among state courts whose decisions have been cited at least five times by out-of-state courts.[42]

Putting this in a historical perspective, Stephen Choi, Mitu Gulati, and Eric Posner indicated that between 1870 and 1970, leading state courts were those of New York, California, Massachusetts, and Illinois. However, they found that, between 1945 and 1970, there was a significant shift: "California emerged as a star. New Jersey, Texas and Illinois also were among the influential states."[43]

In its transformation into an independent, activist state court after adoption of the 1947 constitution, the New Jersey Supreme Court had some notable advantages over other state courts. In addition to the method of appointment and the commitment to judicial independence already mentioned, other important factors included the absence of initiative and referendum (I&R). In a number of states with I&R, particularly California and Florida, when the state supreme courts issued decisions some deemed to be liberal and activist, movements were spawned to reverse or limit the effect of those decisions by means of constitutional amendments via voter-initiated I&R. In New Jersey, by contrast, a constitutional amendment can be placed on the ballot only if both legislative houses vote in favor of it by 60 percent majorities in one year, or if they vote in favor of it by simple majorities in two successive years.

A second distinctive New Jersey factor that contributed to the development of the supreme court's activist tradition was the existence of an executive branch public advocate whose role was to represent the public interest by, among other things, initiating or participating in groundbreaking litigation. No other state has ever had such a high-level state government official.

The Department of the Public Advocate was created in 1974 by Governor Brendan Byrne, a Democrat, and persisted for twenty years during the gubernatorial tenures of Republican Thomas Kean and Democrat James Florio. It was dissolved in 1994 under Republican governor Christine Todd Whitman but restored in 2005 under Democratic governor Richard Codey. It remained in place during the term of Democratic governor Jon Corzine and was eliminated by the Republican governor Chris Christie, although some of its functions were assigned to other offices within state government.

During the twenty-five years the Department of the Public Advocate was in existence, it evidenced a strong liberal activist tendency in New Jersey that permeated the legislative and executive branches. New Jersey governors who served while the public advocate was in place were considered to be moderate to liberal, and so, too, was the state's electorate. In fact, it was common wisdom, borne out by real electoral results, that when Republicans picked a strongly conservative candidate for governor that person would lose, usually overwhelmingly, and when they picked a moderate he or she had a very good chance to win.

In 2009, by contrast, the New Jersey electorate may consciously have chosen a more conservative Republican in Chris Christie, a former U.S. attorney. That hypothesis may be suspect, however, both because Christie presented himself as being relatively moderate on many issues and because Jon Corzine, the incumbent, was seen as such a deeply flawed candidate. Further compounding the analysis was New Jersey's perilous fiscal situation.

Yet another factor contributing to New Jersey's activist judicial tradition relates to the appointment system in New Jersey. The fact that both the state's attorney general and prosecutors are appointed by the governor rather than having to stand for election, as is the case in many states, meant they were not directly involved in political campaigns and were spared from having to campaign against some of the courts' generally liberal criminal law decisions.

Finally, the New Jersey Supreme Court has the authority to carefully control its docket, and it has exercised that authority. While the constitution provides for an automatic right of appeal to the supreme court in constitutional cases and in cases where there is a dissent in the appellate division, in virtually all other cases the supreme court must grant certification for the case to be heard. The court limits its grants of certification so that it can carefully scrutinize those cases it hears. Consequently, many opinions of the New Jersey Supreme Court are lengthy and fully analyze the area of the law. Some read almost like treatises on the legal issue involved. This has resulted in a number of legal opinions that have become models for other states.

Many of the cases highlighted in this book are a result of the 1947 constitution's pathbreaking innovations, which made it possible for New Jersey's courts, and especially its supreme court, to become bold and creative. Those innovations were augmented by the distinctively New Jersey factors I have described.

Major changes may be coming.

Governor Christie has made no secret of his desire to refashion New Jersey's judiciary. During his 2009 campaign, Christie promised that if elected he would change the direction of the New Jersey Supreme Court. That was particularly a response to the court's decisions in *Robinson* and *Abbott*, which required the state to provide most of the funding for the poorest urban school districts in New Jersey.[44] Many asserted that those decisions had contributed to the state's fiscal crises since education funding is the largest single item in the state budget, as well as in local budgets.

Once elected, Christie sent out a clear message that he planned to reshape the court. The message was communicated by Christie's action toward Justice John Wallace.[45] Wallace had been appointed seven years earlier and could not continue to serve unless he was reappointed. In his case, though, reappointment would only enable him to serve for twenty additional months, at which time he would reach the mandatory retirement age of seventy. Christie decided not to reappoint him, emphasizing that he was seizing the earliest opportunity to start changing the character of the court. His decision not to reappoint represented the first time a governor of either party failed to reappoint a sitting justice since the adoption of the 1947 constitution.[46]

This action became a major source of consternation and concern in the legal community. Although Christie had his supporters, eight former justices

joined many other prominent lawyers and public figures in criticizing the decision. Steven Sweeney, president of the state senate and a strong supporter of
John Wallace, indicated that he would not hold hearings on Christie's nominee
for the court, Anne Patterson, until after Wallace, who had been nominated
and confirmed, would have had to step down because of age more than twenty
months in the future.

Sweeney's action seemed to have little to do with Patterson's qualifications
and more to do with Christie's efforts to diminish the court's independence.
Wallace had hardly been a leading figure on the court regarding school funding reform, yet Christie couched his decision in terms of Wallace being part of
the problem Christie was determined to solve. There is concern that Christie's
action may have a coercive effect on other probationary justices due to come up
for reappointment during Christie's term.

Subsequent to the actions of the governor and the president of the senate,
the chief justice elevated the presiding judge for administration of the appellate
division, Edwin Stern, to fill in temporarily. That was consistent with decisions
that previous chief justices had made. However, some years earlier a law review
article suggested that it violated the New Jersey constitution to designate a judge
to sit on the supreme court unless the court lacked a constitutional quorum of
five justices.[47] Chief Justice Rabner read the language differently and made the
temporary appointment. As chapter 10 of this book indicates, this issue loomed
large in the most recent of the many supreme court decisions in *Abbott v. Burke.*

In the first case in which Judge Stern authored an opinion, the *Henry* case,
Justice Roberto Rivera-Soto wrote an abstaining opinion in which he accepted
the argument that it was unconstitutional to bring up anyone when there was
an existing quorum.[48] In a subsequent opinion issued the same day, he also
stated that he would not vote in any cases in which Judge Stern participated. He
eventually modified that position to abstain only when Judge Stern's opinion
was necessary for a majority.

The constitutional language at issue is: "The Supreme Court shall consist
of a Chief Justice and six Associate Justices. Five members of the court shall
constitute a quorum. When necessary, the Chief Justice shall assign the Judge
or Judges of the Superior Court, senior in service, as provided by rules of the
Supreme Court, to serve temporarily in the Supreme Court."[49]

The supreme court also had adopted a rule providing that "[f]ive members
of the court shall constitute a quorum. When necessary to constitute a quorum,
to replace a justice who is absent or unable to act, or to expedite the business
of the court, the presiding justice may assign one or more retired justices of the
Supreme Court who are not engaged in the practice of law and who consent
thereto or the judge or judges of the Appellate Division, senior in length of service therein, to serve temporarily in the Supreme Court."[50]

The chief justice, in his concurring opinion in *Henry,* wrote a defense of his decision to make the temporary appointment by referring to the history of other chief justices making temporary appointments—one of which lasted more than two years.[51] He also described the extensive workload of the court and the need to have a seventh member of the court to deal with the large number of cases, certification petitions, ethics cases, and other matters.

The chief justice's concurring opinion was joined by three members of the court. Judge Stern did not join in that opinion and Justice Helen Hoens wrote a "dubitante" opinion essentially showing the difficulties in the positions taken by both the chief justice and Justice Rivera-Soto.[52]

Subsequently, Justice Rivera-Soto announced that he did not wish to be reappointed. At that point Senator Sweeney and the Senate agree to hold hearings on the nomination of Anne Patterson as a replacement for Justice Rivera-Soto. She was confirmed by the Senate.

Judge Edwin Stern, who had been assigned by the chief justice to sit temporarily, reached mandatory retirement age, and Judge Dorothea O'C. Wefing, then-presiding judge for administration of the Appellate Division, was assigned by the chief justice to sit on the supreme court. Shortly thereafter, Justice Virginia Long reached mandatory retirement age and had to step down. That left one additional open seat. At that point Governor Christie nominated two people to fill the empty seats. After a rather contentious series of hearings neither of those candidates was confirmed by the Senate.[53]

Another issue raised further concerns about the relationship between the branches of government and, more particularly, about judicial independence. Since the election of Governor Christie, he and the legislature have been attempting to rein in the costs of pensions and health care for state workers. The Democrats and Republicans reached some consensus and enacted legislation (the Pension and Health Care Benefits Act),[54] which reduces benefits and increases costs of state workers. The legislation included judges and increased rather drastically the amount judges would have to pay for their retirement benefits, amounting to $17,000 or more per year after a phase-in period, and without any corresponding salary increase assured.

One judge, Paul DePascale, sued, arguing that such increases violated the New Jersey constitution. The New Jersey constitution of 1844 had contained a provision similar to that in the United States Constitution designed to ensure judicial independence and that provision was carried forward to the constitution of 1947. The provision prohibited the diminution of judges'salaries while they served in that capacity.[55] This was the basis of the decision in *DePascale v. State of New Jersey,* which overturned the statutory increases for judges. The supreme court then took the case directly, skipping the appellate division. In a three-two decision written and signed by its three tenured members, the court affirmed the lower court decision ruling that the state constitution prohibited the contribution increases because they reduced the judges' salaries.[56] (At the time there were only five justices and one temporarily assigned appellate division judge sitting on the court, and Chief Justice Rabner had recused himself.) The majority buttressed its constitutional ruling by referring to the historical record in which other increases in contributions by judges were always combined with salary increases that covered the added costs.

The two dissenting justices, by contrast, argued that deference had to be given to the legislature's decision and that the presumption of constitutionality also weighed against the majority's conclusion. The dissenters also argued that the change in the wording of the 1844 constitution from "compensation" to "salary" was intended to have a significant effect while the majority thought that the constitutional drafters were using those terms interchangeably.

After the supreme court decision in *DePascale,* the legislature placed on the ballot a question to amend the constitution to essentially overturn that decision and permit the legislature to raise contribution levels for judges at will. It read "Do you approve an amendment to the New Jersey Constitution, as agreed to by the legislature, to allow contributions set by law to be taken from the salaries of Supreme Court Justices and Superior Court Judges for their employee benefits?"[57] This provision does not mandate that increases in judicial contributions be part of a comprehensive plan to increase contributions for all state workers, although part of the dissenters' argument was that in the statute before the court that was the case.

One of the chief concerns about the impact of this constitutional amendment was that it might empower the legislature, if it did not like a decision of the supreme court, to increase judges' contribution costs to a confiscatory level, thereby rendering the provision of the 1947 constitution, which sought to ensure that reductions in judges' salaries could not be used to pressure the judiciary, totally irrelevant.

While the provision itself is unclear about whether it can be applied retroactively, the interpretative statement indicates that it can have that application. In that event, judges could be required to pay the back contributions that have been stayed by court orders.

The timing of the legislative decision to include sitting judges among the state workers whose contributions could be increased raises serious concerns about judicial independence. The bill's original language excluded judges because of the constitutional impediment. As introduced on February 23, 2011, the bill stated that the higher contribution rates would only apply to new members of the judicial retirement system. The statement accompanying the bill said, "The increase in the contribution rate for members of the Judicial Retirement System should be implemented in a manner to conform to a prohibition in the State Constitution against reduction in the compensation of a judge during the judge's term of appointment."[58]

In June 2011, a new version of the bill was introduced, which applied the increases to sitting judges. While it is hard to determine why the bill was so drastically changed, one possible, if not probable, explanation is that in May of that year the court rendered its most recent decision in the long line of *Abbott v. Burke* decisions.[59] That decision mandated the state to increase by hundreds of millions of dollars its funding of the so-called Abbott districts—the poorest urban school districts in New Jersey. This was a highly unpopular decision for Governor Christie and a number of legislators.

Thus, it is possible that in the future whenever the governor and a majority of legislators strongly dislike a judicial decision they could increase the contributions of the judges in retaliation. That is exactly what the drafters of the United States Constitution and of New Jersey's 1844 and 1947 constitutions feared when they protected the independence of the judiciary. Given the public's embrace of the constitutional amendment at the November 6, 2012, election,[60] the risk is real that New Jersey courts will no longer have substantial protection from retaliation by the political branches of the state. It is premature to make a definitive judgment as to whether this constitutional amendment will contribute to a substantial decline of the independence and excellence that has characterized the New Jersey Supreme Court since New Jersey adopted its 1947 constitution. To a greater extent than before, however, that power now may be in the hands of the other branches of state government.

NOTES

1. Carla Vivian Bello and Arthur T. Vanderbilt II, *Jersey Justice: Three Hundred Years of the New Jersey Judiciary* (New Brunswick, NJ: Institute for Continuing Legal Education, 1978), 16–17.
2. The 1776 constitution also provided for judges of the supreme court, judges of inferior courts of common pleas in the several counties, and justices of the peace. New Jersey Constitution, article XII (1776).
3. The council was essentially a legislative body as described in Article VI of the constitution of 1776.
4. New Jersey Constitution, article XII (1776).
5. Arthur T. Vanderbilt, *The Challenge of Law Reform* (Princeton, NJ: Princeton University Press, 1955), 17.
6. *In re Yengo*, 72 N.J. 425 (1977).
7. Bello and Vanderbilt, *Jersey Justice*, 19.
8. New Jersey Constitution, article VI, sec. 1 (1844).
9. See generally Robert F. Williams, *The New Jersey Constitution: A Reference Guide* (New Brunswick, NJ: Rutgers University Press, 1997).
10. That clause can currently be found in New Jersey Constitution, article VIII, sec. 4, par. 1.
11. See Alan Tarr and Mary Porter, *State Supreme Courts in State and Nation* (New Haven, CT: Yale University Press, 1988).

12. Arthur T. Vanderbilt II, *Changing Law: A Biography of Arthur T. Vanderbilt* (New Brunswick, NJ: Rutgers University Press, 1976), 128.

13. Stewart G. Pollock, "Celebrating Fifty Years of Judicial Reform Under the 1947 New Jersey Constitution," *Rutgers Law Journal* 29 (1998): 675.

14. See Vanderbilt, *Changing Law*, 162.

15. John B. Wefing, "State Supreme Justices: Who Are They?" *New England Law Review* 32 (1997): 47.

16. See Stephen J. Ware, "The Missouri Plan in National Perspective," *Missouri Law Review* 74 (2009): 773n82.

17. That appointee had been primarily criticized for activities he carried out as attorney general prior to his appointment to the court. When it became clear that he would not be reappointed, he resigned from the court before his term ended. Ironically, in the legal community he was highly regarded for his service on the court.

18. The original order also excluded lawyers from serving as the public members on the theory that lawyers had their say through the New Jersey State Bar Association. In the Christie change, though, lawyers were permitted to serve as public members.

19. For an in-depth discussion of the issue of senatorial courtesy see *DeVesa v. Dorsey*, 134 N.J. 420 (1993).

20. The constitution of Delaware mandates bipartisanship. It provides: "First, three of the five Justices of the Supreme Court in office at the same time, shall be of one major political party, and two of such Justices shall be of the other major political party." Delaware Constitution, article IV, sec. 3.

21. The temporary appointee, Edwin Stern, was a Democrat.

22. Arthur T. Vanderbilt, *The Challenge of Law Reform* (Princeton, NJ: Princeton University Press, 1955), 32–33.

23. Ibid.

24. Arthur T. Vanderbilt, "Assignments of Superior Court Judges," *New Jersey Law Journal*, September 16, 1948.

25. Delaware joins New Jersey in this requirement, but by constitutional rule. Delaware Constitution, article IV, §3.

26. New Jersey Statutes Annotated, sec. 2A:3–14.

27. New Jersey Laws of 1981, chapter 462, section 57.

28. It should be noted that Eisenhower was specifically looking for a Catholic who was already a judge for the position. Bernard Shanley, of the former Newark firm of Shanley and Fisher (now Drinker Biddle), was serving as appointment secretary to Eisenhower and knew Brennan and supported his candidacy. For more detail, see David Alistair Yalof, *Pursuit of Justices: Presidential Politics and the Selection of Supreme Court Justices* (Chicago: University of Chicago Press, 1999).

29. 5 N.J. 240 (1950).

30. New Jersey Constitution, article VI, sec. II, par. 3 (emphasis added).

31. See Pollock, "Celebrating Fifty Years," 682–688.

32. John B. Wefing, "The New Jersey Supreme Court 1948–1998: Fifty Year of Independence and Activism," *Rutgers Law Journal* 29 (1998): 701.

33. Subsequent to Chief Justice Weintraub's tenure, the New Jersey Supreme Court embraced far more liberal interpretations in the search and seizure area, using the New Jersey constitution to grant greater rights to defendants in criminal cases than the United States Supreme Court had done under the U.S. Constitution. Robert Williams discusses this in chapter 6 on *State v. Hunt*.

34. See generally John B. Wefing, "Search and Seizure—New Jersey Supreme Court v. United States Supreme Court," *Seton Hall Law Review* 7 (1976): 771.

35. See generally John B. Wefing, *The Life and Times of Richard J. Hughes: The Politics of Civility* (New Brunswick, NJ: Rutgers University Press, 2009).

36. Glen R. Winters, "New Jersey Goes to the Head of the Class," *Journal of the American Judicature Society* 31 (1948): 131.

37. New Jersey Constitution, article IV, sec. 3, par. 2. The supreme court also has a role in the reapportionment process with regard to congressional seats. There is another commission for that process consisting of six members of each party. If they are unable to agree, they are charged with selecting a tiebreaker. If they cannot agree on that selection, the supreme court is authorized to choose the tiebreaker. New Jersey Constitution, article II, sec. 2, par. 1 (c). That provision was enacted in 1995. In the redistricting after both the 2000 and 2010 censuses, the twelve members of the commission were able to agree on a tiebreaker, so the supreme court did not have to act.

38. Other New Jersey Supreme Court decisions rankled Republicans, particularly the conservative branch of the party. A notable example was the court's decision in *New Jersey Democratic Party v. Samson*, 175 N.J. 178 (2002). In that case, U.S. Senator Robert Torricelli, a Democrat and candidate for reelection, was under investigation by the Senate ethics committee. Evidence from that inquiry was damaging to Torricelli and it appeared he would be defeated by his Republican adversary, who focused much of his campaign on the ethical lapses. The Democrats then chose former Senator Frank Lautenberg, who had great name recognition in the state, to take Torricelli's place on the ballot. The Republicans sued, arguing the relevant state statute clearly provided that after a certain date there could not be a substitution. The New Jersey Supreme Court, however, found that the constitutional right to vote trumped the statutory provision.

39. Gerald Russello, "The New Jersey Supreme Court: New Directions?" *Journal of Civil Rights and Economic Development* 16 (2002): 655.

40. Tarr and Porter, *State Supreme Courts*, 184.

41. Kevin M. Mulcahy, "Modeling the Garden: How New Jersey Built the Most Progressive State Supreme Court and What California Can Learn," *Santa Clara Law Review* 40 (2000): 863. See also Michael P. Ambrosio and Denis F. McLaughlin, "The Redefining of Professional Ethics in New Jersey Under Chief Justice Robert Wilentz: A Legacy of Reform," *Seton Hall Constitutional Law Journal* 7 (1997): 351.

42. Jake Dear and Edward W. Jessen, "'Followed Rates' and Leading State Cases, 1940–2005," *U.C. Davis Law Review* 41 (2007): 683; Jake Dear and Edward W. Jessen, "Measuring the Comparative Influence of State Supreme Courts: Comments on Our 'Followed Rates' Essay," *U.C. Davis Law Review* 41 (2008): 1665.

43. Stephen Choi, Mitu Gulati, and Eric Posner, "Judicial Evaluations and Information Forcing: Ranking State High Courts and Their Judges," *Duke Law Journal* 58 (2009): 1313.

44. There were seven supreme court decisions in *Robinson v. Cahill* and twenty-one in *Abbott v. Burke*.

45. Justice Wallace had served in the judiciary for many years and had been on the appellate division when he was appointed to the supreme court.

46. Justice Wallace was the only African American serving on the supreme court, and Governor Christie nominated a white woman to replace him. Ordinarily, the addition of another woman to the court might have been seen as a strong statement in favor of gender equality since it would have resulted in a majority of female justices. In this

case, however, the racial issues raised by Governor Christie's action overpowered the gender dimension.

47. Edward A. Hartnett, "Ties in the Supreme Court of New Jersey," *Seton Hall Law Review* 32 (2003): 735. Hartnett serves at Seton Hall Law School as the Richard J. Hughes Professor of Constitutional and Public Law and Service.

48. *Henry v. New Jersey Department of Human Services*, 204 N.J. 320, 354 (2010) (Rivera-Soto, J., abstaining). Justice Rivera-Soto attached to his abstaining opinion five appendices categorizing more than two thousand decisions of the New Jersey Supreme Court and consuming 153 pages of the court's opinions in the Henry case.

49. New Jersey Constitution, article VI, sec. 2, par. 1

50. N.J. Sup. Ct. R. 2:13–2(a).

51. *Henry*, 204 N.J. at 340 (Rabner, C.J., concurring).

52. *Henry*, 204 N.J at 525 (Hoens, J., dubitante).

53. One candidate was an openly gay African American who had been a transactional attorney and was considered to have insufficient court experience to serve on the supreme court. The other candidate had difficulty because of problems his family business had experienced and because he had only recently moved to New Jersey, where he registered as an Independent despite having been registered in New York as a Republican.

54. Law 2011, chapter 78.

55. This provision provides that judges "shall receive for their services such salaries as may be provided by law, which may not be diminished during the term of their appointment." New Jersey Constitution, article VI, sec. 5, par. 6.

56. 211 N.J. 40 (2012).

57. Senate Concurrent Resolution 110 (introduced May 14, 2012) (proposing an amendment to the New Jersey Constitution, which became Question 2 on the November 6, 2012 ballot).

58. New Jersey Assembly Bill No. 3796 (introduced February 23, 2011).

59. 206 N.J. 33 (2011).

60. Matt Friedman, "Voters OK Measure to Make Judges Pay More for Benefits," November 6, 2012, http://www.nj.com/politics/index.ssf/2012/11/nj_ballot_question_2_result.html,; see also "Election Results: New Jersey Ballot Questions," November 12, 2012, http://www.nj.com/politics/index.ssf/2012/11/election_results_new_jersey_ba.html, (reporting that 83% of New Jersey voters supported Question 2).

NOTES ON CONTRIBUTORS

PAUL W. ARMSTRONG has been a superior court judge in Somerset and Hunterdon counties since 2000 with a special focus on drug issues and treatment, an adjunct faculty member at Rutgers School of Law–Newark, and a longtime practicing lawyer. In the last capacity, he was a pioneer of patients' rights, representing patients and their families in a number of important, high-profile cases, including *Quinlan*. Judge Armstrong also served as chair of both the New Jersey Bioethics Commission and the New Jersey Governor's Advisory Council on AIDS.

RONALD K. CHEN is a graduate of Rutgers School of Law–Newark who moved over to the faculty and administration. He is currently vice dean and a clinical professor of law. Starting in 2006, he served for four years as the Public Advocate of New Jersey. Throughout his career, Chen has been deeply engaged in litigating civil rights, civil liberties, and other constitutional law cases, and his commitment and excellence have been widely recognized.

RICHARD H. CHUSED joined the faculty of New York Law School in 2008 after a thirty-five-year career at Georgetown Law School, but it all began at Rutgers School of Law–Newark, where Chused was on the faculty from 1968 to 1973, when *Marini* was decided. Throughout his career, he has focused on property law and gender and law in American legal history. Cases such as *Marini* have particularly attracted him because of his interest in housing for the impoverished. He wrote the definitive history of *Javins v. First National Realty*, a sister case to *Marini*. Not surprisingly, Chused's interests include *Mount Laurel*, about which he has written a contrarian article, like his chapter on *Marini*, arguing that *Mount Laurel* was, in some ways, wrongly decided. In March 2010, he lectured about the *Marini* case as the first Allen Axelrod Visiting Scholar at Rutgers School of Law–Newark.

CAITLIN EDWARDS is a 2011 graduate of Rutgers School of Law–Camden.

JAY M. FEINMAN is a senior faculty member at Rutgers School of Law–Camden, where he is also a member of the Rutgers Center for Risk and Responsibility and a longtime teacher of tort law. He is a member of the prestigious American Law Institute and an adviser for the Restatement Third of Torts: Liability for Economic Loss. Feinman is the author or editor of seven books and more than fifty scholarly articles.

FREDRIC J. GROSS returned to Rutgers School of Law–Newark after being an academic in anthropology; graduated with honors and hung out a shingle. More than thirty-five years later, he continues to litigate important public interest cases, such as *Lehmann*, largely as a solo practitioner. He also is coauthor of the now-outdated ACLU handbook, *The Rights of Veterans* (1978).

ROBERT C. HOLMES is the deputy director of the Rutgers School of Law–Newark Clinical Programs and director of its Community Law Clinic. Between 1971 and 1987 he served in a series of public positions that related to housing in New Jersey, including being executive director of the Newark Housing Development and Rehabilitation Corporation, assistant and then acting commissioner of the New Jersey Department of Community Affairs, chief executive of the Newark Watershed Conservation and Development Corporation, member of the original State Planning Commission and a member of a task force charged with drafting the 1985 Fair Housing Act.

SUZANNE A. KIM is a member of the faculty at Rutgers School of Law–Newark. Her work focuses on intersections of family law, gender, culture, work, and critical theory. She has won or been nominated for several prestigious national awards for articles about marriage, parenthood, and family privacy. She is currently at work on a book about the social relationship between marriage and gender in same-sex couples. Kim offers many thanks to Heidi Arnesen, Carlys Lemler, Timothy Pedergnana, and Mia Volkening for their excellent research assistance.

ROBERT S. OLICK, who has both a J.D. and a Ph.D., is a professor at SUNY Upstate Medical University where he directs the Ethical, Legal, and Social Issues in Medicine component of the first-year curriculum. He also served previously as executive director of the New Jersey Bioethics Commission and as chief consultant to the New Jersey Governor's Advisory Council on AIDS.

DEBORAH T. PORITZ is a retired chief justice of the New Jersey Supreme Court. She began her legal career in the New Jersey Department of Law and Public Safety, where she served as assistant attorney general and director of the Division of Law from 1986 to 1989. She left to become chief counsel to Governor

Thomas H. Kean and then was a partner at Jamieson, Moore, Peskin and Spicer from 1990 until 1994. In 1994, Poritz was named attorney general by Governor Christine Todd Whitman and served in that role until her appointment as chief justice of the New Jersey Supreme Court in 1996, a position in which she served for ten years. She was the first woman to hold both positions. The recipient of many prestigious awards, Poritz is now Visiting Jurist Emerita-in-Residence at Rutgers School of Law–Newark and Rutgers School of Law–Camden and of counsel at Drinker Biddle & Reath, LLP. She also serves as chair of the board of trustees of Legal Services of New Jersey, vice chair of the board of Princeton HealthCare System, and as a member of the board of the Fund for New Jersey.

LOUIS RAVESON is a member of the Rutgers School of Law–Newark faculty and a graduate of the law school. Raveson was deeply involved in the development of the school's clinical legal education programs. He directed the Urban Legal Clinic for eight years and established the Environmental Law Clinic in 1985, when it was only the second such law school clinic in the nation. Both before and during his service as a law professor, Raveson has litigated countless trials in state and federal courts and pursued numerous appeals before the New Jersey Supreme Court, the federal circuit courts, and the United States Supreme Court, including *Right to Choose* where he was one of the plaintiffs' attorneys. Raveson would like to express his sincere thanks to Ola Akache, Xavier Nunez, Zaara Bajwa, Jessica Schreckengost, and Caroline Young for their exceptional assistance.

PAUL L. TRACTENBERG is the Board of Governors Distinguished Service Professor and Alfred C. Clapp Distinguished Public Service Professor of Law at Rutgers School of Law–Newark. For most of his forty-four-year career there he has been deeply involved in pursuing state constitutional claims, including *Robinson* and *Abbott*, on behalf of disadvantaged and disabled students in the New Jersey courts, and especially in the New Jersey Supreme Court. In 1973, Tractenberg established the Education Law Center in Newark and Philadelphia and was its first director for three years. In 2000, he established the Rutgers–Newark Institute on Education Law and Policy, and he continues to co-direct its interdisciplinary research program.

JOHN B. WEFING is the Distinguished Professor of New Jersey Law and History at Seton Hall University School of Law, where he has taught for the last forty-four years, and previously served as associate dean and acting dean. Wefing is the author of many law review articles, as well as *The Life and Times of Richard J. Hughes: The Politics of Civility*, published by Rutgers University Press and chosen as a 2010 Honor Book by the New Jersey Council for the Humanities. He has served on a number of state committees and is currently a member of the Governor's Higher Education Council.

ROBERT F. WILLIAMS, a senior member of the Rutgers School of Law–Camden faculty, is among the nation's leading experts on state constitutional law. Williams is the associate director of the Center for State Constitutional Studies at Rutgers–Camden and author of dozens of articles and numerous books on state constitutional law. Prior to starting his association with Rutgers in 1989, he worked in Florida on revisions of its state constitution, both as a legislative aide and on behalf of clients. Williams has participated in a wide range of state constitutional litigation, lectured to hundreds of judges and lawyers, and produced a TV documentary marking the fiftieth anniversary of New Jersey's 1947 constitution.

INDEX